Also by James M. Jeffords
My Declaration of Independence

An Independent Man

Adventures of a Public Servant

Senator James M. Jeffords

*with Yvonne Daley
and Howard Coffin*

Simon & Schuster
New York   London   Toronto   Sydney   Singapore

SIMON & SCHUSTER
Rockefeller Center
1230 Avenue of the Americas
New York, NY 10020

Copyright © 2003 by James M. Jeffords
All rights reserved, including the right of reproduction
in whole or in part in any form.

SIMON & SCHUSTER and colophon are registered
trademarks of Simon & Schuster, Inc.

A leatherbound signed first edition of this book has been published by Easton Press.

For information about special discounts for bulk purchases,
please contact Simon & Schuster Special Sales:
1-800-456-6798 or business@simonandschuster.com.

Manufactured in the United States of America

1   3   5   7   9   10   8   6   4   2

Library of Congress Cataloging-in-Publication Data

Jeffords, James M.
An independent man : adventures of a public servant / James M. Jeffords ;
with Yvonne Daley and in collaboration with Howard Coffin.
p. cm.
Includes index.
1. Jeffords, James M. 2. Legislators—United States—Biography. 3. United
States. Congress. Senate—Biography. 4. Republican Party (U.S. : 1854–)—
Biography. 5. United States—Politics and government—1945–1989.
6. United States—Politics and government—1989–
7. Vermont—Politics and government—1865–
I. Daley, Yvonne. II. Coffin, Howard, date. III. Title.

E840.8.J43 A3 2003
328.73'092—dc21
[B]   2002030330

ISBN 0-7432-2843-X

All insert photographs courtesy of the author except the *Newsweek* cover
© 2001 Newsweek, Inc. All rights reserved. Reprinted by permission.

"Song of the Open Road," copyright © 1933 by Ogden Nash, renewed.
Reprinted by permission of Curtis Brown, Ltd.

Author's Note

I did not write this book alone. Many people helped in so many ways. Most important are my two coauthors, Yvonne Daley and Howard Coffin.

I must first pay tribute to the work of Yvonne Daley. Yvonne was the glue that held this book together. Her talent as a writer is obvious, but it was her tenacity and her ability to draw out the personal stories and memories from those who have been a part of my life that make this book so special. I owe her a great debt of gratitude.

I especially want to thank Howard Coffin. Howard, a Vermont historian, has detailed the tumultuous years in Vermont's history, and in particular, my personal and professional experiences as Vermont's attorney general. Howard, who has been a friend for decades, lived those exciting times with me. His perspective, research, and writing were invaluable in bringing this book to life.

Also a special thanks to Rayne Guilford who worked with me from start to finish.

To my wife, Liz Daley Jeffords.
The life I lead has made sustaining a marriage difficult,
but she has made it possible.
And
to my children
Leonard Olin Jeffords
and
Laura Louise Jeffords
who have graciously endured the fallout from
their political dad.

Contents

1 On the Street Where I Lived 1

2 Leaving Home 24

3 Ships at Sea 30

4 Love and Law 46

5 A Short Primer in Vermont Politics 64

6 Maverick Republican 72

7 Making Environmental History 85

8 David and Goliath 105

9 The Realities of Power 117

10 After Nixon 130

11 The Walking Wounded 140

12 Leo Ryan, Baby Seals, Solzhenitsyn, and Energy Wars 152

13 Musical Homes 168

14 Trickle-Down Economy, the Contras, and the Evil Empire 174

15 The Second Time Around 188

16 Protecting Tradition, "The October Surprise," Clarence Thomas, and Working for an International Nuclear Test Ban 193

17 Building the Case for Education in the Shadow of Gingrich's Contract with America 209

18 Again the Maverick: Health Care and Impeachment   231

19 The Singing Senators   248

20 The Days Before the Switch   253

21 Making History   273

22 The Reaction   278

23 September 11   284

24 My Challenge to the Country   292

Afterword 301

Appendix: My Declaration, May 24, 2001,
Burlington, Vermont   303

Acknowledgments   307

Index   309

An Independent Man

CHAPTER 1

On the Street Where I Lived

My wife likes to say I was born into an Andy Hardy movie and remained out of step with contemporary times, that there's something inherently naive about me that keeps me from seeing things as they really are. There's a lot of truth to that statement, but if I were to pick the movie that feels most emblematic of my life story, I would choose *Mister Smith Goes to Washington,* or some other wholesome film that shows what life was like before we became so obsessed with speed and consumption, a time when your word meant something and people were driven by ethics more than money—or, at least, most people were.

I'd also want a story with so many other interesting characters that I could step into the background and watch it all unfold. Like most people, I like to be in the limelight—but only on occasion. I have been blessed with leadership roles and important challenges. Recent events, especially my decision to leave the Republican Party in May 2001, and my integral role in protecting Americans after September 11 as chair of the Senate Environment and Public Works committee, have cast me into the national spotlight. But the best of life, I learned at an early age, is being part of something larger than yourself. My decision to become an Independent was prompted by that sense of public responsibility, something I've been trying to explain to folks ever since I made it.

I'm sure it was growing up in Vermont, where my father was the chief justice of the Vermont Supreme Court and so many of our family friends were in public service, that brought me to this understanding. I was born in Rutland. Although it was the state's second-largest city until recently, it was—and remains—a place where everyone on your street knew you and you knew them. There's an inherent bond among Vermonters that's hard to explain to people from other places. It comes from our small size, both in terms of population and actual acreage. When I was growing up,

Vermont had roughly 400,000 residents; we shared a value system rooted in hard work, perseverance, and a respect for the individual. Today, even in Vermont's larger cities, most folks know something of their neighbors. And today, with only about 600,000 state residents, Vermonters still regard their politicians with a sense of ownership and expectation that comes out of a neighborliness that seems quite natural—a respectful familiarity, albeit, but a sense of ownership nonetheless. Because of all of this I grew up with a security and sureness of purpose that too few people experience.

There are, of course, downsides to being known too well, and of people having expectations of you. There have been times when I have felt as if my life was preordained, or that people who thought they knew me sought to make me someone I was not. But, for the most part, I count my birth in the Green Mountain State and my childhood there as gifts that provided me with a foundation on which to build an independent nature. And from very early on in life, I knew that I would serve my community and state. Like Jeff Smith of the Capra film, I grew up a wide-eyed, innocent idealist who went to Washington expecting to actually get something done and to represent the average person rather than the rich and powerful. I just didn't know any better.

I was born May 11, 1934, and came to age during World War II, a time when there was little question about who the enemy was and how to define valor. Then, as now, Rutland's population was a little more than 20,000. Located in a pretty valley rich in natural resources, Rutland was the hub of commerce in my neck of the woods. We were not a hick town, nor can I describe my childhood as a rural one, although I spent most of my free time in the outdoors. The Rutland of my youth was a bustling community. People came here on Friday night and Saturday to shop, go to a movie, or simply to walk the city streets and converse with neighbors. This was the time of soda shops and specialty stores, where the shop owner knew your name and probably your size.

Rutland has always been one of Vermont's most important cities. The state's two main roads intersected here. (Now interstate highways bring many out-of-staters elsewhere.) A railroad that served the entire Northeast was based in Rutland in my youth; many of my neighbors worked for it or traveled by way of it. The city had an odd mix of sophistication and working-class values, grounded in its Yankee heritage and enriched by an interesting overlay of ethnic diversity brought to us by French Canadian, Irish, Italian, Polish, Greek, Jewish, and the few African-American families who settled in Rutland and the surrounding area.

Our city was the county seat, home to some of the state's oldest industries, including the Howe Scale Works, once one of the largest factories in the country, a foundry, dressmaking, and machine-work shops. To the west, the towns of Proctor and West Rutland had some of the nation's most productive marble quarries, finishing sheds, and artisans' shops. And all around us were wonderful mountains and woods, family farms, orchards, and sugarbushes.

A boy could find much to do here—skiing down Kingsley Avenue and Country Club hill or, later, Pico Mountain in winter; fishing and swimming in rivers and lakes in summer; hiking at all times of year.

But it was our street that was the center of my universe. My parents had met in Rutland. My mother, Marion, was a talented pianist who had grown up in Glen Cove on Long Island and attended Syracuse University before moving to Rutland to teach music and art for the entire school system. My father, Olin, was a Vermont native in a long line of Vermont natives. He had grown up in Enosburg Falls, a town way up north by the Canadian border. There, his grandfather had been a minister and his father a pharmacist. Jeffords Drug Store closed thirty-one years ago despite my efforts to save it after my aunt, Cora Jeffords Pratt, died in 1966. Father graduated from Boston University Law School, where he taught law for a couple of years before moving to Ludlow, Vermont, to work at the law firm of Stickney, Sargant, Skeels, and Jeffords. John Sargant took a leave of absence to join Vermont's President Coolidge as the U.S. Attorney General.

Later, Father was asked to join the firm of Fenton, Wing, Morse, and Jeffords in Rutland. Like many young single people of the time, he took a room at a rooming house, in his case the Brock House, where my mother had been living for several years. Over time, a friendship blossomed into a romance, but I know little about their courtship. My parents weren't much for talking about themselves. One of the few stories they told of these years was that my father came into a sizable inheritance, promptly proposed to my mother, and bought a plot of land on Kingsley Avenue, across the street from where Leonard Wing Sr., his law partner and best friend, lived. They married in 1928.

My mother's father, my grandfather Nicholas Hausman, designed my parents' house. He was a clever man, an architect, who taught me much about life and labor in a way that my busy father never had the time to do. The house, built near the top of Kingsley Avenue, was a lovely wooden colonial, painted white with green trim, with a center staircase, bird's-eye maple floors, and a practicality that pleased all the adults in my life. I still own that house, although I live in Shrewsbury, a rural mountain village south of Rutland. I can't bring myself to sell the family home; I doubt I ever will. We rent it out, of course, because being a politician is not the lucrative occupation some folks think it is.

Everything about that house, the street, the town, seemed perfect to me as a child. If there were things in my environment that were wrong, I never knew about them, except, of course, the life and death events that no one can avoid. Arthur Guild, the principal of Rutland High School, lived at the top of our street. His sons, Malcolm and Jim, were among my best pals and have remained so throughout adulthood. Jim and I spent most of our early years together. Sadly, he passed away a decade ago of cancer.

Next door to the Guilds was a duplex owned by Otis and Ethel Edson; their son Alvin, older than me by eight years, was a budding engineer and one of my early mentors. He was an inventor and for a while I toyed with the idea of becoming an inventor myself when I grew up. The Edsons' tenants were William and Cecelia Paul and their two daughters, Lillian and Dorothy, who were part of our gang. Next to them lived the Wings and their three children—Leonard, Patricia, and Bruce, all much older than the rest of us kids but friends nonetheless.

Two brothers, Rex and Ned Shaw, had built houses across the street from each other just down the street from us. Rex and Betty's son, Harlow, was also part of our gang.

Also living on our street was Lou Salander, the man behind the politicians and railroad magnets of Rutland, and Harold "The Hawk" Nichols, a railroad dispatcher who became a popular city mayor. I still cherish the days when I visited Nichols's railroad office. He kept track of the Rutland Railroad trains on a big master board. My desire to bring back the railroads to ease truck traffic on Vermont highways, an effort I'm involved in to this day, probably started right back there in his office.

To cap off the experience of growing up in this close-knit neighborhood, Bob Stafford, my political mentor and predecessor in both the U.S. House of Representatives and U.S. Senate, lived a stone's throw away, across Main Street.

There was a vacant lot next to our house where we played a gazillion games of football and baseball and where we organized circuses in which I got to be master of ceremonies, play the clown, or try a few feats of daring. The lot is still empty but kids don't play there much anymore. That's too bad, isn't it? We had no TV or computers. We made our own fun. Mother sometimes made me practice the trumpet, but when we weren't in school or at church and if it wasn't pouring or a blizzard, we spent most of our free time outside. Parents back then were not ever vigilant in the way they are today. They didn't have to be. All the moms were home and someone was always aware of what we were up to—and not afraid to set us straight if our mischief got out of hand. I feel sorry for today's kids, having so little time to develop imaginative games and leadership skills without the constant supervision of adults.

My sister Mary was eighteen months older than I was and we were very close. When I was born, she took on the role of mother's helper. Mary and I have remained close over the many decades. She was quite popular, and as we got older, she played more and more with the girls and I played with the boys—that's how it was back then.

By the time I was old enough to know what my father did, he was already on the state superior court, requiring him to rotate around the state's courthouses. He was often in the state capital of Montpelier, about sixty miles from Rutland, especially after he became chief justice on the Vermont Supreme Court. All told, he was rarely home during the week, and even on the weekend, he was often away from the house.

My mother was bright, fastidious, organized, and very involved in the community. She cooked our dinner and was always home to make sure we did our homework and ate together. But it was Edith Fuller, the woman who lived with us in the early years of my childhood and did most of the housework, who bestowed hugs and kisses—and Band-Aids for the occasional boo-boo.

The long and short of it was that I spent most of my spare time alone or with the other boys on our street, outdoors or at their houses. I didn't mind being alone; indeed, I have always enjoyed solitude. I like to say it's when I get my best work done—in my head.

• • •

I have a few foggy memories of early birthday parties and wagon rides, but the first vivid memory of my youth took place a few days before Christmas 1939, when I was five. We had spent the day decorating the Christmas tree, a fresh-cut balsam that stood, year after year, in its appointed place in the corner of the roomy, formal parlor. Mother probably had 78 rpm albums of her favorite Christmas carols playing on the record player, but every once in a while she would pause from putting up the decorations to play a carol or two herself on the piano. Her favorite was "Silent Night." I loved this moment every year, as we placed the metallic glass balls, the strings of popcorn, and the tinsel on the tree and hung our stockings on either side of the mantel. But this particular Christmas I was in agony. Aldo Merusi, a photographer from the *Rutland Herald,* had come by to take a picture of Mary and me standing in front of the fireplace with our stockings hanging on either side of us. All the while I tried to ignore the growing pain in my stomach. At first we thought it was the dreaded grippe, but by the time I was doubled over in the bathroom, Mother realized I was really sick. She called Dr. Ed Hines, who came over right away. I can still see his kind face as he bent over me while I lay on my white chenille bedspread. The model airplanes I had hung from my ceiling were spinning around and around and I was crying softly, too weak from pain and fever to wail, although I felt like it. He poked for just a minute, then announced that we had an emergency and he had to get me to the hospital immediately. I don't know where Father had been but suddenly he appeared in the doorway, already wearing his overcoat. Mother dressed me in my new pajamas and Father picked me up and carried me down the stairs, something I can't remember him doing before or after. As we went through the door to our shiny new Buick, I turned back toward the tree, lit up as if nothing were amiss, and said softly, "Good-bye Mister Christmas Tree."

As you might have guessed, my appendix had burst and I was in deep trouble. Fortunately, new sulfa drugs and penicillin treatments had recently been introduced, and Dr. Hines had refreshed his medical training so he knew what to do. He told my parents that had my appendix burst six months or a year earlier, he might not have been able to save my life. This, of course, became a family myth, told and retold, about how the boy that I was whispered "Good-bye Mister Christmas Tree" on his way to the emergency room. Curiously, my father, who was neither an overly affectionate man nor a sentimental one, was the one most apt to retell the story.

Father—yes, he had a big influence on me. Of course I admired him. I knew he was an important man and that he had values. Others saw him as entertaining, a storyteller, and a rock of dependability. I saw these things, too, but I also felt his unhuggableness. I can picture him now in his dark suit with his stark white shirt and his conservative tie, making it clear that whatever he was telling me was the law and not to be argued with. He never raised his voice nor did he ever strike me. He didn't have to. All he had to do was give me his stern look and utter the words "Your mother tells me . . ." and I'd be shaking. I rarely could come up with the right answer to his "And what do *you* have to say for yourself?" Even when I came upon him asleep in his chair after he had returned from playing pinochle at the Masonic Hall, or when he took me on our annual fishing trips to Lake Champlain or along the Missisquoi River, I found him formal and distant.

One of my other early memories is what I call my first honesty test. That new Buick was Father's pride and joy; he kept it nicely polished. One day, just fooling around like any kid will, I took some dirt and rubbed it on the fender. Don't ask me why, maybe just to see if I could get away with it. Later, I was outside playing in a puddle, making a dam with twigs. I had all but forgotten about the dirt on the fender when Father came outside and saw this affront to his precious Buick. Of course, he knew how it had gotten there, but he asked me anyhow. His voice was even and his hazel eyes intent upon me, but he did not yell. I was tempted to lie but Mother had taught me it was wrong to not tell the truth, so I admitted what I had done. He came over, knelt down in front of me, and praised me—a rare happening. Part of me was listening to his words, but most of me was simply scrutinizing him, looking intently at his face, the fine hairs in his nose, the earnestness of his gaze, the lines on his soft face. It's an odd thing, but to this day, I always feel good when I come out and say what I know to be true, even when it makes someone else angry.

It's not just that my father was distant with me. My parents were formal with each other. I do not recall them ever arguing, but I never saw them exchange physical affection either, other than an occasional peck on the cheek. I imagine now, looking back, that my mother had made some concessions to her husband and was happy enough with them. He had told her before they married that Saturday night was his card game night. He was a man's man, and although my parents had a circle of loyal friends, they weren't much for entertaining. And so my mother developed her own women friends, with whom she often lunched or played bridge, and she had her volunteer activities. And my father worked or went to one of his clubs.

Our world was relatively free of turmoil, other than the occasional appendicitis, of course. That tranquillity came to a sudden end on December 7, 1941. My father had gone to the Rutland Country Club to play cards. I was playing in the backyard, enjoying my time alone. The sun was out; I remember it vividly to this day. Suddenly, my father drove back to the house, hours before his usual return. I immediately sensed something was wrong. He told me in a voice I'd never heard before to get my sister and come into the house. There, we found Father and Mother already gathered in front of the Magnavox cabinet radio in the living room. The Japanese had bombed Pearl Harbor and we were at war. We sat together and listened to the radio for hours.

The radio was a fixture in our lives. On Sunday nights, we usually ate a light supper of cornmeal mush with milk and butter, popcorn and corn bread and maple syrup—Father liked corn; this was his favorite meal of the week—and then we retired to the living room to listen to Jack Benny and Charley McCarthy, George Burns and the like. My father would sit in his favorite chair, a deep Morris-style with wooden arms, and laugh and laugh at the programs. He loved the radio. After Pearl Harbor, the radio took on a new significance. It, the *Rutland Herald,* and letters from the front became our links to the people on our street who were fighting in the war. The war may have been very far away, but at the same time it was right there on Kingsley Avenue.

My father's best friend, Leonard Wing Sr., was among those fighting overseas. Major General Wing was a large man with red hair—his friends called him Red—and he was the head of the Vermont National Guard. Within days of Pearl Harbor, he was called to active duty and eventually made commander of the 43rd Division of the army, which was comprised of New England men serving in the Pacific. His son, Leonard Wing Jr., was fighting in Europe. At one point, Leonard Junior was imprisoned in Poland and then escaped safely. Our next-door neighbor, Natalie Shaw, had married army pilot Hugh McLeod. During the Battle of the Bulge he was grounded by fog and taken prisoner by the Nazis, but came home safely. Meanwhile, General Wing was leading his division in battle after battle. We followed the drama as best we could, piecing together the various stories from news accounts, newsreels, and letters home. Jim Guild and I were convinced that we needed to train to fight the Japs and Krauts. We all talked like that. Those words were used in headlines in the papers and in the newsreels that we were finally allowed to see at the downtown cinema. I once made myself sick eating Pep cereal because I was trying to save enough box tops to earn a model airplane. I spent hours in my room building warplanes and daydreaming of fighting the enemy. In my daydreams I was a hero like General Wing.

I saw my father even less during the war. By this time he had been appointed to the Vermont Supreme Court. Each Monday he took the bus to Montpelier, where he stayed at the Pavilion Hotel while court was in session. His stated reason was gas rationing, but it was a habit he continued long after the war ended. Simply put, my father was a frugal man, and it was less expensive to stay in Montpelier than to travel back and forth—both in terms of time and money. Another way he sought to save money was to raise laying chickens in a coop we had in the backyard during the war. The problem was he wasn't around to clean and tend the chickens; I was.

When letters arrived from General Wing, there was often a message for me, wishing me a happy birthday or telling me some little story about the general's exploits. I had to wait until Father got home to open them, of course. I still treasure those letters from the Philippines or New Guinea, with their six-cent bomber stamps and the general's hand-penned message at the top. On one, dated August 14, 1944, the general had drawn a tropical scene and written, "From under the Southern Cross." Another, sent from Guadalcanal, told of how he had cut his leg while opening K rations with his knife. He warned me to be careful when I used my knife. His letters provided lots of grist for the mock battles the neighborhood kids fought.

There was a feeling of danger and excitement to the war years. At its height, most of the kids on our street, including my sister Mary, the Guilds, Jean Nichols, and Tom and Dot Paul, organized a circus to raise money for the Bundles for Britain relief. Mary, Tom, and I were clowns in the circus, which got a big write-up, complete with photographs, in the *Rutland Herald*.

When General Wing arrived home on November 5, 1945, the city held the largest parade in its history. There had been parades for the 43rd Division all over New England, but this was the culmination, the grand finale: The general was home. Reporters from Boston and Providence covered the event. General Jacob L. Devers, chief of the army ground forces, flew to Rutland to personally bestow the Distinguished Service Medal on General Wing. In the parade, I carried the flag for the local Boy Scout troop—even though I was still a Cub Scout. I'm sure the general or my father had something to do with that. But my friends didn't suspect any favoritism and were mightily impressed when, as we passed the grandstand, the general shouted out, "Hi there, Jimmy."

In the weeks after General Wing's return, my father often visited with him at the Wing home or at the country club, or the general would stop by our house. I was in awe. Once, father brought me to a camp on nearby Lake Bomoseen where General Wing, exhausted from the war, was resting. I was so overwhelmed by the man that I couldn't say a word. I froze. I was a quiet kid anyhow, and the fact that I was standing in front of the great commander, my hero, didn't help to loosen my tongue. Father was disappointed in me, as he sometimes was, but I suspect he was also a little pleased that I had shown so much respect for the general.

About this time the *Rutland Herald* ran a photo of me, Malcolm, and another friend, Jackie Stetson, digging a foxhole in the Wings' backyard. The caption said, "When these three Kingsley Avenue admirers of Maj. Gen. Leonard F. Wing learned that their idol was experiencing trouble in resting well since his return home, they produced shovels and dug a foxhole in the garden of the Wing home. They figured he'd be more comfortable sleeping outdoors than in a soft bed. The idea appealed to the Vermont hero apparently, for he is shown supervising the project." In the photo, I'm wearing a navy sailor's hat that, at the time, was a favorite possession. Another was the Japanese sword that the general had brought back from the war. I gave it to my son, named Leonard in the general's honor, when he reached high school.

Not long after he arrived home, General Wing passed away. Dead of a presumed heart attack. I was lying in bed not yet asleep although it was about ten P.M. when I heard the phone ring downstairs, then the slamming of the front door. I raced to the window and saw the door closing at the Wings' home across the way. A car arrived and a man ran into the house, carrying a bag. Much later, a van arrived and two men went into the house carrying a stretcher. When they finally came out, there was a shape on that stretcher covered with a blanket. No one had to tell me my hero was gone. But much later, when I was a military man myself, I got to see the Philippines that General Wing had written me about. During a two-week tour of active duty thirty-five years after General Wing's death, in January 1981, President Ferdinand Marcos and his military advisers told me personally of their appreciation of the men of the 43rd Division and of General Wing in particular.

But there was little solace for my family and me that year. At Memorial Day, when a special service was held at the cemetery on Main Street, I was the one asked to play echo to the taps. I was ready to break down but I kept playing without making a mistake. I remember the day so vividly that in my mind I often compare it to the day we heard of the bombing of Pearl Harbor. Both were clear, blue-sky days, but on this day all the veterans were gathered around us, row after row of them, crying for General Wing and so many others.

What is there to say of school? I was a good student. I didn't dare not be. But I wasn't a studier. Fortunately, I didn't really need to be. I spent fourth grade in the closet, being punished along with some of my pals from Kingsley Avenue. Over the course of the year, we got rid of four teachers—all young and inexperienced, and we took advantage of each and every one of them, throwing things, sitting on our desks and refusing to get down, laughing when they cried. We were downright cruel. It's not a proud chapter in my life. What can I say? I was skinny, gangly, and the ringleader of a bunch of rascals. My mother adored me. My father wasn't often home. Luckily, I eventually got over pulling those pranks.

Maybe it was the steadying influence of Grandfather Nicholas. He taught me how to use all sorts of tools, not just saws and hammers but drafting tools as well. I loved working with my hands. With his help, I converted part of the basement of the Rutland house into a woodworking shop and my obsession with model airplanes turned into a full-blown hobby. The other boys and I built planes with rubber-band engines that became more and more sophisticated the older we got.

My mother, sister, and I visited my mother's parents every summer. Their house in Glen Cove was small, like an English cottage. My grandmother Laura Hausman was a great cook with a big heart, very warm and affectionate. The atmosphere in their house was very different from ours, more relaxed and warm. Every day my grandfather and I would walk to Hempstead Harbor to look at boats or dig for clams. He loved to sketch boats going in and out of the harbor while I watched. I wanted to be an architect just like him. Designing runs in our family. One of my great-great-uncles was Baron Haussmann, the designer of Paris. How's that for a claim to fame, many times removed? When and if I retire, I plan to research the history of this ancestor.

If I had any philosophical conversations as a child, they were with my grandfather. Our talks never felt contrived or forced; I knew intrinsically that I could trust him with any confidence. I was a big Brooklyn Dodger fan in part because my great-grandfather had been born on a Brooklyn farm. My grandfather took me to my first live baseball game—in Brooklyn at Ebbets Field.

My relationship with my grandfather gave me practical aptitude, but the Hausmans, including my mother's sister Doris, spoiled me a little, too. Their only son had lived just eighteen months, so I was particularly special to the family. When I was about eleven, I wanted a dog in the worst way, but my father had said no. One day, Aunt Doris called to say she had put a dog on the train and that I was to have it for my birthday. My father would have nothing to do with it but somehow she prevailed. I met that train with all the excitement of a boy with a dream come true. There was a Kerry blue terrier, full grown but still young and, best of all, already house-trained. Two weeks later the dog started turning wildly in circles. When we took him to the veterinarian, we were told he had distemper and had to be put down. I was heartbroken and cried for weeks, but no other dog was allowed in our household. I did get to keep a cat, an orange tabby and Persian mix named Patrick that I loved with all my heart. Father hated that cat, and the cat must have known it. Patrick's favorite chair was Father's favorite chair, and Patrick's long hair did not go well on Father's wool suits. Father was always swatting a sleeping Patrick out of his chair. One day he came home and found that Patrick had peed on his seat. He discovered this by sitting down. Father was so livid he chased Patrick through the house, but I caught him and hid down in the cellar with him in my arms until Father had calmed down or gone to play cards.

I don't mean to say that my father was a tyrant. He was simply a man who had an important job to do and wanted to spend his spare time as he liked, with as little stress or bother as possible. As I've said, he did take me fishing on occasion. He'd wear his fishing outfit, complete with waders and fisherman's vest; I'd be in my regular clothes, freezing as I waded into the frigid water but loving the brief moments of camaraderie. We once went on a fishing trip way up north along the Missisquoi River, a wild place full of rattling woodpeckers and grouse with the river sinewy and rich with fish. That was a good time, the most time we ever spent together. I think my lasting love of the outdoors is in part mixed up with those brief moments of intimacy with my father. At the same time, however, I know that my father's inability or lack of desire to communicate with me and his deficiency when it came to showing affection or intimacy contributed to my own shortcomings in this area. I've been told many times that I lack the simple ability to carry on a social conversation. It's true. I don't like chitchat. Nor am I very adept at expressing my deepest emotions, even when I sorely desire to do so. Perhaps I should blame my father, but I don't. He was who he was and I am who I am. So many events outside our control make us the people we become; by the time we're adults it's often too late to really change.

Father believed in the value of work. I got my first job at age nine, opening doors during the Christmas shopping season at Wilson's Clothing Store downtown. I wore my brown suit and my galoshes over my shoes, looking quite grown-up. Wilson's was a fantastic place with the heads of all sorts of exotic animals mounted on the wall at ceiling height. My job was to greet people and tell them where they might find an item. But I was still a kid, and would sneak away from the front door on occasion to gawk at the animal heads or to put my feet in a kind of X-ray machine they used to see if a shoe fit properly.

I had a lot of jobs growing up. It was the only way I had pocket money. Besides Wilson's, I worked as a stock clerk in Rudolph's Jewelry Store and as a bicycle delivery boy. When I was older, I ran the refreshment stand at the skating rink at Rotary Field. I may have been a bit too thrifty and sometimes kept the hot dogs overlong. I'm lucky I never poisoned anyone. Once, when I was about fifteen, I got a call from the football coach that Norman Rockwell wanted a model. Would I like to pose for the famous painter? I told the coach I couldn't do it; I had to work. When I saw the final result I was glad I hadn't given up a day's pay to model. There was my pal Billy Farwell immortalized by Rockwell as a youngster with big ears and a big nose, which Billy did not have. He was a good-looking boy. I figured Rockwell would have had a heyday with my awkward looks. Actually, I wasn't as bad-looking as I imagined I was. When I look at photographs today of myself as a kid, I'm always surprised to see that I wasn't homely at all. Reality matters little in these situations, however. It's what you believe that matters. I learned early to accept my ungainliness.

Sports gave me a place to feel good about myself, especially as my parents were far from athletic. I skied early, by age seven or eight, first going down Kingsley Avenue on skis that were quite primitive by today's standards. Later, when a group of ski enthusiasts put a rope tow down Pico Mountain, the Guild boys, the Shaws, and I spent whole days pulling ourselves up and skiing down the mountain.

I loved to hike and camp. And my friends and I went on long treks into the woods. I wasn't much for studying but I enjoyed reading about the outdoors and Vermont history. Often, when we set off on a hike, we were in search of some place we had read about. We hiked to Rocky Pond and Muddy Pond in Rutland, to North Pond along the Long Trail, the oldest hiking path in America, and to lakes and ponds and battlefields as much as forty miles away. I had learned to camp and hike under the tutelage of Craig Perkins, our Troop 9 Boy Scout leader. Everyone called him Pinky, Pinky Perkins. Later, when I was in Congress and placed in charge of helping to get the District of Columbia schools back on track, I used Pinky as my role model of a good teacher. He was a very thoughtful man who never talked down to the troop members. Everything he had us do was a learning experience. If we were at Chittenden Dam, he would ask us whether there would be more energy generated from taking water from the top of the dam or the bottom. We would have to come up with the answer then defend our thought process. He was one of the first people who impressed me not only with the idea that learning could be fun and useful but that young people would perform better if treated with respect.

In sixth grade I was the captain of the baseball team and arranged an interschool competition. My friend George Hansen, whom I had met in Sunday school when we were in kindergarten, loves to tell the story of our early competitions in these sixth-grade matches. I went to Lincoln School near my home; George attended Dana on the other side of Main Street. My team was really up for the game. Unfortunately we were a little too up. The game was called at 49-0 with my team having the 49. George has never let me forget it.

By the time we got to Rutland High School our teams were often the winners of the state championship, or in the running, year after year. I particularly liked football and track and field and also played on the basketball team. All this, as you might guess, was routinely recorded in the *Rutland Herald.* Later, when I began my political life, I came to appreciate the name recognition that came from all the articles that had been written about me and not simply because I was my father's son. Or maybe that was the illusion I allowed myself to harbor. Perhaps I wouldn't have received so much press attention if I'd been someone else's son. Regardless, it's fun to read those articles now. In one, I'm described as someone "who would never be chosen as a 'typical athlete' on appearances." It goes on to say that I "was a Rutland first stringer just because [I] didn't know what it meant to quit." I think that was meant as a compliment. In another article, I'm shown in my football gear in the hike position with the caption, "Gentleman Jim." The accompanying article says, "When Jim first reported for varsity athletics as a freshman four years ago, the coaches were tempted to pass him by. He didn't appear put together the right way to make a good athlete. But at long last Jim has pulled himself up by the bootstraps. He has what it takes."

As for girls, I had female friends with whom I hung out at the Teen Center, which my sister and I had helped create by convincing the local Rotary Club to let us use a clubhouse they owned. And I loved the dances—I thought I was a good dancer, I've since been informed differently—but I never had a steady girlfriend. I was awful shy, and sometimes I'd cover up for that with an odd bravado. Besides, I thought going steady was silly—and a waste of money. After all, I was my father's son.

By high school, I and the other boys from Kingsley Avenue, joined by Hansen and a few more, had a political gang we called The Machine. I ran for class president at Rutland High School four times, and despite our confident moniker, I lost all four times, though never by more than six votes. One of my opponents during these years was Bernie Rome, who later became a personal friend and strong ally in the Republican Party. So I had political ambitions even then, but I always made it a point to never say anything bad about my competition. My campaign signs said it all: "If you can't say something nice, don't say anything at all."

Maybe my classmates didn't know what to make of me. I never wanted to be a Goody Two-shoes and had a bit of the rebel in me. Once I set off a stink bomb in a class and then ran to the bathroom. My father had pushed me to go to Phillips Exeter Academy, his alma mater, but I had refused. Perhaps it was an aversion to following in his footsteps. Or, perhaps, it was that I felt comfortable where I was, that in Rutland I could pull off the balancing act of being the good son and occasionally allowing the scamp in me a little free rein. Still, it's clear I got away with a lot. For example, for reasons I no longer recall, but no doubt because of some shenanigan, I had been blackballed from going to Boys State, the annual mock senate and leadership conference that a select group of high school boys are sent to. But Principal Guild got the parent-teachers' association to send me anyhow as an add-on.

Still, I couldn't push it too far. I was always very aware of my father's position as the top judge in Vermont—and so was everyone else. Our license plate was simply the number 9. In Vermont, like most states, the governor has license number 1; the lieutenant governor has 2 and so on to show the order of power. Number 9 definitely caught too much attention for a young man who was still getting over his awkwardness at the wheel. I agonized over picking up a girl with that car.

Sports and music provided me with my own identity. In my senior year we were not only state champions in football and basketball but also runners-up in baseball and track. In track, I placed second in the mile and third in the half mile. Our biggest thrill was when our team was chosen to represent the north in the North-South High School football championship to be held in Atlanta, Georgia. Unfortunately, or probably fortunately, our football team was also our basketball team and we were in full season and therefore unable to attend.

I got my love of music from my mother. I played baritone horn and also sang at the all-state music festival. My love of singing remained a lifelong hobby, straight through to my tenure with the Singing Senators, that quartet of Republicans who came to a sad ending shortly before I announced my decision to leave the Republican Party. In high school, four of us guys—John Hartigan, George Cady, Al McPherson, and myself—formed a kind of barbershop quartet that we called the Harmogenizers. We got paid $10 a performance—that's $10 between the four of us. We sometimes sang for the men's club dinners, like the Elks and the Eagles, or at local parties. Times were easy then, or at least they appeared to be.

I don't know where I got it into my head that I had to go to Yale. Yale had a fantastic football team, although I didn't harbor any illusions on that regard, and I had been cheering for The Eli from almost as soon as I could differentiate one team from another. Because of my admiration for my grandfather, I wanted in the worst way to be a civil engineer and architect, and Yale had a great reputation as an engineering school. But I think I was simply taken with the idea of Yale. I never considered applying anywhere else. Today, I can see how young and certain I was, thinking that believing a thing made it so. From this vantage point I also see that there is great truth to that notion. Belief in one's dreams is a powerful tool, one I took to instinctively but later came to rely on with greater consciousness.

Of course, if I had followed Father's recommendation and attended Phillips Exeter, my entrance to Yale would have been almost guaranteed. Instead, I waited expectantly for my admissions letter and was absolutely thrilled when it came. I felt I had achieved that goal entirely on my own.

One of the downfalls of growing up in a fairly insulated place was that one could sometimes be overly trusting—some would call it naive—about human nature. My first big lesson in this regard occurred shortly after high school graduation, when a harmless outing with one of my pals almost ended not only my chances of going to Yale but also my life.

My friend Fred Hyland had been admitted to Cornell and asked me to accompany him on an orientation visit. I was always up for a road trip, so we set off, thumbing across Vermont and into New York. We had gotten a few short rides that took us toward Ithaca when a hardtop convertible with three teens pulled up next to us and offered us a ride all the way to Cornell, which we thought was great luck.

I waited in the library while Fred registered, then we went back to the highway to hitchhike back to Vermont. Lo and behold, who came along but the same three teenagers in the hardtop convertible.

"Well, where're ya' going now?" one of the teens asked. They said they would take us to Albany, which was a good deal, as the New York state capital was an ideal place from which to get rides north to Vermont.

I was sitting center front between the driver and one of the passengers, Fred was in the back, and we were sailing along. I was a little concerned about the speed but I was trying to be cool and kept my thoughts to myself. We stopped for gas and then very quickly got back on the road. But now I had a queasy feeling. I didn't remember seeing anyone pay for the gas. We were on a three-lane highway, not the big interstate that now runs up New York's eastern border. Everyone was chatting away but I had my eye on the speedometer as it climbed—60, 70, 75, 80, 85 miles an hour. We were going 90 when we came to a red light. Damn if the driver didn't speed right through. I was really worried now, squished down in my seat, when in the rearview mirror I saw a motorcycle policeman chasing after us. I was thinking surely the driver would stop now; I for one was going to get out of the car and not get back in. But no, he didn't stop. The driver seemed to know his way around, or at least I thought he did, because he was taking back roads at breakneck speed with the motorcycle cop hard on our heels. Then we lost the cop. I started praying the driver would drive a bit down the road and stop so Fred and I could get out.

All of a sudden we screeched to a stop. We had driven down a dead-end street. The driver threw the car into reverse and started backing up, driving like a madman. We hadn't lost that police officer; he'd known all along we were headed down a dead-end street and had simply parked his motorcycle to block our exit. When the driver careened out of the dead end, he almost hit the cop. I dove out of the way of the window when I saw the police officer pull out his gun and start shooting. I was yelling, "Look, he's shooting at us." I was flabbergasted by all of this but, like an idiot, I had no sense of fear. Everyone else was ducking while I was watching the officer shoot at us. Fortunately, he was aiming for our tires. The last thing I saw was the speedometer hit 80 as we spun out on the dirt road and went rolling. The car landed upside down and kept going on its hood for what seemed an eternity. When it finally stopped, we couldn't get out. We had to break a window. My heart was pounding and I was probably pretty shook up, but I wasn't thinking about any of that; I was just glad we had finally stopped. Next thing I knew, the three teens were running away and yelling, "Scram, it's a hot car."

Fred and I decided it was best to get ourselves back to the highway and hitchhike as far away as we could, but then we realized that the police would be looking for the driver *and* the passengers, and that meant us, too. We soon found we were right. Hiding behind some bushes, we could see police everywhere. We crawled through a culvert to get to the other side of the road, where we hunkered down in the damp pipe, quaking in our shoes and trying to figure out what to do next. Finally, Fred said, "We haven't done anything wrong. Let's just give ourselves up." I hesitated at first—what if my father found out?—but after some thought I agreed.

We hailed down a police cruiser and tried to tell the officers we were simply hitchhiking back to Vermont when we got involved in the whole mess. One cop yelled gruffly, "Get in" as he pushed us roughly into the cruiser. Another officer grabbed my arm and twisted it behind my back, hurting me something wicked as he screamed right in my ear, "Where are those other guys?" I was trying to tell him I didn't even know who they were but he wasn't listening. I hated to use my father's name and truly refrained from doing so, but I considered this an acceptable exception and so I told him my father was a Vermont Supreme Court judge.

The next thing I knew we were driving into somebody's yard and getting pushed into a house. At first I thought, great, they believed me and now they're getting us to a phone or a safe place for the night. It was midnight by now and both Fred and I were exhausted. As it turned out, we were at the home of a justice of the peace and he wasn't interested in our story any more than the cops had been. He kept telling us to quiet down and not wake his family. Within minutes we were charged with attempted murder of a police officer, resisting arrest, grand larceny, leaving the scene of an accident, and Lord knows what else. We protested our innocence but the JP just told us to shut up, then ordered the cops to take us "to the hotel." There was a brief moment of hope before we realized "hotel" was a euphemism for the Albany County Jail.

Now, you've got to imagine what this jail was like. Here we were, two seventeen-year-olds from Rutland, Vermont, who thought we were old enough and savvy enough to hitchhike around New England but in reality we were just two young sprouts still wet behind the ears, and now we were being thrown into dark, individual cells no bigger than closets, each with a bed covered with a stinky mattress, a sink, and a toilet. I was getting more concerned and frightened all the time as the men around us yelled out, "Hey, number twenty-three, what are you in for?" Fred started yelling back, "We're innocent," but I quickly hushed him, thinking our charges might offer us some protection if our fellow inmates thought we were tough characters. Thus, when they asked me, "Hey, number ten, what are you in for?" I responded, "Attempted murder, grand larceny, and resisting arrest." All the while, I was thinking about my stern father back in Rutland but also cracking up because my number on the Rutland High School football team had been ten!

You know the story about having the right to one free phone call? We didn't get ours. Eventually, overcome with fatigue, I stretched out on the bed, hoping to sleep until the morning. But within minutes I began to itch like crazy. It wasn't my imagination: The bed was infested with bedbugs. I sat up the rest of the night on the toilet. At 6:30 A.M. all the cell doors opened and a prison guard called us to breakfast. Fred and I filed out and joined the other men, an assortment of different colors and sizes that were a bit beyond the scope of our usual companions, at a long steel table on which each person had been doled out cornflakes and water, white bread and jelly. I wasn't exactly eating at warp speed when a huge hand grabbed me by my neck and dragged me back to my cell. Breakfast was apparently over. "Where's my phone call?" I asked as the metal door slammed shut behind me. "You're not allowed one," the guard said and stomped away. When the doors opened again for our brief time outdoors, the other inmates immediately gave us nicknames. Fred was Shorty and I, of course, was Slim. Fred was a little slow on the uptake—forgive me

Fred, but it's true—and he kept saying things that upset the other inmates. I was simply trying to keep a low profile while I figured out how to get us out of there. I was mulling this over when I heard a shout and ran to find that this big, 250-plus-pound inmate had Fred hoisted over the bars with his own belt—they hadn't taken ours away—around his neck. Fortunately, I got help from the other inmates and got Fred down.

I don't know if it was true or not, but one of the other inmates told me the guy had killed someone just a month previously and that no one dared squeal on him. By now I was feeling pretty desperate and for the first time began to understand the meaning of freedom. But again fortune was with me. I made friends with one of the inmates, a quiet guy who was due to get released that day. I got some paper and an envelope and wrote a letter to my father that said:

> Albany County Prison
> Waterviliet, NY
> July 31, 1952
>
> Dear Dad,
>
> Fred and I have been detained in Albany County Prison. Coming home from Ithaca we were picked up by 3 boys in a stolen car. Outside Schenectady, NY, this car was pursued by police and was in an accident from which we escaped unhurt. It was at this time we learned the car was stolen. As we did not desire to be left with this car when the 3 boys ran, we also went, running in another direction and were stopped by police. We told them what we knew concerning the matter. For obvious reasons we were placed in jail awaiting a grand larceny charge.
>
> We have written this letter in the event that if we do not reach you by phone, we trust you will know what to do.
>
> James Jeffords

I had no money to give to my jail buddy for his help in mailing the letter, but he had taken a liking to the sports shirt I was wearing. I literally gave him the shirt off my back in return for the promise that he would get a stamp and mail my letter to my father. I had just a T-shirt on but it was July so I wasn't concerned.

About five P.M. we were taken out of the jail by a police officer. He didn't tell us where we were going, just drove about ninety miles an hour to the courthouse, where our charges were read again and we entered our pleas. Once again I told our story, who we were and so on. They must have believed us this time, because the judge just gave us a lecture about hitchhiking and then simply released us. We had to hitchhike home, of course.

By now our story had been on the front page of the *Knickerbocker News*, under the headline "Five Seized in District Gun Chase." The sub-head read, "Patrolman Says Stolen Car Tried to Injure Him." The article said, "Five youths were being held at three communities today for questioning in the theft of two cars and a spectacular escape under gunfire of a Schenectady motorcycle patrolman whom they allegedly tried to run down when he cornered them momentarily at 1:30 A.M. today."

It went on to explain the dramatic episode that followed our accident, alleging that the car we had been in, which had Missouri plates, had been stolen two days previously in Lake George, a resort community near the New York/Vermont border. After our car wreck, the three teens had stolen yet another car, one belonging to a motor route carrier for the *Knickerbocker News!*

By the time we were on our way home, our names had been released to the press and we were being described as two Rutland youths who "inadvertently [got] involved in the affair when they hitched a ride in the allegedly stolen car. . . . Hyland and Jeffords were released Thursday afternoon after questioning by authorities established they were hitch-hikers who did not know the car was stolen. The adventure is a reversal of the usual hitchhiker complaint," the story concluded. "Traditionally, the ride-thumber is the one who gets the driver in trouble."

A friend of my father's had read of our ordeal and called him, so by the time we finally arrived home, he was fully aware of our misadventure. He lectured us about the dangers of hitchhiking and made us promise not to do it anymore. Of course, I didn't stop. I hitched all over the country in the next few years and nothing like that ever happened to me again.

But the event did come back to haunt me. Later that summer I had to return to Albany for a military physical because I had been selected for

Navy ROTC at Yale. I couldn't lie when I read the question "Have you ever been arrested? If yes, provide details." It took me awhile to put it all down. Hours later, the military was still checking my story. Plus, I had felt a cold coming on that morning and had drunk a lot of water. When the medic finally tested my urine, he loudly proclaimed, "Damn, I think we hit a spring. Boy, you're pissing water." They ended up keeping me overnight so they could check out my story and my urine. Eventually, both cleared the test and I was on my way to the next phase of my life.

There was, however, a happy outcome to the event. My trust in human nature was restored when the letter I had written my father arrived at my parents' house. I've kept it to this day as proof that trust is often rewarded.

CHAPTER 2

Leaving Home

I WAS MISERABLE my first months at Yale. It wasn't that I missed home; I was more than happy to step out on my own. What I missed was the sense of surety that I had had on Kingsley Avenue in Rutland, that small circle of friends who had known me all my life and whom I knew as well.

Maybe I missed the playing fields where I knew every inch of real grass, and the classrooms, small and humble as they were, where I had excelled without really having to try. Yale was quite different. Of the Guild boys, Jim had been my best friend growing up, even though he was a couple of years older than I. Now I was glad to have Malcolm also traveling to Yale. We had agreed not to room together our first year to give us both the opportunity to meet new friends and spread our wings, but as I felt more and more uncomfortable among the rich prep kids around me, I realized how lucky I was to have a friend like Malcolm on campus. Malcolm and I both received ROTC scholarships but Malc also had an athletic scholarship as he was All New England in high school, thus he was busy those first few weeks as I struggled to find my place. I found my fellow students snobbish. All they seemed to care about was where you'd gone to prep school and whom you knew. I had no interest in going out for a fraternity—maybe that was self-protection, as I probably didn't expect to get chosen for one. I guessed my father had known what he was talking about after all.

There was, of course, the issue of money. My father's salary as supreme court justice wasn't much more than Yale's tuition, and my sister, Mary, was attending Wheelock College in Boston. I had earned a full scholarship and received a little spending money—I think it was $50 a month—from NROTC. So if I wanted pocket money I had to earn it, which I did by raking leaves or shoveling snow for professors. Meanwhile, my roommate, a kid from Danbury, Connecticut, studied all the time and went home on weekends. He simply wasn't much company.

I soon learned that Yale was more demanding than Rutland High School, where I rarely studied. I got a reality check early on when my first calculus midterm grade came back with a grade of 20. I ended up with an 80 average in that course.

But my early unhappiness at Yale involved more than just having to study harder. It was something bigger. It had dawned on me that I was never going to be a part of Yale, at least not in the way I had been a part of Rutland, Vermont. I'd achieved my dream but the dream turned out to be a bit different from what I had imagined. I think it was my first major disillusionment. But, low as I often felt, I never thought of quitting. That was not an option, not for Judge Jeffords's son.

In the end, I found a way to make it work for me—by working hard enough at my studies so that I could take Fridays off. I spent most of my weekends on the road, hitching to the University of Vermont to visit Billy Farwell or George Hansen, to Cornell where George Cady and Fred Hyland were going to school, to Middlebury to visit John Webber, or to MIT to hang out with John Hartigan and Al McPherson. I planned these weekends around dances and parties; my buddies were nice enough to make sure I had a date.

I also eventually gave up my goal of becoming an architect. I did best in statistics. The subject just worked with my brain and seemed like such a useful tool to have. As time went on, it became apparent to me that my natural ability was in management and business, and I eventually switched my major from engineering to industrial administration. That meant, of course, that it would be unlikely I would follow in my grandfather's footsteps, yet I had come to terms with the fact that I just didn't have a natural aptitude in that regard.

By the end of freshman year I'd developed a cadre of Yale friends. I played tennis and basketball on intermural teams. My grades continued to improve, and I adapted to the Yale culture. Well, at least I adapted enough to fit in.

I was nonetheless quite happy when summer finally arrived and with it my plebe training with the navy on the destroyer escort the USS *Thaddeus T. Parker*, which took us on a month-and-a-half-long cruise to Rio de

Janeiro, stopping along the way at ports in Trinidad and Colombia. I loved life on the ship even though I was slow to accept the principle of doing what I was told. My independent streak got in the way of taking orders or following protocol. But I had luck on my side.

The night of July 3, for example, we were invited to a party where young women would be wanting to dance with us. I loved to dance and this party was great fun. Sometime about nine P.M., one of the young women's chaperones announced, "Tomorrow is your Fourth of July. We've got a celebration planned for you." I knew we were supposed to be back on ship by ten P.M., but I didn't want to leave the party, especially with our hosts recognizing our Independence Day. So, I didn't leave. A bit later I realized that most of the plebes like me had left and it was primarily upperclassmen from the Naval Academy who had remained, and none of them was from my ship. Nonetheless, the upperclassmen told my shipmate and me not to worry; they'd make sure we didn't get in trouble. Not wanting to chance it, my shipmate returned to the *Parker.* I stayed. I justified my presence by saying it would be insulting to my hosts to leave.

When I did arrive back on ship in the wee hours of the morning, dog-tired but still full of life, I was greeted by the officer in charge who ordered me to captain's mast in the morning to answer to a lieutenant. I was charged with a Class-A offense. That was fairly serious; you can get thrown out of the navy for a Class-A offense. Fortunately, one of the upperclassmen who had been at the party came to my defense and I was eventually cleared.

The next fall, however, when we went back to school and looked at the list of all NROTC members and their status, I read that J. M. Jeffords had been disenrolled. I really freaked out. I thought it had something to do with the charge that had been dropped. I later found out it wasn't me who had been disenrolled but someone with the same initials and last name who attended the University of Virginia. With an uncommon name like Jeffords, having two joining the navy was an incredible coincidence. I'm going to trace him down some day.

I had promised Aunt Doris that I would visit her friends in Rio and got permission to do so. But on the way back to the ship, I got a little lost. Fortunately, I ran into a Brazilian marine who said he would show me the way to my ship. We got on a trolley car with big metal wheels that ran on a rail. The trolley was full so I found myself standing on the front of the car when the marine suddenly realized we were on the wrong car. He jumped off and I went to follow him. But as I jumped, the car made a sudden turn. When I landed, I pitched forward and fell onto the tracks. I looked up and saw the big steel wheels of the trolley about to crush me, but my uniform coat was caught by a protective bar, like a cattle guard on a railroad engine, and I was dragged in front of the wheel. Even today, I can close my eyes and see that wheel about to crush me. Finally, the driver stopped the trolley. I yanked my coat free and waved it as the trolley full of people stared, mouths open, while I walked away. The marine took me back to the ship where I promptly went into shock. It was the only time in my life when I came close to fainting. I knew that I had closely escaped a brutal death.

There were other shocks in Rio, but they were of the culture variety—and I shared them with the other plebes: prostitutes, poverty, the disparity between the haves and have-nots. The first time some child ran up to me and shouted, "Sister suckie for a dime," I was shocked. I was still very wet behind the ears, but even so, to see a child offering his sister for prostitution was beyond anything any of us were prepared to see or hear.

But as we traveled from port to port, I also got to see many sides of many different cultures. It all made a great impression on me.

By the end of the summer I had learned how to be an enlisted man. I had scrubbed the deck. I had chipped paint. I learned navigation and spent many hours in the engine room. I took my gunnery practice. And as we crossed the Equator, I officially became a shellback. They kept you busy. The food was bad and the living conditions spartan—a bunk, no private toilets. I loved every minute of it.

I grew up that summer. When I returned to Yale in the fall, I was much more worldly. I had fallen in love with the idea of the world, with its diversity, with travel, and with the concept of experiential learning. I also felt comfortable in my own skin. I had nearly lost my life; I'd spent the summer working hard with other men on a ship. I felt confident about my presence at Yale and began to really get into my classes. Malcolm and I also had decided to room together. Jim Glenn, our other roommate, is still a good friend. Through another Yale friend, Jim Donne, a student from England, I had become a member of the Yale cricket team. Ours was not an official college squad, but we had interesting times playing teams organized by several foreign embassies and U.S. cricket teams from

Philadelphia and Staten Island, New York. My only claim to fame was that I was never wicketed, if there is such a word. If you know cricket, you know that means I was last in the batting order. Some would consider that the worst position, but I took it as a lucky break since the batter before me always got out first.

During the second summer the navy sent me to Corpus Christi, Texas, to learn how to fly. I enjoyed it, but I knew by the end of the summer that I was not cut out for flying. I had started thinking about law school and maybe some sort of public service. My ideas were still forming but I knew I wanted a leadership role and began to explore what that might be. It had begun to dawn on me that serving as an officer on a ship might provide the experience I would need if I decided to go into politics.

The best experience of these years was my third summer, when I was assigned to a navy cruiser patrolling the Mediterranean. During that summer we got a week or two off in Europe. I spent it mostly by myself, hitching around and exploring places I'd only read about in my history books. I was looking for experiences I couldn't have in Vermont—flamenco dancers in Barcelona, riding a bicycle around Majorca, eating in an outdoor cafe in Milan. I was constantly amazed at how receptive people were to me, even though I didn't speak their language.

Back at school, I was even more comfortable with myself. People sometimes look down on these ROTC experiences, but I think they can do as much, if not more, to educate a person about the ways of the world as college courses. Of course, I'd found other ways to fit in as well.

During my final year of college I was finally in a situation economically and gradewise where I felt I could actually do what most college students took for granted—take part in Spring Break. I owe my great experience to my friend Peter Caldwell, who had grown up in New York City and had become a very good friend by senior year. We hitchhiked one weekend up to MIT, where my friends had fixed us up with dates. While there, our dates told us they were going to Spring Break in Daytona Beach and invited us to visit them if we could make our way to Florida.

We decided to take them up on it. Peter and I, along with some other friends, went car hunting. Following my motto of never spending more than necessary or of doing things the easy way, we found a 1937 Chrysler four-door sedan for sale for $35. We learned quickly that we needed a lot of tire repair equipment along with us. Every few hundred miles we'd blow a tire. Our rear tires had more patches than tire, but we made the trip and met up with our young lady friends, who, after some time, allowed us to bring our sleeping bags into their beach motel rooms. We had a great time of course and, believe it or not, limped back into New Haven driving that same car, albeit with several more blow-out patches. We then sold the car for $35.

During the last months of my senior year I began making plans for the next six years of my life. I would first complete my naval duty, something I was certainly looking forward to after all these years in school. But then it would be more schooling for me. I had decided to become a lawyer and had been accepted to Harvard Law School.

I should mention one social area where I did excel at Yale, and that was in the drinking contest held at the end of the school year between two competing colleges. I lived in Silliman College from my sophomore year on. Our rival was Timothy Dwight College. My position was anchor-man. The anchorman takes the first drink of beer, slams his glass down hard, and sends the glass to the next teammate, who then gulps his beer as quickly as possible. The anchorman also drinks the last beer. I had a special talent in this regard. I could straight throat the entire eight ounces of beer in one continuous swallow, making me near impossible to beat. My teammates discovered my skill the second year of the competition and put me in the anchor position from then on. We won the next two years.

I told you I hated to lose.

CHAPTER 3

Ships at Sea

IN JULY 1956 I received orders to board the USS *McNair* DD679 in New-port, Rhode Island. I drove my 1952 blue Plymouth from Rutland to Newport arriving sometime around midnight. After parking the car, I made my way to the ship, which was secured beside one of its sister ships, the *Sullivans*. As I approached the *McNair*, I saw on deck two rather large and angry sailors engaged in a serious knife fight. When they finally were separated by the ship's crew, Lieutenant Tom Topping drew a line across the deck to keep them apart, ordering one to stay forward and the other aft until they reported to captain's mast. I could not recall anything dur-ing my four years of NROTC training that covered how young officers should handle these types of situations. I concluded life aboard ship would not be boring.

The first thing I did was to go to the wardroom to get a cup of coffee. There, the duty steward informed me that I could make my own cup of coffee; he wasn't going to wait on me. I soon learned that discipline was not the only problem aboard the *McNair*. Operating efficiency and morale were also rather poor.

I was accustomed to the competition inherent in navy training and behavior aboard ship. Ships of each type are ranked within their squadrons and in the entire fleet. Each strives to be the best, earning the prized efficiency award, referred to as the Big E. Each department aboard a destroyer (gunnery, engineering, operations, and supply) vies for its own efficiency award. The combined rankings of all departments are weighed, with the ship having the overall best performance rating being designated the top ship in its squadron. Not only did the *McNair* rank last in its squadron of eight destroyers, but it was somewhere near the bottom of the whole U.S. Atlantic Fleet. Lucky me.

Whether it was coincidence or intentional on the part of the naval higher-ups who had observed us during the last six months, but there was a complete changeover in our roster of officers. These changes meant we had the opportunity to turn the *McNair*'s reputation and rating around—something that interested us greatly.

A number of the other junior officers reporting aboard shared my Ivy League background, and we got along very well socially and in the business of operating the ship. We shared college stories, hoisted brews together, and learned that the expertise each of us had acquired in ROTC allowed us to mesh together into a competent team. Collectively, without exactly putting it in words, we were determined to improve our ship's rating so we could earn the Big E.

The *McNair* was a 2,100-ton Fletcher-class destroyer that had been launched in November 1943. It had served in the Pacific Theater during the latter stages of World War II and had been decommissioned in May 1946, having won eight battle stars. It was recommissioned in July 1951 and operated briefly on the West Coast before coming to its home port of Newport, Rhode Island. I was assigned to the Gunnery Department and was an officer of the deck divisions. This meant I oversaw a crew of sailors who handled mooring lines, manned the guns, and did a lot of the seemingly endless chipping and painting that keeps the main deck and most visible parts of a ship looking good.

Ships are like any organization in which people have to rely on one another and tend to form a close camaraderie based simply on the fact that you're spending a heck of a lot of time together. Nicknames are common. My shipboard nickname was Jeff. Ships also have social order. One of the officers in my department was not an Ivy Leaguer. Salvatore Acquilino, who came aboard a month after I did, was what the navy calls a mustang—that's the term used for those who start as enlisted men and come up through the ranks. Sal had been involved in the Seaman to Admiral Program, joining the navy in 1946 and eventually being accepted to Officer Candidate School (OCS). He reported aboard the *McNair* immediately upon graduation and was assigned to head the Gunnery Department. In navy slang, he was the Gun Boss.

I mentioned earlier that the ship had not distinguished itself in performance, and nothing illustrated that better than the Gunnery Department prior to Sal's arrival. That summer, during training exercises, when the order was barked "Commence firing," not a sound could be heard from any of our five-inch guns. That was most embarrassing. Sal was adamant about changing that—and very quickly. He held constant drills, ensured that equipment was properly maintained, and made us proud to be a part of it. He would frankly have loved nothing better than to deploy his department's weapons under real battle conditions, and so we nicknamed him Salvo Sal.

Another major change in our officer corps was our new executive officer, the second in command aboard ship, Lieutenant Commander Thomas Harbin. He was also a mustang, but he had had submarine as well as destroyer experience, and quickly distinguished himself as someone we could look up to and admire. He had a can-do attitude and made sure that temperament was instilled in all of us.

Another thing the young officers admired about Harbin probably related to our not-too-distant college days and our macho attitudes. He could down a greater quantity of alcoholic beverages than we could, and yet still, at 0615, he'd be the first one up at reveille.

We also had a new commanding officer take over the ship that fall, Commander Wesley Gebert. Gebert was a graduate of the U.S. Naval Academy, where he had been a star quarterback. He had been commissioned just after the breakout of World War II, and served aboard ship in the Pacific. During the latter stages of the war he entered flight training, earned his wings, and served in a fighter squadron before returning to the shipboard navy for a few years, and eventually taking command of our vessel. The leadership of Gebert and Harbin was undoubtedly a significant reason our ship quickly began to climb from the bottom of the squadron.

That fall I was dispatched to antisubmarine warfare school for a few weeks to qualify as the ship's new ASW officer. Since locating and destroying enemy submarines and protecting other surface ships was a primary mission of the U.S. Navy's destroyer fleet, it was a big responsibility. To be honest, I was both pleased and a bit overwhelmed. I often had the added responsibility of shore duty, which meant that it fell on me to settle disputes, large and small, that occurred in our various ports. My acceptance to Harvard Law School had been noted. I took these responsibilities very seriously, both when I was judge or played the role of defense counsel.

After surviving a damp, windy, and cold winter in Rhode Island, mostly with the ship tied to the pier in Newport, we were looking forward to its deployment to warmer climes. We were initially scheduled to sail to the western Mediterranean in May, but the ship's orders were changed several times so that we traveled to the Azores, back up to and through the Straits of Gibraltar, and then through the western Mediterranean. There, we conducted numerous naval exercises at sea, and enjoyed stops in Palma, Majorca, and Piraeus, Greece, which afforded the opportunity for culture-embracing visits to Athens and its wonders. The *McNair* then had the distinction of becoming the first American warship to enter the Suez Canal since the canal had been closed by Egypt earlier in the year following the objections of France and Great Britain to that country's taking over its operation. We passed through and entered the Red Sea from the north.

When we reached Port Said, the Egyptian police contacted me late at night because a British seaman had had his knife stolen by a young Egyptian kid. The sailors were insisting that the kid be arrested and prosecuted. The Egyptian police explained that, under their laws, if found guilty, even for a first offense, the youngster's left hand would be cut off. I had no stomach for that outcome. So, given the assignment of convincing the British seaman to drop the charges, I put my relatively untested persuasive skills to the task. Fortunately, I was successful, but not until I spent several tedious hours pleading with the British chap who had charged the kid and patiently waiting for the booze in him to wear off.

While in Iskenderun, a port in Turkey, I had further opportunities to practice my negotiation skills, albeit in a situation for which I was not prepared. We had been told over and over again that Mustafa Kemal Atatürk, the founder of the Turkish Republic and its first president, was a hero to the Turkish people. The commanding officer and the embassy people had told us, "For God's sake, don't let anyone show offense to Atatürk." Wouldn't you know it, one of the sailors from another ship got loaded and pissed on a statue of Atatürk located in a local park. I had the job of negotiating him out of jail.

We also had stern instructions to stay away from houses of prostitution and were told the Turks would be quite insulted if we did anything sexual to a female, even suggestive. We had one fellow who apparently did not understand this or got it reversed. He fondled a woman's breasts. Within moments there was a near riot with about a hundred people shouting and screaming to hang him. The local authorities were ready to put him in jail for five years. I had to promise that we would punish him quite severely when we got him back to the ship. He was punished, but not as badly as he would have been treated in a Turkish prison—if he had survived.

Besides the chance to hone my negotiation skills, this portion of our cruise also afforded us the opportunity, one not particularly relished, to visit the port of Massaua in Eritrea, which we found somewhat hotter than most of us had envisioned hell. A side trip up the scenic railroad to Asmara for a brief escape from the desert heat was one of the few highlights of our visit to that port.

Four of us had the opportunity to go on a taxi safari into the desert to hunt trip gazelle. Our guide was a young boy of about twelve years of age. We got the driver of a 1937 German Maxwell taxicab to take us to the desert. To say we were a bit nervous with the enterprise—taking essentially what was a trail rather than a road into the desert to hunt one of the fastest animals on the planet—would be an understatement. Our confidence was badly shaken when our guide yelled, "Ariel, ariel, ariel," over and over, which we thought was their word for gazelle. I took out my binoculars excitedly, only to discover that the animals he was shouting about were actually donkeys. We proceeded on with the engine so overheated it was steaming. Eventually, ahead of us stood four gazelles, looking docilely at the four of us. We carefully got out of the cab, raised our rifles, and all fired on signal. My gun misfired. I was saved from the embarrassment of having missed as we watched the animals race away unharmed. Later in the day, though, my fellow *McNair* mates did shoot two gazelles. At the time, I was disappointed that I hadn't shot one; now, I'm glad I missed.

Hunting is one of those areas where my ideas have evolved over the years. I think it's fine to hunt for food if you need it, or to shoot overpopulated animals like deer to keep the herd healthy. But as I've matured, I've come to realize that simple sport-hunting and hunting for animals whose numbers are decreasing is just plain wrong.

It's hard to imagine today how nerve-racking and important it was to be the first U.S. military ship to navigate the Suez Canal. We did it on September 23, 1955. We expected to be received as heroes since it was the United States that had convinced the British to give up the canal. Instead, we had to fight off hundreds of Egyptians who came on board shouting, "Our canal. Get out." Ironically, a second mob of vendors also charged about the ship to sell everything from camel saddles to opium pipes. Out came the fire hoses. Finally, the police arrived. Things calmed down and only the vendors were allowed to stay.

The CIA came on board and tried to look like tourists rather than spies, taking photographs of defense positions along the canal. Why they thought tourists would look natural on a navy ship is beyond me. Our ship's pilot was on to their ruse and humorously started suggesting better vantage points for their photos. We got a good laugh at the CIA's expense.

We alleviated the tension with daily softball games between the officers and crew, boxing and basketball competitions against the crews of other destroyers as well as some of the larger tenders, oilers, and aircraft carriers we were periodically escorting. I volunteered to work with our basketball team and became the low-scoring player-coach.

I had invested my law school money in stocks and continued to save money from my pay toward my Harvard education. Shortly after our crossing through the Suez Canal to the Red Sea, I began to get nervous about the market. Being in the middle of momentous occasions made me realize that the market might not be as stable as I once thought it was, and I remembered that I had never put a stop-loss order on my stocks to protect them in case the market fell. I sent a message to my broker to do so, but, alas, my instincts were off by a few days. While my stop order was being processed, President Eisenhower had his heart attack and the stock market fell by 10 percent. Under the rules, the brokerage had to sell my stock at 10 percent loss. When President Eisenhower was out of danger, the market went back up, but I was already out a bunch of money. Great instincts; lousy timing.

Things turned much more positive when we left the Red Sea. During a visit to Venice, our officers and crew donated 100,000 lire to the children of an orphanage, and we were able to host forty of the children aboard ship for a party one afternoon. It's hard to explain how much a morale booster something like this can be after the tedium of days at sea.

But life aboard ship rarely remains dull. Before departing the Mediterranean we engaged in some very hairy day and night antisubmarine warfare exercise patrols, cruising perpendicular in a dense fog through the heavy traffic passing through the Straits of Gibraltar. Being senior watch officer, I had a lot of pressure on me and found the experience terrifying.

After final recreational stops in Barcelona and Gibraltar, we headed home, unfortunately by way of Argentia, Newfoundland. Our departure from that far-northern port was in a prolonged and violent storm that tested the stomachs of all onboard. To complicate matters, a lot of the officers and crew were not feeling well anyway, because the major souvenir we were able to bring back from this cruise was the Asian flu. Once a bug like that starts going around within the confined spaces of a destroyer, virtually everyone becomes infected. Our chief hospital corpsman, who was single-handedly trying to soothe and cure scores of fairly sick people, posted a bedsheet sign that read Saint Mary's Hospital in one of the sleeping compartments, where many of the crew were virtually unable to get out of their bunks.

All in all, the deployment had more enjoyable moments than depressing ones, and many of them were recorded in the Cruise Book that I and some others put together about our five-month adventure.

After our cold days at sea and in Newport, we were looking forward to a short reprieve from the weather. We were being sent to the base at Mayport, Florida, to conduct training maneuvers. The day we arrived in port, it was 40 degrees in Boston and 17 in Jacksonville! As soon as we tied up, a large contingent of officers and crew became engaged in a game of flag football that was so quickly becoming dangerous for all players that our executive officer wisely decided it should be shut down.

That was a good thing because only minutes thereafter the *McNair* received orders to depart immediately on a search-and-rescue mission for a downed fighter pilot somewhere off the coast. Everyone scrambled back aboard and we steamed out into a very dark night in exceedingly heavy seas to join another destroyer in the search. By the time the flier was located, the ocean had become so rough that we could not get our whaleboat alongside him to accomplish the rescue, but we were close by when a navy helicopter lowered a cable and plucked him from the sea.

Unfortunately, he slipped loose of the harness and fell back into the water, severely injuring his back. A second try was successful and he was secured and hoisted to safety.

One of our sailors, named Regan, had volunteered to go over the side of the ship, swim to the downed aviator, and help in the rescue in spite of the terrible weather conditions. Regan was utterly fearless in such circumstances and dedicated to duty, which otherwise could be described as a very likable discipline problem. He had a number of years of service behind him but was always getting into trouble of one sort or another, and thus losing any opportunity for advancement in the ranks. One time he was accused of leaving the ship without permission, a charge he fought vigorously until the captain noted the distinct automobile tire tracks across the back of the shirt he had worn the night before, which he was completely unable to explain. We had an interesting time trying to figure out how he'd managed to get tire tracks on his clothing while drinking in Newport until we learned he had taken the shirt off and laid it on a lane through the brush while he caroused nearby with a young woman he'd picked up.

On another occasion Regan stayed out past curfew but somehow climbed up to the crow's nest, emerging in the morning to claim that he had spent the night there and had not been late at all. This unlikely excuse might have been reluctantly accepted except that our executive officer noted that it had rained all night and Regan's clothing was dry.

Despite his behavior, there was no man on that ship who was more efficient in his duties or who had a bigger heart. It's men like him that made my years of active duty so interesting and taught me to be circumspect in judging character, a lesson I have never forgotten.

On our journey back north we encountered a very severe late-season hurricane off the Carolinas. We were one of eight destroyers escorting a small aircraft carrier, retaining our circular formation around the larger vessel. We were taking a tremendous pounding from the waves (the ship rolled, at one point, nearly forty-five degrees), and again we had a lot of seasick personnel. Furthermore, one of the bos'n mates had neglected to secure the hatch covering the chain locker in which one of our two anchor chains was stored. As a result, in the turbulent seas, that compartment became filled with seventeen feet of water, making progress more difficult. The captain ordered our damage control officer to carefully monitor the situation, going all the way forward where the pitching of the vessel was most severely felt, and returning every few minutes to the bridge with a status report. The DCA lengthened each trip somewhat between his investigation and report phases by stopping in the head to discharge what little was left in his stomach.

Meanwhile, Commander Gebert repeatedly asked the captain of the aircraft carrier to let us cruise independently, remaining close by, but on a course that would be more comfortable and safer for the *McNair*. The request was always denied, and we remained in the middle of the hurricane, making just eight knots of speed (the storm was moving at about the same rate and in the same direction) for a very miserable two days.

Each squadron has an officer as its medical doctor who splits his time among eight ships. Ours spent this cruise aboard the *McNair*. At the first hint of rough seas, his bunk became the doctor's office from which motion sickness pills were distributed. There were only three things we could do, with the third being decidedly the best: stand our four-hour watches on the bridge; try to eat; or stay in our bunks. I aimed for the latter whenever possible as the ship would ride high on the crest of one wave, each time with forty to fifty feet of its keel out of the water. Then it would crash down, and the next wave would wash well over the bow, flooding the forward part of the main deck. Heavy spray would inundate the open wings of the bridge. The chest-high sides of the open bridge were thirty-four feet above the main deck, and we were repeatedly drenched. Nonetheless, we had to stay outside, because the water hitting the enclosed pilothouse reduced visibility inside to nearly zero. My job was to make sure that the ship stayed in formation, so there was no release from the difficult conditions. Fortunately, my bout of seasickness was less severe than that of most of my mates and, obviously, I survived.

We returned to our mooring in Newport for the year-end holidays. The balance of the winter and early spring was divided between days moored to the pier in Newport, training exercises of various lengths, and some short cruises. One executive officer who came on board after Tom Harbin left was very different, to say the least. He spent a lot of time in his state-room reading sex-oriented paperbacks, emerging periodically to walk around the ship offering criticism of personnel. His pettiness was quickly recognized by his junior officers, who felt we were doing a pretty good job *without his help,* in bringing the ship's performance up to where it should be. While showing him the respect due a senior officer, it was not particularly sincere, and we all agreed, without specifically discussing it, that we could pretty much run the ship efficiently on our own, and really did not need to consult with him or pay an overwhelming amount of attention to him.

At one point he nearly caused a disaster for the ship, and greatly embarrassed our captain. We were engaged in what was called a "full power run"—with all eight ships in our squadron steaming side by side, 2,000 yards apart. Our engineering department had geared up for the fastest possible speed we could make—in the range of 33 to 34 knots—and there was a matter of pride among the eight engineering departments, and the ships in general, as to which would be the leaders in the "race." I was on the bridge as officer of the deck when suddenly our ship banked sharply in a tight turn to the left. We had completely lost steering, and were making a wide, fast circle, as the seven other ships raced straight ahead.

Every warship has a small compartment below decks at the stern called the "after steering," where a couple of men on watch are stationed. They can steer the ship from there in the event of an emergency, rather than it being done by the helmsman on the bridge. A frenzied call came from the sailor on the phones in after steering as soon as control was lost. Before we could even ask for an explanation, he blurted out, "The exec pulled the pin!" Our executive officer, during a routine tour of the ship, had ventured into that compartment and noticed a "nonregulation" toggle pin had been inserted in the mechanism that kept the rudder control in its proper position. With no discussion, he had bent down and pulled out the pin, whereupon the rudder swung completely to one side and all steering control was lost. He just about put us on a collision course with a tanker.

Fortunately, within a few minutes the manual rudder control was wrestled into the proper position and the pin reinserted, restoring our steering capability. Then, over the ship's loudspeaker, came a stern order: "The executive officer report to the captain on the bridge immediately." Our normally mild-mannered commanding officer was rather red in the face as he escorted the chagrined XO into his stateroom, just behind the bridge, for what we assumed was a not particularly friendly chat.

As we prepared that spring for another deployment to the Mediterranean, our commanding officer, seeking to avoid trouble on the cruise, scanned the ship's roster and made provisions for anyone who was likely to be a discipline problem to be sent to the brig or otherwise detained in Newport rather than be aboard when we set sail.

A new captain came aboard to relieve Captain Gebert that July, just after we had entered the Mediterranean—Commander John Gano, also an Annapolis graduate. Likable, dedicated, fair, and reasonable, he instantly earned the respect of the entire ship's company.

The *McNair* and its squadron engaged in fairly routine antisubmarine warfare and other naval exercises, including some with the Italian navy and Great Britain's Royal Navy, before pulling into the port of Naples for a few days of R&R.

Upon arrival in Naples, I was anxious to get our uniforms to a local laundry. Before I could retrieve them, however, we were suddenly dispatched to the eastern Mediterranean because of what came to be known as the "Lebanon Crisis." This was to be as close as the *McNair* would come to a wartime situation during my time aboard.

All of us were anxious and excited. You train for years for this moment. When it comes, the excitement keeps increasing. I reported to the wardroom with the other officers. There we were informed that Communist forces were gathering to invade and seize Lebanon. There was also evidence that the Lebanese air force may have defected. The *McNair* had been ordered to proceed at once to Cyprus to receive on board members of the U.S. State Department, including high-ranking military personnel and foreign diplomats, who were coming in for a high-level strategy meeting. I had been assigned as the Underway Officer of the Deck, the person in charge of ship safety and navigation—substantial responsibilities.

During this crisis, message traffic coming to the ship was encrypted. That means everything, including weather reports, had to be decoded via machine by one of the ship's department heads, sitting at a typewriter-like device in the cramped code-shack, which was roughly half the size of your normal bathtub. At one point a message came through indicating that four enemy aircraft had been dispatched from Lebanon to strafe the anchored U.S. ships.

As we got under way for Cyprus, Lieutenant Fitz Lufkin, the navigator, joined me on the bridge where we broke out the charts and plotted our course. It was a beautiful, warm, starlit night, too tranquil for the circumstances as we sailed along at 25 knots into the unknown. As we had Cyprus in view, I was told that an aircraft was approaching our ship. Using my binoculars, I sighted the plane, alerted the lookouts, bridge, and combat information center. I reminded everyone that we had been told that the Lebanese air force might have defected. As the plane neared our ship, I announced, "Look, he dropped something." Every man but me hit the deck, even the helmsman. It obviously was a British patrol plane releasing a flare, but I received a lot of kidding for being the only one stupid enough to stay standing. I knew that in time of war, I would have either been a Medal of Honor winner or, more likely, dead.

We were directed to a motor launch to pick up the delegation, which boarded our ship and spent the next few hours discussing war preparation plans. Later, as we sailed into Beirut, I looked with my binoculars at the shore and found myself staring at nine large guns pointed at us from the cliffs. I immediately called the officer in tactical command and asked, "Are those guns friendly?" I got the worse possible reply: "What guns?"

With that scary lack of intelligence we pulled into Lebanon. Gunnery Officer Sal Acquilino had spotted an Israeli PT boat coming toward us. He immediately sounded "general quarters"—summoning all ship's personnel to their battle stations. We had had countless "general quarters" or full-alert drills and were well trained to respond quickly, but when the G.Q. alarm comes unexpectedly, people really move. The Israeli vessel came close, but no harm was done. We pointed out to Sal that Israel was an ally, not a potential enemy. His response was, "They were at general quarters so I thought we should be, too!"

Captain Gano met with a top officer of the U.S. 6th Mediterranean fleet, and was advised that we would be one of the key gunfire support ships to be anchored in Beirut Harbor. While anchored there a junior officer constantly circled the ship in our motor whaleboat, on guard for enemy frogmen who might swim underneath and attach explosives to our hull.

U.S. Marines were already on the ground in Lebanon, and Sal went ashore to meet with their officers, who would coordinate targets for us if we had to turn loose with our five-inch guns. Sal, of course, was hoping he *would* have the chance to fire them.

Every Sunday aboard ship, whether under way or in port, religious services were held on deck. Attendance doubled during the time we were in Beirut Harbor. Actually, things quieted down very quickly in Lebanon, and we were able to leave without further incident after only about a week. But it was one heck of an interesting week.

We then proceeded to Izmir, Turkey, where I again drew the assignment as shore patrol officer. The only instance of real trouble from our crew onshore was when a young sailor again made an unwanted pass at one of the local girls. The local gendarmes arrested him and we had visions of his spending twenty years in one of the country's infamous prisons. Fortunately, he escaped that fate, but the incident was a black eye for the U.S. Navy.

Our crew was allowed to stay ashore in Izmir throughout the evening, reporting back aboard ship by midnight. The officers, on the other hand, were allowed out until three A.M. One time, I was scheduled to go wild boar hunting in the nearby Turkish foothills—an experience a kid from the country might dream about but never imagine experiencing. I had shore patrol the night before the hunt. When I got off at eleven P.M., I met up with Fitz Luftkin to have a few drinks. We joined a couple of Brits over gin and tonics and promptly got into a fierce argument over the Suez Canal. I kept trying to break away, since the hunting party was picking me up at five A.M. but it wasn't until one-thirty in the morning that I finally got back to my hotel room.

Right on schedule, Tom Kharl, my hunting buddy, woke me and off we went, with me rather hung over, to spend the next few hours in an old bus filled with dogs and native people, making what felt like a tremendous amount of noise. The natives carried beaters that they would use to scare the hogs from the underbrush and direct them toward the hunters. I made friends with the dogs, hoping that would improve my chances and impress the lead guide. It must have worked, because when we reached our destination the head honcho took me aside and said, "Come with me. I get boar to come to you." We broke away from the rest of the party. He took me a hundred yards up a hill and sat me down under a tree where I could see what was going on below. After my late-night revelry, however, I promptly fell asleep. I was woken by the sound of dogs yapping and saw a wild boar running right at me from the bottom of the hill. I shot over his head. Fortunately, the boar turned left rather than continuing straight at me. I could see him intermittently running between the bushes. I fired again and hit him right in the heart. The party came running up and the chief guide told me, "You shot good." Little did they know that I had simply been the recipient of good luck. The boar weighed something like 450 pounds. We tied it onto the bus and brought it back to the ship. The ship's crew couldn't cut it up or store it properly, so we gave the meat to the Turks. I still have the tusks and photographs of me standing beside this huge, dead animal—the great white hunter.

After more operations at sea we returned to Naples, and found our laundry still waiting for us. The last day there, three of us officers, along with a group of enlisted men, had the opportunity for a trip up to, and a tour of, Rome. Most headed back in the early evening, but our trio was more interested in exploring additional cultural opportunities (i.e., nightlife) of the Eternal City. We arrived back in Naples disturbingly close to the time our ship was scheduled to depart, constantly assuring one another that the ship could not possibly leave without three of her qualified officers of the deck.

When we reached the pier the *McNair* was already under way, but our whaleboat was waiting for us. Except for having to endure the captain's withering glance, no harm was done.

Before we departed the Mediterranean, we were advised that our Gunnery Department, and, more important, the ship, had been awarded the "E" for efficiency . . . putting the "Mighty Mac" at the top of the squadron. We were particularly glad that our Gunnery Department had received this recognition, because the person most responsible for it, Salvo Sal Acquilino, was scheduled to depart the ship in October. When he left, I assumed the position of gunnery officer.

• • •

One Sunday after our return to Newport we decided to have a "family cruise" so that the officers and enlisted personnel could invite their spouses, girlfriends, and in some cases their parents on board. Being unmarried, and not having anyone local to bring aboard as my date, I spent the majority of the cruise as officer of the deck.

One of the things we wanted to show off for our guests was our efficiency at the "man overboard" drill. This exercise consists of throwing a dummy off the stern, to be followed by a call to the bridge that there is a "man overboard." The officer of the deck—in this case me—immediately takes appropriate action, wheeling the ship around sharply in a circle and then, with power greatly reduced, coming up alongside the floating dummy so that it could be "rescued." For some reason, this particular dummy, whom we had named Oscar, was floating with his legs wide open. And my aim was not what it should have been. Rather then bring the ship to rest a few feet beside Oscar, I steered the McNair's prow right into Oscar. The captain, observing the exercise next to me on the bridge, said sarcastically, "Great, Jeff, right in the crotch."

And then, as luck would have it, Oscar drifted down the starboard side of the ship. By then, I'd put the engines into reverse and promptly ran Oscar through the screws. The crew cheered; the parents groaned.

For most of the winter the McNair was scheduled to undergo a major overhaul in the Boston Naval Shipyard, with a considerable amount of the time spent in drydock. Our "home" was destined to be noisy, dirty, and frequently quite cold. We spent our time doing routine ship work, supervising repairs and the installation of new equipment for our departments, and stumbling over the many civilian shipyard workers on board.

It was quite flattering that two of my closet friends still aboard—my suite mates in Boston, Combat Information Center (CIC) Officer Stuart Meeker and Engineering Officer Franklin "Brownie" Brown—kept urging me to extend my stay in the navy to make the summer cruise with them. While I was in no hurry to end my time on the McNair, I had another reason for wanting to extend my tour of duty beyond June: I needed money for law school. I asked the captain if I could stay through to September but the navy personnel department rejected my request.

For the second time in my life I asked my father for help. He reminded me that Bill Franke, the secretary of the navy, lived in Rutland. I drove straight there and Father and I went to the navy secretary's home, a formidable stone fortress–like building on a sweeping hill on the outskirts of Rutland. The place resembled a castle more than a house, but the meeting was very low-key. Franke asked one question: "Does the captain want you?" I told him he did. Franke said, "Don't worry about it." By the time I got back to Newport the orders granting an extension were awaiting me.

The summer cruise was relatively routine, with more antisubmarine and other training exercises off Sardinia and visits to Palma, Majorca, and Lisbon before heading home. We did have an opportunity for an exercise with the USS *Skipjack,* an extremely modern U.S. sub, quite different from the old conventional submarines with which we had been conducting exercises over the last three years. We were quite amazed at what that boat could do. If it had been an enemy sub, we would have been virtually helpless to successfully attack it, even after discovering its whereabouts, which would have been the first challenge.

Two days after we arrived back from our summer cruise, I was scheduled to leave the *McNair* for good. I took my time. Most of my officer friends had already left the ship; some had already left the navy. I went down to say good-bye to the chiefs but found they were all somewhere else. I went into the area reserved for offices but could find no one there either. I chatted with the staff in the wardroom. Frankly, I just was putting off leaving.

Finally, the messenger serving at the quarterdeck came around and informed me that the captain was waiting to say good-bye. This was strange, but I naturally grabbed my bag and hurried to the quarterdeck.

Ordinarily only the captain of a ship is accorded ceremonies when he turns over command and departs his vessel. I was therefore granted a rare honor when the crew, dressed in their white uniforms (rather than the working uniforms usually worn in port) lined the rails to see me off. As the ship's gong sounded, and the bos'n mate of the watch announced "Jeffords departing," I saluted the officer of the deck and went ashore for the last time. To leave the ship in such a manner was an unexpected honor I will never forget.

This was not the end of my navy years. I stayed in the naval reserves for thirty years, retiring as a full navy captain in 1990.

CHAPTER 4

Love and Law

ALL THE TIME that I was aboard the *McNair* I continued my habit of traveling around New England to visit my old high school pals, now in graduate or medical school or beginning their careers, whenever my schedule allowed. I especially liked to spend time with George Hansen, who had plunged into his medical studies at the University of Vermont in Burlington. I was still relatively shy around women; not George. He was a ladies' man—charming, outgoing, courtly. He always had a bevy of lady friends to whom he'd introduce me or arrange a date with when I was staying over, but I was less than interested in getting serious. I knew that the years on the *McNair* would be demanding ones, followed by three rigorous years of law study at Harvard. I was determined to get through them with as little debt as possible. I had neither the time nor the resources for a serious relationship.

One weekend in November 1957, like so many others, George arranged a party at his house and began calling around to the women he knew, inviting them over. One of these young women was Liz Daley, whom George had met the previous spring while he worked his part-time job selling tickets at the Vermont Transit bus terminal. Liz was a lively and attractive woman with her own coterie of friends in and around Burlington. She worked at Vermont Transit's busy travel agency and often joined George on their coffee breaks. Would she come by? No, she said, she had just canceled a date with a jet pilot because she didn't feel all that well; it would not be right to go to a party when she'd stood up her date.

Well, you have to know George and his powers of persuasion. "I've got this navy friend I really want you to meet," he told Liz, and eventually she gave in, got dressed, and came to the party to be my date. What I didn't know at the time, but learned later, was that she had a crush on George and, on the advice of her mother, had accepted the date with me in hopes of making George jealous.

When I say that I wasn't all that interested in settling down, that doesn't mean I wasn't out to make a good impression on this woman, whom George had described as quite a looker. I'd been at sea so much that my hair was quite blond and my skin tanned. I put on my navy whites, even though it was going into winter. I like to think I did it because I knew the white jacket would accentuate my tan, but it might simply have been that the dress uniform was clean. Those who know me will tell you that my sense of fashion and season-appropriate attire is severely challenged, but I insist that the oft-told story about how I wore a black tie with my brown suit to a black-tie event at the White House is total fiction.

Liz was petite, lovely to look at, and interesting to chat with. Unlike so many Vermont women I had met up to that time, she had traveled around the United States, Mexico, Canada, and Europe and enjoyed ballet and Broadway shows. As far as blind dates go, I thought we had hit it off pretty well, and I guess we did because we developed a loose but practical relationship. I'd write or call George or write directly to Liz to see if she was free whenever I planned to be in Burlington. Sometimes she would be; sometimes she would be busy. What always struck me about her was her zeal about so many things—politics, reading, making the world a better place. These were, of course, interests of mine. The problem, however, was that Liz and I were often on opposite sides of the political spectrum. Compared to my father, I was fairly liberal; compared to Liz, I was a stodgy right-winger. Liz was anything but conservative on all manner of things, from labor issues to American foreign policy. We had some lively debates, particularly in regard to Central and South America and the Communist threat from Cuba. Sometimes I would purposely annoy her by, say, taking the side of United Fruit Company when she was inclined to carry the banner of the banana pickers.

But what I liked best about her was that she seemed unlike so many of the other young women I had met. She wasn't interested in becoming Mrs. Anybody. She said marriage was like death; it came to you eventually, and she wasn't going to rush into either one. My thoughts precisely. She loved Hemingway, as did I. She was independent-acting as well. She was thinking of leaving Vermont Transit Travel and starting her own travel agency. I found her intriguing. It wasn't simply that she was opinionated but that she had learned early on that if she wanted to go against authority at home or at school, she'd best have some facts to back her up. I liked arguing—or at least debating—with someone who could give me a run for my money. She was a rarity, all right.

She could be a challenge, though, with her hot Irish temper. Sometimes she'd get so angry over something I'd said that I'd think it best to call it off. She said I was a stuffy old Republican and she didn't know why she spent time with me. At these times I always made matters worse by saying the wrong thing. Yet time after time, these rows would blow over and we'd find ourselves laughing over the very thing we'd just been arguing about.

One of the wonderful things about my blossoming friendship with Liz was that it came about the same time that my father's health began to decline. She was always so generous in listening to my concerns, and I had many. Father was suffering from serious fatigue. The doctor had advised my parents to go to Florida for the winter, hoping that the warmth and relaxation might enable him to continue working and not have to retire. Liz's concern for my parents touched me deeply.

Still, there were conflicts in our personalities. By the standards of the day, she was quite unconventional, even uninhibited. Her big Irish family was loud and fun-loving and they doted on her; in contrast, mine was, as they say in the lexicon of today, rather uptight and certainly not outwardly affectionate. Sometimes her spontaneity would throw me for a loop, like when she'd join arms with a sibling or friend and start singing or dancing down Church Street in downtown Burlington. I'd feel like a self-conscious klutz, hoping no one would recognize me or that they wouldn't expect me to join in. I was uncomfortable about public displays of affection. Liz could be loud. She wasn't shy about expressing her opinions or telling someone if she thought he was being a jackass. I sometimes shrank from these public displays of emotion. My behavior could send her into a tizzy. Lighten up, she'd say, and I tried.

Liz was a stickler for making plans and keeping them; I liked to keep things loose. Once, during the summer before my tour of duty ended, I sort of invited her down to Boston for the weekend. She could provide me with some much needed social life and stay in the nurses' apartment upstairs. Unfortunately, we had a bit of miscommunication relative to firming up her plans. Then I learned at the last minute that my ship had to get under way first thing in the morning for a one-day shakedown cruise to test some newly installed equipment. For that reason my roommates and I had elected to sleep on the ship rather than commute in very early Saturday morning. Unfortunately, I didn't let Liz know of the change in plans in time. That night Liz arrived by bus to be greeted by an empty apartment. Fortunately, she was able to stay with a friend of her boss, who lived in the city. She returned to Vermont the next day, and my roommates, showing their usual degree of sympathy and understanding, said, "You'll never see her again, Jeff!"

But Liz also had a good sense of humor and she got over that gaff. Which was good, because there would be plenty more to come.

Liz and I maintained this loose arrangement throughout 1958 and 1959. Sometimes, as when my ship was touring around Cuba and then the Mediterranean from spring 1959 until well into the fall, we didn't see each other and I didn't write for long stretches of time. But when I did, I often put into words emotions that I shared with no one else. Fortunately for me, Liz has kept those letters, because they give me a glimpse of the young man I was. As in my letter about the week I spent in Zermatt, Switzerland: "a place I shall always hope to return to. I spent several fascinating days getting lost from the world, at times quite literally so, climbing in the Alps. I discovered that my days of dissipation had not lended to my physical endurance. In fact at one time, I became so exhausted I denounced liquor and women forever! I recovered from this ridiculous state quickly and made my way to the nearest establishment and partook of energy (liquor only)-giving substance. The days of spectacular beauty, rest, and the friendliness of the people again endeared me to the land of the Alps."

That letter was as close as I came to eloquence. Most of my missives to Liz involved making plans for future meetings or had me apologizing for not writing sooner or longer or for something I'd said or done. Liz, on the other hand, was a great letter writer. She took to addressing me as Sir Crudess Prudess, referring to my lack of social graces—I'd often show up in jeans and plaid shirts while Liz was quite stylish in the era of gloves and heels and carefully coifed hairdos—not to mention my tightfistedness when it came to spending money. I called her Ma Petite and Princess Lizarina. We were young and silly, a needed antidote to my concerns about my father, whose health had not improved. By September, he'd been forced to retire.

My tightfistedness when it comes to money was part of my overall stoic Yankee upbringing. As a seventh-generation Vermonter, it's just part of my makeup to not complain about the weather or about things I can't control, to not whine when I'm cold or wet or hungry, and to not waste money or resources. As I've been writing this book and thinking about my life, I've realized how much these attributes have influenced my political life as well. So many of the bills I've introduced over the years have been based on my Yankee sense of practicality, efficiency, and acceptance of reality. Some of these bills and provisions have passed, creating new programs in solar energy and research into alternate sources of fuel and energy, but many have been defeated or gutted at the last minute. My Yankee stoicism has helped me to keep a positive attitude about these disappointments, to take hope from the successes, and not complain about the defeats.

And one of the things I liked so much about Liz was that even when she complained that I didn't spend money on dinners or flowers or gifts, she also believed in the rightness of making do with what you had. She liked high fashion and bought nice clothes when she could; when she couldn't, she sewed them. I found this combination of creativity and practicality very attractive.

Meanwhile, I had planned for my official discharge from the navy to take place on September 18, 1959, which also was the first day of classes at Harvard Law School. I knew I was playing it a bit close but I felt that every dollar counted. I lived on campus and worked as a dorm proctor to help pay for my room and board. I had classes six days a week, which meant that I had to seriously change my ways. Instead of partying I would be studying on Friday nights and there would be far fewer weekend sorties into the north country.

After three years aboard ship and away from scholastic study, I found law school grueling. I spent much of my time studying medical tort cases, which intrigued me because I thought medical law would be quite lucrative. In one letter to Liz I called myself a "legal bore" and begged her help in rescuing me from myself. Week after week I'd make a plan of how I'd complete my studies, but there were the usual distractions of college life—primarily golf and parties. In one letter to Liz, written during the second week of classes, I wrote: "My big study weekend was somewhat successful but as usual could have been slightly more efficient. My Law Club threw a cocktail party from 5–7 on Saturday. Since I had paid for the booze through dues, I felt obliged to go for a couple. I got my dues back plus some olives to boot. Law and liquids don't mix. Slept well though."

In the spring of 1960 I went again to visit Liz at her sister Harriet's in Burlington. Harriet, Liz later told me, had taken a shine to me and had taken her kids to the in-laws so that Liz and I could have the house to ourselves. Harriet had even set up a card table in the front parlor and taken out her best linen and china so Liz could impress me. Liz, who wasn't much of a cook in those days, had decided breakfast wouldn't be much of a challenge. She proceeded to burn the bacon, and when she went to serve my egg, it bounced from the frying pan to the plate to the floor. We had a good laugh about that.

As time went by we learned we had even more in common—a love of Vermont and of the outdoors, of camping and hiking through the hills. We also liked a good meal as long as Liz didn't have to cook it. Some weekends the guys would buy the wine and the women would bring the food. Liz surprised us all one night by bringing spaghetti, homemade sauce, and salad. She shut the lights off when she saw that her spaghetti noodles had turned blue. She'd cooked them in a pot that her mother had used to dye a sweater without properly rinsing the pot. I didn't know until she told me months later.

In spring of 1960, at the end of classes, Liz and I took a short camping vacation on Cape Cod. It was pure heaven to be with a beautiful woman, hiking over dunes, and eating lobster. One day we ran into a rather drunk Norman Mailer on the beach. We had both read *The Naked and the Dead* and joined him the following morning for breakfast on the beach for what turned out to be a most interesting conversation, despite our physical discomfort. After our first night of camping, we discovered we'd pitched our tent in a poison ivy patch.

All along, we kept things loose. I'd return to Cambridge and my studies. Liz would return to her work and travels. If she was free, we'd go out on a date or to a party. I liked our arrangement just fine.

But over Christmas 1960, Liz's attitude toward me began to change. The collapse of the summit conference and the growing tension between the United States and the Soviet Union really concerned her. She worried about nuclear war; I, on the other hand, thought we had to take a strong stand against communism. The uncertainties in the larger world began to have their effect on both of us. One night we sat up late talking about our life plans. We admitted we both wanted to marry someday and have children. *The Ugly American* had been published and we were aware that our generation had been charged with making a difference. Our president, John F. Kennedy, had called on us to do so. We shared a sense of purpose and optimism that somehow made our political differences— she had been for Kennedy in the 1960 election; I had supported Nixon— seem unimportant, even though Liz's mother had made me take my Nixon/Lodge campaign button off before entering their home. Liz was sympathetic to Fidel Castro while I was worried about Communist encroachment. What seemed more important was that we shared a belief that many of the world's problems came from misunderstandings between nations and cultures and that these problems could be over- come. By the end of that evening in late 1960, we'd made a kind of com- mitment to each other that we would date exclusively and see where that would lead. I returned to school feeling very warm and loving toward Liz, but she had heard something in my words that I had never said and, six weeks later, when she came to Boston in mid-February 1961, shortly after her birthday, she was expecting me to give her an engagement ring. She was finally ready for a commitment. Problem was, I wasn't. At school, we were in the midst of our moot trial competitions. I felt overwhelmed with work. And I was broke.

Still, that's no excuse for the dunce I made of myself. I met her bus, which arrived in downtown Boston shortly after midnight. I overcame my shyness and greeted her with a long kiss. But rather than take her to a romantic setting, I took her to a fairly seedy all-night hamburger joint. Liz had had a manicure in preparation for receiving a ring, but my present was an envelope stuffed with green stamps. (For those of you too young to know what those were, they were given by merchants and pasted into books that you could trade in for small appliances and sundries.) Being the klutz that I am, I put my foot in it further by giving Liz a card that read, "I'll go to any length to make your birthday a happy one . . . as long as it doesn't cost more than 25 cents."

Liz's reaction came in six words. "You're a son of a bitch."

I can still see her, small in her maroon coat, with me trudging behind in my hooded loden jacket. I'm a good walker and much taller than Liz, but she was so furious that I could barely keep up with her. She was muttering on about my intentions and finally got me so angry that I shouted back, "Who do you think you are to question me? I am, too, an honorable man." It was the first time I'd raised my voice to her. The weekend wasn't a complete bust. We called a truce; she took me to see a play, ironically called *The Devil's Advocate*. But when she got home to Burlington she sent me a Dear John letter and resumed her relationship with an old boyfriend, the helicopter pilot who'd shared her affections off and on during the past few years.

It hit me hard. I had really screwed up and I had only myself to blame. I realized I was deeply in love with this woman. Much as she might drive me crazy, I didn't want to lose her. Once, I called her apartment and the other fellow answered. It wasn't good. Sometimes I felt like I was being played for a chump, that she was purposely trying to make me jealous. Other times I was seized with a panic that I'd never see her again. It didn't make studying any easier. My letters were full of the conflict I felt. "I will neither propose nor depose myself via the postman," I wrote her. "We are young. The coming months will wear us well. The coming years will be ours, I so hope. Please let us not waste one precious moment of them."

Finally, over Easter break, I came to my senses, drove to Burlington, and went to Liz's. She had just poured me a drink when I got down on my knees and proposed. I still didn't have a ring but she accepted.

When I did the honorable thing and went to speak with her father, I came equipped with a paper on which I'd listed my meager resources and my expected income. "That doesn't mean a thing to me, young man," Liz's father said. "When there's love, you'll both find a way." But then he proceeded to give me fair warning. "The question is will you be in love in the future. No one's perfect, and I must warn you that Liz is far from domestic. She doesn't know how to cook. Her room's a pigsty, and she likes to spend her money in foreign countries whenever possible. She has a terrible temper. I'm just warning you."

I thought his "buyer beware" speech was hysterical. But in later years there were times when I wished I had listened more closely to his warning. And, perhaps, Liz did, too. Our marriage has been no bed of roses and we have caused each other great pain too many times. But it has never been for lack of love.

Liz almost called off the marriage over the summer—mostly because of my inability to make decisions over the wedding plans. Her parents' resources were limited; she had the idea of hosting a buffet after the ceremony for the wedding party and the older relatives, followed by an informal outdoor barbecue at her parents' house for the younger crowd. She would write to me for guidance. I'd say something to the effect of, whatever works best for you, dear, whereupon she'd be upset that I wasn't helping with the arrangements.

At the same time, we both believed in the concept of marrying for life and wanted our ceremony to be the best we could afford. And, thanks to Liz, it was—a lovely wedding on August 26, 1961, at St. John Vienney Church in South Burlington, followed by a small reception at the Old Board in Burlington and the backyard party with food prepared by friends and family and enough beer to keep us all happy. I was twenty-seven; Liz was twenty-two. George, of course, was best man.

When I returned for my last year of law school as a married man, it was the first time that I lived off campus. We found a small apartment on Harvard Street, chosen primarily because it had a big backyard. The apartment was truly horrid, with uneven floors, a filthy galley kitchen, and a bedroom that was far from charming. We moved our few possessions down in my old 1952 blue Plymouth. The car had seen better days. The driver's side was all smashed in and the latch didn't fit on the passenger's side. I had to rig the whole thing with ropes to hold the car together. We pulled our few belongings behind us in a rented unit. I put the mattress on the bottom with the furniture on top. To save money I didn't get an enclosed trailer, and as luck would have it, it started pouring along our route. Every time the sun came out in the next few months, we'd drag the mattress outside to air; it took that long to dry completely.

Liz took a job at Cinema Incorporated, a small company on Clarendon Street in Boston that rented out educational films to schools and clubs. She would get up early in the morning; bring me cereal, milk, and the paper; and then go to work while I lolled around in bed until my mid-morning class. I must confess I was spoiled. One day Liz became ill and returned home to find that I had not even returned the orange juice glasses and cereal bowls to the kitchen. They were three deep on the floor, along with several days' worth of the daily newspaper. She was so angry that she short-sheeted my side of the bed, putting the newspapers and cereal bowls and glasses on my side. When I returned that evening very late from naval reserves, I had to crawl through the mess to get into my side of the bed, Liz had hoped to teach me a lesson about cleaning up after myself, but I just pushed everything aside and fell asleep, laughing. I thought she was hilarious.

To make extra money, several of us took jobs managing the production of the law school's annual yearbook. Previous to our doing so, there had been a bit of a scandal in which the yearbook's student managers had been caught skimming money from the profits. Those students were fired and the school asked for volunteers to take it over, along with their outline of how they would manage it. My former roommate Steve Stepanian and I were chosen. Our plan allowed us to take a percentage of the gross income from ads, which turned out to be rather lucrative. We did better than the administration had imagined. Previously, law firms that routinely hired Harvard graduates had sent donations to the dean for students in need; we ended up getting some of these funds in return for ads in the yearbook—a dubious arrangement perhaps, but one that got me through my last two years of law school. Besides, who could be more deserving and needy than the team of Stepanian and Jeffords?

After graduation, Liz and I moved to Burlington where I clerked for Pearly Feen, a well-known Vermont attorney. We slept in Liz's old bedroom on Hinesburg Road. But then in late July, Father broke his hip and we learned he had lung cancer. We returned to Rutland to help Mother adjust.

I got a job clerking for Frederic J. Delaney at Delaney, O'Neill, and Valente, a law firm in Rutland that I hoped to join some day. Ted, as everyone called Delaney, had married my childhood friend Pat Wing, the daughter of General Red Wing, and moved into the Wing house across the street from ours. Ted had movie-star good looks and was a fairly close cousin of John F. Kennedy; actually, he looked a lot like the president. Ted drove a little sports car (sometimes too fast), was very smart, charming, and full of fun. I guess he had some of that famous Kennedy charisma. He was about old enough to be my uncle, and he took a liking to me. He'd grown up in a working family in Boston and enlisted in the navy when World War II broke out. He'd piloted fighter planes in the Pacific and was full of great stories. He had the Irish gift of gab. People loved him. He'd walk into a crowded room and suddenly everybody would be looking at Ted Delaney.

He and his partner Joe O'Neill were not only building a first-rate law practice but had begun venturing into politics. In 1962, Ted ran for lieutenant governor on the Democratic ticket. His running mate was Phil Hoff, the Democratic candidate for governor who was about to pull off the biggest political upset of the century in Vermont. Ted was running strong, too. It was really fun to be around Ted and the excitement he generated, even if he was a Democrat.

By September, however, I was back on the road, clerking for Federal Court Judge Ernest Gibson, repeating my father's habit of spending the week in Brattleboro, Windsor, and Burlington and returning home to Rutland on the weekend. My letters from those times reflect how much I missed my wife and just how penurious I was. Each week I'd send a check for $37—$12 for Mother for board, $10 to pay for the nurse's aide, and $15 for Liz to maintain herself and take care of our needs. To make ends meet, Liz worked one fall as an apple picker, making seventeen cents a box. Mother must have been mortified to have Liz doing manual labor and spending time with the pickers, but work was hard to come by. Eventually Liz got a job at the Rutland credit bureau and assumed a more respectable life, at least by Mother's standards.

It was very difficult to come home and see my father, who had graduated cum laude from BU law school and had retired as chief justice of the Vermont Supreme Court, now so incapacitated that he had to be hoisted from his bed to a wheelchair. Father had smoked three packs of cigarettes a day all his life. I was glad I had never picked up the habit, but Liz still smoked and I often asked her to quit. She finally did, but it took years of trying every program available and every alternative regime she heard of—including acupuncture and hypnosis.

There were hard times ahead. Ted might well have become Vermont's lieutenant governor, but one night that October he and his friend Jack Spencer stayed out late at a meeting. About two in the morning Ted got into his sports car to drive Jack home to Shrewsbury. Three miles down Route 7 his car swerved on wet leaves and went out of control, crashing at the Cold River bridge in Clarendon. Jack survived the accident but Ted died the next day. His name on the ballot still, Ted got more than 50,000 votes. A friend said recently that I might have joined Ted's law firm if he'd lived, and maybe I would have. As to my friend's suggestion that, if I had, I might have become a Democrat a long time ago . . . well, anything is possible. Although my roots were firmly planted in Republican soil, it was hard not to get caught up in the challenge those young Democrats had laid down to the Vermont voters—to prepare for the social and economic changes that the sixties were ushering in so fast: pressures on the environment from developers, an invasion of out-of-staters, and the closing of so many old industries that had formed the backbone of Vermont's economy.

Ted's death had a powerful impact on me, one that made me realize it was time to get my adult life in order—buy a house, start a family, advance my career. I told Liz all this that Christmas. We were saving for a house and we had a plan. One essential element of that plan was a place in the country where I could have a garden and we could raise a family surrounded by nature and friends and share with them the outdoor activities we loved so much.

We had met Joanna Taft Maynard, known locally as Taffy, at a basketball game in the winter of 1963 and she had invited us to stop by her home on the Cold River Road in the mountain town of Shrewsbury. We drove out to see Taffy on a snowy day in January. As it turned out, the Maynards weren't home, but I knew their road went to one of Shrewsbury's small hamlets called Northam. Liz and I decided to continue along for a ride. Shrewsbury is a particularly beautiful Vermont community with steep hills, deep woods, and a fast-flowing river. On the way we saw an empty house that looked desperately in need of an owner—not because it was in disrepair but because it was so lovely. Liz did her research and found that the house had 165 acres of woods and open meadows, gorgeous hardwood floors, and lots of rooms. Liz was especially close to her sister Harriet McGreevy, who at this time was pregnant with her sixth child. Liz loved having the children around and wanted a house big enough that her family could visit regularly.

The house cost $18,000, double what we had budgeted, but we fell in love with it. We bought the house in April 1963. Now we could proceed to the next step in our plan. Liz had begun going to the doctor in hopes of us beginning our family and was busy working as a volunteer at the Rutland hospital. That spring I put in a garden, worked on the house, and built a pond that was fed from a small brook that ran through our property.

Over the summer Harriet and her children stayed with us off and on, and I came out of the funk I'd been in since Ted's death. Liz and I found it easy to be part of this town. Up the street from us, the Pierce family—two elderly brothers and two elderly sisters—ran a general store that had been in their family for generations. Who could forget walking into that store with its shelves stocked with old patent medicines, the antique cash register and woodstove, the penny candy under the counter and Glendon, Marion, Gordon, or Marjorie—all white-haired and shy—greeting you with their warm, welcoming smiles. Although old in years, there was nothing old mentally about any of the Pierce siblings. They loved a good tale and enjoyed gardening and talking politics. The Pierces went back in Vermont to the Revolution and their politics were Republican, of course. Glendon Pierce liked to sit by the store's old iron woodstove and tell stories; his favorite was the one about counting votes in some mountain town in Vermont. One election night, the town clerk, as usual, talked as he took each vote out of the ballot box: "Republican, Republican, Republican, Republican," he said. "Yep, Republican, Republican. What's this now? Democrat? Hmm." And the town clerk put that vote aside, then continued, "Republican, Republican, Republican, yes Republican, Republican, another Democrat? Tear that one up. That son of a bitch must've voted twice." I must have heard Glendon tell that story a dozen times, and every time, he made me laugh.

Within a brief time of moving to Shrewsbury, Liz became a Sunday school teacher and I became a member of the town volunteer fire department. Indeed, our barn soon became Fire Station #2. One of the town trucks, a 1939 Ford with mechanical brakes, was stored there. Once, Hull Maynard, now a state senator, was riding in front of me in his Volkswagen as we sped downhill to a fire. As we came to the blaze, I realized the brakes on the fire truck weren't working and sped right past Hull and the fire, working desperately to keep the truck out of the ditch. It finally stopped when it ran out of gas. Luckily, we had already been running on vapors, so I didn't get very far. To fill the tank on this antique, you had to lift out the seat and take out a big cork, then lean way in and pour. As I was filling the tank from a spare gas can, a man smoking a big cigar stopped by. Leaning over, he asked if he could help. I yelled, "Yes, you can help—by getting the hell out of here with that lit cigar!" We became heroes of a sort when we finally arrived at the fire. The other truck had run out of water and our old truck saved the day.

Each year, the Cold River Northam/Eastham Club held a fair. Along with games for kids and a chance for the locals to compare crops and trade gossip, the women sold craft items and home-baked goods. Marjorie Pierce stressed that the baked goods *had* to be homemade. That first year in Shrewsbury Liz made brownies, a first. I wanted a sample but she wouldn't give me one; I had to buy it. I ended up buying the whole plate. The ladies oohed and aahed to Liz about her doting husband. It wasn't until we got home that I confessed I bought the brownies not because they were so tasty but rather because they were like bricks. She had put in baking soda instead of baking powder.

Shrewsbury was paradise on earth. When I went to work at the Windsor courthouse, I drove on old dirt roads installed by the CCC during the depression. They cut through deep woods where, on any given day, one might come across white-tailed deer or see songbirds like scarlet tanagers and indigo buntings. In September, Art Crowley, Earle Bishop, and I formed the Rutland firm of Bishop, Crowley & Jeffords.

Meanwhile, though we were trying, Liz was not getting pregnant.

Finally, bored with too much time on her hands, she went to work for the Killington Lodging Bureau, the agency that made arrangements for tourists visiting the fast-growing ski area just east of Rutland. I threw myself into my legal work and loved it—a mix of defending indigents and mothers with no money and legal problems to working for the up-and-coming business establishments on the mountain.

By now I was making enough that we were really getting serious about starting a family, but, alas, the doctor told us we couldn't have children. Liz's friend Teresa Tomasi, a social worker, worked at the Elizabeth Lund Home for unwed mothers in Burlington. Liz began talking to her about adopting a baby. The process wasn't as arduous as we had feared and we were approved very quickly to adopt a child from the Lund home. With all the excitement of expectant parents, we began buying diapers, undershirts, nightgowns, and receiving blankets. Our son Leonard was born September 12, 1964, and came to live with us ten days later. The whole town threw us a baby shower.

Father was failing fast but he lived to see Leonard. I can still see him sitting in his wheelchair, holding our son, tears rolling down his face as he thanked me for naming our boy "after me and my best friend." Leonard's full name is Leonard Olin Jeffords. The Leonard, of course, was for General Wing. Father died two weeks later.

I was determined to be a more active father than mine had been. After work, I would read Dr. Spock and play with Leonard. I became an overnight expert on parenting. In retrospect, I did overdo it a bit. I made us both wash our hands and face before picking him up. I made everyone who came by the house, even the road commissioner, look at the baby.

Meanwhile, outside our idyllic Shrewsbury, the world was a mess— the assassinations, the Vietnam War, the political and social unrest, civil rights marches and antiwar marches, drugs. All of it made me worry what the world would be like when Leonard grew up. Liz and I spent many long hours worrying and hoping. Liz was opposed to the war; I believed that we had to continue the fight against communism. I began to talk about volunteering for active duty. By now, I was a lieutenant commander in the naval reserves and thought I could do some good. And I still had those unfulfilled dreams of wartime battle left over from childhood.

One thing I've got to say about Liz, she always supported me. Much as she was opposed to the war, she said, "I know you, Jimmy Jeffords, and you're going to do what you've got to do regardless of what I say."

And despite all this, we began talking about having another child.

Two things kept me from going to war: my mother and my daughter. One day Liz was visiting my mother for lunch. She happened to mention that I was filling out papers for active duty. Mother, a normally quiet and nonconfrontational woman, slammed a wooden spoon on the counter and said between clenched teeth, "He's done his service to his country." Liz repeated my arguments for joining up. Leonard, hearing the adult voices rising, climbed into Liz's arms. My mother, bless her, took advantage of the moment and said, "You wouldn't want your son to go to war, would you? Well, I don't either." That really brought it home.

The clincher was the news from the adoption agency that we wouldn't be considered for a child right then if I were about to go off to Vietnam. I didn't hesitate. It was very important to me to have children while Liz and I were young, unlike my parents. There were other factors at work that made me realize the importance of family and the fact that time was passing quickly. That February, on the very same day my father's sister, my aunt Cora, died, we received the news that Harriet had breast cancer. We immediately went to Enosburg to be with Aunt Cora's family. After the funeral, Liz went to Burlington to be with her sister and family. Thus, when we learned that our daughter Laura had been born, we truly rejoiced. Our daughter was born on Valentine's Day 1966. We had told the whole town that we would name the new baby Laura after my mother's mother, yet when she arrived Liz decided to name her Marion Elizabeth after my mother and herself—all three shared February birthdays. But when we showed up with the baby at the Shrewsbury town meeting on the first Tuesday in March, there was no doubt what her name would be. Everyone in town had already taken to calling her Laura.

That's the kind of place Shrewsbury was and continues to be.

Certain days of our lives we always remember. In late July 1966 I got a call that would change my life. It was from Roland Q. Seward, the owner of the biggest dairy operation and milk production plant in the area, along with a popular icecream stand and restaurant. Roland Q, as everyone called him, was a bigwig in the Republican Party, a maker and breaker who was about as close as you got to a political boss in Vermont. Would I run for state senate as the Republican candidate from Rutland? Would I? You bet I would. Roland Q said the Republican Party needed me. He had been on the phone talking to people about running on the Republican ticket for hours, with no success. I wasn't his first choice, but he promised he would help me and said it looked like I could win the Republican primary in September without a contest. Call me back as soon as possible, he urged, because time was getting short.

The first person I needed to talk to was my wife. She sometimes resented how much my work took me away from home. Although she loved living in the country and being a mother, Liz felt spending time alone with her was not a priority with me. Serving in the Vermont Senate would mean even less time together and more work for her. And there was also the question of money. What would Liz say, now that I'd just begun bringing home a decent income?

I drove home that afternoon a little faster than usual, but the ten miles from Rutland to North Shrewsbury seemed to take forever. Liz and the children were out in the sunshine on the little patch of sand I'd had trucked in that summer as a beach for the pond. Liz's sister Harriet and her children, who were spending the month of July with us while Harriet's housekeeper was on vacation, were out on the pond also. Harriet seemed to be doing well after her operation, and Liz really enjoyed her company and being able to help out.

The whole crew had been in swimming and were as relaxed as could be when I showed up, fairly excited to share my news, but also a bit concerned about Liz's reaction. Right away I told Liz about Roland Q's call. She asked me only one question: Did I truly want to run? I said I thought I did, and she said, "That sounds really tempting." We talked more about it that night and decided I'd talk with Art and Bish.

The next day I went to work, excited to share the prospects with my partners and hopeful they would support my venture. But here, too, I knew there were obstacles: The new law firm of Bishop, Crowley & Jeffords was just beginning to make money. The legal work was coming in as fast as we could handle it. I knew my partners would not be thrilled that I wanted to get into politics right now. And what if I won? I knew that serving in the senate was nearly a full-time job for about four months of the year. State Senator Bob Bloomer, another Rutland lawyer, had decided not to run for reelection. That's why a senate seat was open. Ironically, he had told Roland Q that he needed to spend *more* time in his law office. Still, here, obviously, was the great chance and I told my partners I wanted to take it.

They said in no uncertain terms that they couldn't possibly handle all the work without me. Then Bish explained that if I were lucky enough to get elected, I'd have to quit the firm. He was under contract with Congressman Stafford to handle his Vermont legal work. Federal law precluded an elected official from working for a law firm that represented a U.S. Congressman. I was crestfallen.

I left work a little early and drove home to my wife, upset to think that I'd have to turn down this unexpected opportunity for public service. Liz was out on the pond again with the children. I joined them briefly, then walked a few paces down the shore and sat down on a large rock beside the water. I was trying to sort out the whole situation. Liz saw that I was worried and came over to join me. When I told her the story, she looked at me and recited a line from the Disney movie *Matterhorn*, "A man must do what a man must do to be a man." We had recently taken the children to see the film and the older kids had been reenacting the exciting parts ever since. Our niece Kathleen would say with great gusto, "A man must do what a man must do to be a man." So when Liz used it in the context of my dilemma, we both started laughing. Yet she had made the point that it was up to me.

It wasn't so complicated. I would run for office and, if I won, find a new law firm to work for. The important thing was that Liz was behind me, 100 percent.

CHAPTER 5

A Short Primer in Vermont Politics

DESPITE MY FRIENDSHIP with Ted Delaney, there really was no question that I would run as a Republican. Indeed, Republicanism was so integral to my understanding of politics that I had little choice. As I've said, my father's family had been steadily Republican for generations, and their affiliation with the Grand Old Party had served them well. In that, as in so many other things, my parents were typical Vermonters. Rutland County was, and long had been, a Republican county. Oh, there were a good number of Democrats in Rutland City, because it was a manufacturing town and a lot of union members lived there. But the rural areas were solidly Republican and voters there easily outnumbered the city's Democrats.

Indeed, Vermont had been Republican for more than a hundred years, since before the Civil War. In 1854, Vermont was the second state in the union to get a Republican Party organized. And it would have been first in the nation if a state meeting planned that year for July 4 had been held instead of postponed for a week. The party really got going during Lincoln's presidency. Vermonters loved the American Union and hated slavery. Slavery is outlawed in the Vermont Constitution. Thus, when the Confederate states declared their independence in 1861, Vermonters willingly made a huge contribution to Lincoln's armies, sending the second highest number of troops, per capita, among all the states to fight in the Civil War. Vermont gave Lincoln a majority of its votes in 1861. Even in 1864, when he was opposed by a native Vermonter, Stephen Douglas, the state still voted five to one for Lincoln.

Shrewsbury was also about as Republican as any town in Vermont. It was just over the mountains from Plymouth Notch, where Calvin Coolidge had grown up and then had been sworn in as president in 1923 at the family homestead. At the time, Coolidge was vice president under

President Warren G. Harding. He happened to be at the family home when Harding died of "apoplexy," what we today call a stroke. Since Coolidge's father was a justice of the peace, he administered the oath of office right there in the kitchen by lamplight because, as he said, "Nobody told me I couldn't." Coolidge's sister Abigail once taught school in Northam, a mile up the road from our house and not far from Pierces' Store.

By 1966, when I threw my hat into the ring, some deep cracks were showing in the Republican domination. The party's control had once been so strong that for almost a century the governorship was passed back and forth from Republicans on the east side of the Green Mountains to Republicans on the west side. The party fathers picked a candidate, alternating sides of the state. The people went along and elected him to a two-year term. He'd serve his two years, then some Republican would be chosen from the other side of the mountains to serve his two years. The voters stayed in step. They called it the "Mountain Rule" and because the Green Mountains ran almost the whole length of the state, it kept people on both sides happy.

Since there was no serious Democratic opposition, and the elections were foregone conclusions, Vermont voters never got a chance to vote on how good a job a governor had done. He just served two years and went home. Republican politics was run like a private club. All that time the Democrats seemed to be more interested in getting their share of political appointments than in winning high office. After all, what chance did they have? They were so outnumbered. Looking back, it makes you wonder just how independent those famous "independent Vermonters" really were, at least in terms of their politics.

But toward the middle of the twentieth century things really began to change.

Some people say it started with the influx of out-of-staters, "flatlanders," as they were called, and all those hippies who came in the 1960s. But it really started with George Aiken, a native son, tree farmer, and wildflower expert from Windham County in the southern part of the state. Aiken was a progressive, what you'd call today a liberal Republican. He was a handsome, quiet man who looked a lot like Robert Frost. He had a shock of white hair and he talked in a Vermont twang. In the mid-1930s, Aiken went around the state talking about wildflowers and planting trees, all the while building a formidable political coalition of farmers and working people.

My old friend and former law partner Art Crowley says, "Before George Aiken came along, the way to get elected in Vermont was to be a Republican and go on bended knee to National Life and Vermont Marble and ask their permission. They asked you some questions. If you answered them right, you were on your way." The Republican Party, like Art says, was dominated by big business. Still is, for that matter. But it's no longer the dominant party.

George Aiken turned Vermont Republican politics upside down. With the help of his workers and farmers, he won the Republican nomination for governor in 1936, taking on and beating the old and very conservative machine. Aiken then easily won the general election. He was reelected in 1938, all the while bucking the conservative Republican leadership. In 1940, when Aiken's close friend and Windham County neighbor U.S. Senator Ernest Gibson died in office, Governor Aiken appointed the senator's son Ernest Gibson Jr. to the Senate to serve out his father's term. During his brief time in Washington, young Gibson became a close friend of his Senate seatmate, Harry S. Truman of Missouri. Gibson didn't run in the special election held a few months later to officially fill his father's Senate seat because he and Aiken had an agreement. Aiken ran instead, and was easily elected. George Aiken served in the Senate until 1974, and got to be Senate dean, even chair of the Foreign Relations Committee. Gibson went off to war for four years. He came home from the army in 1945, side by side with the man on whose staff he'd served, my neighbor in Rutland, Major General Leonard F. Wing.

Later, President Truman, the Democrat, made Gibson, the liberal Republican, a federal judge. That's the same Ernest Gibson for whom I clerked. And that also is Vermont politics. There is no denying that I have benefited from those age-old alliances and that those benefits and the awareness of them made my decision in May 2001 to leave the party all the more difficult. But none of this could have been foreseen.

I grew up in the moderate Aiken/Gibson wing. The party was so strong in his day that they used to say that when you ran for governor in Vermont, you spent $30,000 to beat the Aiken/Gibson wing in the primary, then a nickel in the general election. The Aiken/Gibson people changed state politics not just because they divided the Republican Party, but also because they made Vermonters think about political issues.

Meanwhile, the Democratic Party was beginning to make serious election efforts, and in 1952, Robert Larrow of Burlington got 40 percent of the votes in the election for governor. Two years later, a Democrat came within 5,000 votes of winning. In 1958, Bob Stafford beat Democrat Bernard Leddy, another Burlington man, by a mere 700 votes to take the governorship. That same year, history was made when Vermont sent a Democrat to Congress. William Meyer went down to Washington and supported a nuclear weapons test ban treaty and the diplomatic recognition of Communist China. That was a little too radical for Vermonters and they brought him back home after just one term. In 1962, with the interstate highways being built and with more and more out-of-staters coming here to live, a young Democratic member of the Vermont legislature from Burlington was elected governor. Philip Henderson Hoff, originally from Massachusetts, was Vermont's first Democratic governor in more than a hundred years. He served three two-year terms, winning despite the death of his popular running mate, Ted Delaney.

So politics was a lot less predictable by the time I decided to run for the state senate that summer of 1966. Old party operators like Roland Q. Seward, so important in the party organization and able to raise a lot of money, couldn't be ignored. Roland Q had nary a moderate bone in his body.

I went to work that next morning ready to call him and say, "Yes, I'll run." But first I had to tell Art and Bish. I must say they took the news better than I'd expected. After all, they both understood politics and knew I had a real opportunity. They wished me well. But they said again that I'd have to leave the firm if I got elected. Bish remembered that Roland Q had once predicted, "A governor will come out of this office some day." After the meeting with my partners, I picked up the phone and called Roland Q.

I knew him pretty well. Our firm handled a lot of his legal matters, which brought him to the office frequently. We often chatted about things other than the law. There was nothing Roland Q liked to talk about more than politics, unless, possibly, it was the Boston Red Sox. Same for me, though in 1966 the Sox were on the way to finishing next to last in the American League. Our only consolation was that the Yankees finished last. Roland Q was a colorful fellow with a quick wit, a sharp tongue, full of jokes, very thick eyeglasses, and he always wore a bright bow tie. As a boy playing baseball, he'd taken a fly ball on the bridge of his nose and the fracture still showed, the crooked nose made more obvious by a receding hairline. He'd grown up on a farm in East Wallingford, a dozen miles south of Rutland, and graduated from the local high school. He liked to tell how he'd gotten up well before dawn each school day to load milk cans onto the Boston freight train. After a year at Rutland Business School, he went back to East Wallingford and took over the family farming business at just nineteen and turned his dairy farm into a dynasty.

Roland Q was a born entrepreneur. Seward's Dairy Bar on Main Street in Rutland was the centerpiece of his empire. The place was a moneymaker, the home of a clever invention, the Pig's Dinner. People came for miles to eat the giant banana split heaped with toppings and served in a wooden dish shaped like a pig's trough. Get a Pig's Dinner down (lots of people couldn't) and you won a button that said "I ate a Pig's Dinner at Seward's." Roland Q really was a self-made man; he thought that if *he* could make it in life, *anybody* could if they worked hard enough. He was a Republican capitalist, believing in a small government that stayed out of the way of private enterprise. He thought welfare was a waste of tax money and he worked tirelessly for his beloved Republican Party. He was on the county and state committees for years, and it had become a fact of political life that if you wanted to run for office, particularly in southern Vermont, you'd better get to know Roland Q. Seward.

Right off the bat, he offered his advice: get out into the county and get myself better known. For damned sure, he said, the county Democrats were going to field a candidate against a newcomer like Jeffords. He thought the three incumbent county senators—Andrew Orzell, George Cook, and Ellery Purdy (Ellery had taught me history at Rutland High)— were all shoo-ins. I went home that night and told Liz I'd have to start campaigning right away, and she said she'd help all she could. Then I called my mother and she said I was getting into politics a little too early in life. But she didn't try to stop me.

The campaigning began in less than a week. While I kept working at the law office on weekdays, Liz spent three afternoons a week going door to door, starting in Rutland. Right off she learned that people in the solidly Republican section of the city would tell her "Of course I'll vote for Jeffords; he's a Republican," and that was that. In the Democrat sections, especially in the Italian neighborhood located down along Otter Creek—called The Gut because it was lower than the rest of town—people would ask my wife questions about me, want to know my stands on the issues. Oftentimes they asked her to come inside to talk. My Democrat wife loved it.

We had a good campaign plan for Saturdays and Sundays. Harriet, her husband Paul McGreevy, and their children went on the road with us. We had flyers printed that said, "Please vote for my uncle Jim." Laura and Leonard were still in diapers but the other kids went door to door, handing out the flyers. We spread out and worked hard in all sections of the city, then went out into rural Rutland County. We went to every chicken pie and baked bean supper we could find. I think I gained ten pounds. We rang doorbells in the college towns of Castleton and Poultney over in the slate-mining country along the New York border. We campaigned the maple-shaded streets of the white clapboard villages of Brandon and Pittsford. We seemed to get a good reception everywhere, particularly in the little mountain places like Chittenden and Mendon, all strongly Republican. Early on I'd been up the road to visit with the Pierces in North Shrewsbury and they put one of my flyers in the store window. Shrewsbury was solidly with us, not for the least of reasons that I was Republican town chair.

We worked hard, but in the primary election in early September I got the fewest votes of the four Republican senate candidates. But I still didn't lose—there were four openings for candidates. The general election turned out to be a lot tougher.

The Democrats in Rutland County put up just one senate candidate, a fellow I knew well, Joseph O'Neill, the late Ted Delaney's partner. O'Neill had become well known in the country for his brilliant defense of Jeffrey Peter Aldrich, the son of the Rutland Congregational Church's minister who had been charged with first-degree murder after he stabbed his stepmother with a kitchen knife when she told him he couldn't go out one evening. It was a compelling, if gruesome, case, but it had garnered lots of publicity. The odds against young Aldrich had been pretty steep, but Joe was a master defense lawyer who really knew his way around a courtroom. After a long trial the jury found Aldrich guilty by reason of insanity (for better or for worse), not of murder in the first degree. Aldrich went to a mental institution, somewhere out of state, not to prison for life.

Everyone knew Joe—and not just because of the Aldrich case. He was a shrewd lawyer, especially in court, where they used to say he was of the old school that "tried the policeman, not the accused."

Joe had bright blue eyes and carefully combed, wavy gray hair. He was a sharp dresser who also liked polka-dot bow ties. Most evenings after work he held court in a Rutland watering hole called the Carriage Room, entertaining fellow lawyers and anyone else who happened in with an endless supply of Irish stories and courtroom tales. Then he'd suddenly stand up and sing Irish songs, soft and sweet. Joe wasn't known as the world's hardest worker, but in 1966 he put a good bit of energy into his senate campaign.

Cigars were popular in those days, and one of the popular brands was White Owl. The advertisements said, "Smoke the Big O." Joe twisted that into his campaign slogan: "Vote the Big O." Joe was a crowd-pleaser. One evening Liz and I were campaigning in Brandon, a good-sized town north of Rutland, and we stopped at the Veterans of Foreign Wars club. As we walked in the door, I heard a very familiar voice. Joe was on stage, telling a story, and when he finished he launched into "My Wild Irish Rose," or some such song of the Old Sod. After listening in the back of the room for a few minutes, I said to Liz, "Come on, let's get out of here." We just turned around and left. I knew that as long as I lived, I could never compete with that kind of style.

But we kept on campaigning, in our own way, shaking hands and talking issues, all over Rutland County, every moment we could.

Election Day was cloudy and cool when Liz and I voted at the old white Shrewsbury Town Hall surrounded by big, bare maples. That night I went by myself to the county Republican headquarters in Rutland—we couldn't find a baby-sitter. Roland Q was there, and my running mates, and maybe a hundred other party faithful. The beer flowed and a good time was had by all. Governor Hoff's expected election to a third term over Republican businessman Richard Snelling hardly slowed things at all. Fairly early in the evening I was able to call Liz and tell her I'd won, finishing fourth, but beating Joe by about 1,000 votes. I started home as soon as I could. Across town, Joe got the bad news, then got up and sang a few Irish melodies, I'm sure just as soulful as ever. Then he told a few stories that got the Carriage Room crowd laughing. The Democrats' party, I'm told, really took off when the news of Hoff's victory came in.

CHAPTER 6

Maverick Republican

I SAID GOOD-BYE to Art and Bish, and joined another Rutland law office, one headed by old Clayton Kinney, who'd been a friend of my father's. We moved out of our beloved Shrewsbury home, renting it out, and rented ourselves a home in Montpelier for the legislative session. The house was about a mile east of the State House along the Winooski River. It was next to a motel that had a wooden replica of the State House in the front yard to attract business. For the next four months I was hardly ever out of sight of a State House.

We arrived with the children at our new home on a cold day at the start of 1967. As we walked in the door, we smelled something awful. I turned on the garbage disposal, which made a funny noise and then flooded the kitchen floor. I grabbed some cloths from the nearest packing box and began mopping, not noticing they were Liz's hand-embroidered towels. We weren't off to a good start in Montpelier.

Of course, I was familiar with the capitol having visited it many times with my father when he worked next door in the Vermont Supreme Court building. But the feeling of walking into the great golden-domed building, filled with mementos of Vermont's remarkable history, as an elected member of the legislature was almost overwhelming. The Vermont State House was built just before the Civil War, of Barre granite, on a hillock just west of the Montpelier business district. In its hallowed halls the legislature had gathered in special session in 1861 and voted the unheard-of sum of $1 million to start Vermont's Civil War effort. In the lower hallway is a bust of Lincoln by Vermonter Larkin Meade, who sculpted the statues for the Great Emancipator's tomb in Springfield, Illinois. In 1927, when Vermont was almost washed away by a flood, Governor Weeks addressed the general assembly in the Vermont House of Representatives hall, declaring that "Vermont will take care of its own." Vermont refused federal aid; independence has always been our hallmark.

As Nazism spread across Europe, members of the legislature met here to declare war on Germany even before the U.S. Congress did in June of 1941. The walls are covered with portraits of famous Vermonters, including Calvin Coolidge and Admiral George Dewey, the hero of the Spanish-American War. A statue of Vermonter Ethan Allen demanding the surrender of Fort Ticonderoga from the British in 1775 decorates the portico. Nearby, there's a brass cannon captured by John Stark's men at the Battle of Bennington in 1777. The place is so full of history that, on the legislative session's opening day, I was feeling the weight and privilege of my new office.

I was sworn in as one of thirty members of the senate by an old friend, Lieutenant Governor John Daley, also of Rutland, who presided in the senate. Jack Daley grew up in Rutland and starred in football at Mount Saint Joseph's Academy, the Catholic high school across town, and had taught history at my alma mater, Rutland High School. After my membership in the legislature's so-called upper house was made official, the senators paraded into the Vermont House of Representatives to join its 150 members for the governor's inaugural address. Governor Hoff told the packed hall that the legislature should approve a record budget to meet the state's fiscal needs. He proposed a radical change in Vermont's method of taxation and talked about the need for a sweeping reform of the state's public welfare system. Many of my fellow Republicans grumbled about Hoff being a free-spending Democrat with wild, progressive ideas. But I'd known Phil for several years and I liked him. I was determined to keep an open mind.

I was assigned to three committees. As one of three lawyers in the senate, I was, of course, put on the Judiciary Committee. I was also named to the important Finance Committee and to the much less influential General Committee.

Over in the State House, the doling out of committee assignments had produced a heated controversy. Though Vermont had a Democratic governor, the house and senate still had clear Republican majorities. Republican legislative leaders hoped to derail the governor's legislative agenda. The new house speaker was Richard Mallary, scion of a prominent and wealthy old Vermont family. Mallary wanted loyalty from the

Republicans in the house and he decided to replace the chairman of the powerful tax-writing house Ways and Means Committee, Reid Lefevre, with a friend of his, Representative Emory Hebard. Reid was a lifelong Republican but rather independent-minded; Mallary wanted someone he knew and could trust. So Lefevre was stripped of his old job and put in charge of the far less important Social Welfare Committee. Reid protested in an emotional speech on the house floor. In tears, he said he had no skills for the new job. It didn't do any good. Off he went to the Welfare Committee. But there was no quit in Reid Lefevre and he was nobody's fool.

For many years Lefevre had been one of the best-known and best-liked politicians in Vermont. Round and jolly with a lot of chins and a ready smile, he looked like Santa Claus without a beard. He had a shrewd political and business mind. Everybody knew him as King Reid, because he owned the famous King Reid Shows, a big-top circus that traveled up and down the East Coast. One time King Reid brought his performers into the Vermont State House and put on a free show for the local folks and legislators in the house of representatives. *Life* magazine ran five pages of photographs of Reid's acrobats, contortionists, and wild animals performing in the Hall of the People. Reid was generally conservative, but in revenge for his demotion, he entered into an unspoken alliance with the Democratic governor.

Governor Hoff was determined to completely change the state's system of taking care of its poor and disadvantaged. For generations, doling out money to the needy had been the job of local officials. Each of Vermont's 251 organized towns and cities elected an "overseer of the poor." Most did a good, conscientious job. But others were stingy with funds, and the needy in some Vermont towns didn't get all they needed. At best, the system was uneven. Hoff introduced legislation that would change all that by getting rid of the local overseers and bringing welfare under the control of a state Social Welfare Agency. Republicans screamed about Democratic big government taking away local control. King Reid probably would have been hollering with them under ordinary circumstances. But he felt wronged, and pretty soon it seemed the more Reid learned of the welfare changes, the more he liked them. Despite Republican protests, King Reid stayed on Hoff's side.

So my first legislative session started with quite a stir, and certainly nobody was paying much attention to the junior senator from Rutland County who, in the early going, kept his mouth shut and listened, and learned. Still, I had my hands full. Not only was legislating nearly a full-time job, but in the evenings and on Mondays, when the legislature didn't meet, I did legal work for my new firm. On weekends, Liz and I drove to Rutland to work in the law office. We spent weekend nights at my mother's house. Liz helped in the office, particularly with preparing clients' tax returns. More than once, I found my exhausted mother of two sound asleep with her head on the typewriter.

Despite these demands, we also kept an ear on the national news. Early 1967 was a very important, even alarming time in history. The Lyndon Johnson administration was sending more and more troops into South Vietnam, and by January 1967 about 400,000 Americans were there. Casualties increased at a proportional rate. Late in January there was a tragedy at Cape Canaveral when the entire crew of an Apollo space mission burned to death in their capsule. Then, at home, our family confronted a sad personal tragedy. In mid-January, Liz learned that her beloved sister Harriet now had a cancerous brain tumor. To Liz's tasks of full-time mother and part-time legal secretary were added frequent trips to Burlington to help, as Harriet waged a brave but long-odds battle against the relentless disease.

In the senate, my days of quiet learning came to a close. As a member of the Finance Committee I was suddenly in a position to determine if one of the most important pieces of legislation passed or failed. In his opening address, Governor Hoff had proposed a radical tax change. The governor wanted the Vermont state income tax to be attached, or "piggy-backed" as he called it, to the federal income tax. Instead of the legislature setting the income tax rate, Vermonters would pay the state a fixed percentage of the income tax they paid to Uncle Sam. Hoff argued that it would simplify things for the Vermont Tax Department, and make Vermont's income tax "more progressive." In other words, wealthy Vermonters would pay more state taxes, and poor Vermonters less. Republicans bristled and called it Democratic big government and socialistic. But the more I heard of the idea, the more it made sense to me. The proposal got referred to the Finance Committee, which had three Democratic members and four Republican members, one of them being me.

Opinions were divided along party lines. But it started to dawn on some of my colleagues that I was listening to the Hoff administration's arguments. I got some talking-tos from my fellow Republicans. The committee vote on the bill was much anticipated. The morning it was to happen, I found myself facing some lobbying I didn't expect. Mavis Doyle, the tall, bespectacled, formidable woman who was the dean of the State House press corps, cornered me outside the committee room, put an index finger in my face, and told me in no uncertain terms that I had better vote for that bill. I told her in equally certain terms that I would do what I thought was best for Vermont. Mavis, still a legend in Vermont journalistic circles, had a rather unorthodox manner and sometimes got carried away on issues that affected the poor and the disenfranchised. On these issues, she was far from neutral.

In committee, we had a final lengthy discussion of the tax plan's merits. Then we voted, with me casting the deciding vote, joining with the three Democratic committee members to send the bill to the senate floor with a favorable recommendation from the Finance Committee. I gave my first important speech as a legislator in the senate chamber in support of the tax bill. The piggyback tax proposal passed the senate and became Vermont law. It still is. Suddenly, Vermont's tax system went from being one of the country's most regressive to one of its most progressive. Years later, people would say that was the first time I broke with my party. They could be right. I look back from the vantage of four decades and see that the pattern had begun.

I also got in a tangle with Republicans on a bill concerning the state's only horse-racing track, located in the southwest corner of the state where the Vermont, Massachusetts, and New York borders meet. Green Mountain Park, in the tiny hill town of Pownal, had fallen on hard times. There had been high hopes for the track when it had opened a few years earlier. The out-of-state owners thought they'd make big bucks from customers from as far away as Albany, especially when the famous Saratoga track wasn't operating. But the crowds stayed small, as did the amount one could win. Certainly, tight-fisted Vermonters didn't spend much money on betting. The track's owners hired lobbyists who came to the legislature seeking help. They asked us to decrease the percentage of the track's betting take that went to the state's general fund. I didn't like the idea. After a long debate, the racetrack bill was passed and Vermont's income from the tax was cut. I voted in the minority against the tax cut and spoke in the senate to say that the state had been "outshrewded" by the track owners and lobbyists. Veteran senator Edward Janeway, who was Vermont's Republican national committeeman, told the senate, "I think Senator Jeffords should be complimented. He coined a good word." Here again, another Jeffords pattern had begun, my occasional bending of the English language. But you know exactly what I mean, don't you?

Late in the legislative session I managed to get an amendment attached to the big tax reform bill that gave a tax break to Vermont taxpayers who were also students. And I voted for the big social welfare reform bill that Reid Lefevre got passed for Governor Hoff. By the end of the session, the press was calling me a "maverick Republican." I suppose I was.

When the legislature adjourned, the media voted a "legislator of the year" award. The prize went, as it should have, to Reid Lefevre. I was named the best first-year legislator, or rookie of the year.

During the session, I became good friends with a lively young member of the house, Theodore Riehle from Burlington. Ted Riehle was a wealthy young Republican who spent summers on his own island in Lake Champlain, complete with a private airstrip. He'd gotten it into his head that Vermont should try to get rid of what he thought were eyesores all over our lovely landscape—billboards. Ted tried unsuccessfully to get a law limiting outdoor advertising through the 1967 session. As soon as the legislature went home, Ted set off throughout Vermont to sell his idea to the public. He didn't need to convince me. I told him that in 1968 I'd do all I could to help him and, if he could get the bill through the house, I'd lead the fight for it in the senate.

The summer was an incredibly busy one. In addition to my legal work, Roland Q insisted that I chair the Republican Party's big autumn fundraising dinner. We spent the summer at our Shrewsbury home, with Liz often traveling to Burlington to be with Harriet and her family. Then, in July, Liz's father, John Daley, died of a heart attack. Liz took comfort that he'd died while in church, a fitting ending for a devout Catholic who had once studied to be a priest.

As fall moved toward winter, politics was in the air with a presidential election drawing near and a new session of the legislature approaching. It was hard to concentrate on such things considering what Harriet was going through; she died that October. Liz was grief-stricken—not just losing a sister but a best friend.

Nonetheless, she was at my side just a few weeks later for the Republican State Committee dinner that I had put together. It was held at the biggest hall in the state, the University of Vermont's Patrick Gymnasium in Burlington. Liz and I joined forty-eight others at the massive head table, seated before fifteen hundred Republicans dressed in their Saturday evening best.

The guest of honor was Republican presidential candidate George Romney, governor of Michigan, who gave the keynote address. But the show was stolen by the man who had just become the GOP state chairman, Elbert G. Moulton—a man with a broad and engaging smile, an ample midriff, and a contagious laugh, the quintessential political tub-thumper. After the distinguished Governor Romney declined an invitation to do so, Moulton came riding into the big hall sitting atop an elephant. Behind him walked two manure scoopers dressed up to look like Governor Hoff and Lieutenant Governor Daley—Democrats. It brought the house down. After Al dismounted, with some difficulty, he gave a rousing pitch calling for a big party effort in the coming year to recapture the governorship for the Grand Old Party. The applause was loud and long, and when the dinner proceeds were counted, they came to a Vermont record $27,000. I was introduced to the crowd and received a nice round of applause. Liz said afterward that people were calling me a rising star of the party, and I didn't disagree at all. Back home in Shrewsbury, my phone rang for several days with thanks and congratulations from fellow Republicans. This was a unique experience, but at the time I did not know it would be a nearly once-in-a-lifetime one.

There were other things that I had taken for granted. In the earliest years of my political life, my wife and I had been a well-tuned team. I have mentioned how much she threw herself into my campaigns, but I don't think I ever considered how much fun Liz, Harriet, the nieces and nephews, and our own children made of the campaign trail. They joyously hit the road, putting miles on the car and on foot as they passed out homemade campaign posters and stumped for my cause.

In retrospect, I can see that I took much of that for granted and too infrequently asked Liz what she wanted to do, about her hopes and fears, her dreams and disappointments. I was a man on a mission. Liz had told me she was with me through thick or thin. What more was there to talk about?

There had been signs even before Harriet's death that Liz was suffering from the lifestyle I was imposing on her. I was often so busy that we didn't have substantive talks for weeks on end. We had arguments instead; often, that was how things got decided.

How brave she had been to sit there so soon after Harriet's death and laugh while Al Moulton rode around on an elephant and people glad-handed one another. It must have seemed banal to her but she was proud of the job I'd done to organize the big campaign event. I never thanked her for simply being there. Or perhaps, I just assumed she knew how I felt and didn't have to announce my appreciation.

To fight off the depression that she had experienced with Harriet's and her father's deaths, Liz had been prescribed tranquilizers. She also sometimes self-medicated herself with alcohol. A problem was developing but neither of us saw it. I was too busy with my legal and political career; and she was just trying to hold herself together, be a good mom and a good partner to me.

The historic year of 1968 began with a buzz of political activity both nationwide and in Vermont. As Lyndon Johnson failed to significantly decrease the level of fighting in Vietnam, maverick Minnesota Democratic U.S. Senator Eugene McCarthy announced that he would oppose Johnson in the important New Hampshire presidential primary. In Vermont, attorney Thomas Hayes of Burlington, a former aide to Vermont senator Winston Prouty, said he was a candidate for lieutenant governor. Thus the first member of what the Republican Party in 1968 would call its "Team for the Times" had come forward.

The new legislative session was barely a week old when a surprise announcement came from an old bastion of Republican political power, the National Life Insurance Company. Former company president Deane C. Davis, now chairman of the board, held a press conference to say he was running for governor. Davis, sixty-seven, had been a major player in the party for years. He was staunchly conservative, from an old Vermont family, and a friend of Roland Q. Seward. Davis had lived in Rutland years ago when he was a municipal judge. In fact, he'd lived in our neighborhood and he and my father were friends and occasional golf partners. Always well dressed, with a neatly trimmed mustache and a fondness for tweeds, Davis was graceful, well spoken, and a bit of an aristocrat. He'd been a lover of horses since he was a child in Barre, and he raised and trained prized Vermont Morgans.

Davis's entry into the governor's race set up a classic Republican primary. Attorney General James Lowell Oakes was already running for governor. Jim was a Harvard graduate, a moderate Republican identified with the party's Aiken/Gibson wing. I didn't know Davis that well, but Jim Oakes was a friend of mine and I'd helped him get several law enforcement–related bills through the senate. I found myself in a situation I had to get used to and quick—sometimes taking a stand against those who had been my father's friends and political supporters. I privately supported Oakes.

As January ended, sad news reached the State House from the coast of Maine. While on a weekend trip to Portland, the old showman King Reid died of a heart attack.

Back in the legislature, much of the state's attention was focused on the state's roadsides, as well as its roadways. Ted Riehle, having found strong support in the hustings for his antibillboard law, was moving it through the Vermont House despite strong opposition from the outdoor advertising interests and their lobbyists. When it passed the house, I took over the bill's management in the senate. The lobbyists took their fight to me. I thought the billboard bill was an idea whose time had come. The views along Vermont roadways were blighted with big advertising signs, while the state's economy depended so much on attracting tourists. One of the clever devices used to promote the Riehle bill was a rewording of a bit of Ogden Nash verse:

> *I think that I shall never see*
> *A billboard as lovely as a tree.*
> *Perhaps unless the billboards fall,*
> *I'll never see a tree at all.*

Late in the session the billboard bill became law. It not only made Vermont more beautiful, it got people thinking about other conservation matters. The Riehle Bill continues to be law to this day, which is one reason why Vermont is so unique. The borders to the state, especially on the New York side, are crammed with billboards. Then you drive into the Green Mountain State and your view is unobstructed from border to border.

In March, Eugene McCarthy defeated Lyndon Johnson in the New Hampshire primary. The president's popularity was in sharp decline as the Vietnam War raged on. In the same primary, Richard Nixon beat Nelson Rockefeller, making him the favorite to win the Republican presidential nomination. As the legislature neared adjournment in April, I supported Governor Hoff's call for a state constitutional amendment that would give the governor, and other constitutional officers (including the attorney general) four-year, instead of two-year, terms. The amendment failed. A tax increase favored by the governor was passed, but only after the senate reduced it a good deal. I tried, in the last hours, to restore it to the level the governor wanted, but I just missed getting enough votes. Many of my Republican colleagues were not pleased. I should say that during my first two terms in the senate, I voted with the Republican majority most of the time. But sometimes I broke ranks. I heard the word *maverick* used more and more to describe me.

Throughout the session, Liz continued taking prescription drugs for her nerves, but I thought it was a temporary problem, a response to the loss of her father and her sister so close together. I hope my lack of concern was from ignorance and my busy schedule rather than inattention. In retrospect, I see how involved I was in my work as a legislator, making new friends and feeling so much a vital part of change that I was just barreling through life. I felt these losses that Liz took so acutely, of course, but I was not one to dwell on them.

Part of it has to do with personality and upbringing—those old influences again. Liz had been brought up in a family with a father who worked from nine to five and then came home. If Liz's father was away from the house, he was at church. I had been raised with a father who was seldom home and who valued public service and work as a top priority. She had been raised in a family that openly shared emotions; mine shouldered through adversity. That same Yankee stoicism has allowed me to continue fighting for a national bottle bill or for protections for the small dairy farm, despite more disappointments than I would care to count. But those attributes alienated me from my wife. She had been through a lot—as had I—but my way of dealing with things was to plunge on while what Liz needed was a partner who would pay her more attention. She began having nightmares and sought relief in growing numbers of prescription medicines that included Librium and sleeping pills, and more and more alcohol. It got so bad that she actually began to have hallucinations. And the worse the nightmares and hallucinations became so, too, the feeling of abandonment.

In truth, I didn't know what depression was. She was angry with God. She was lonely. And she felt that her opinion had ceased to matter to me. It was not a good time. What made it worse was that Liz knew that I had worked hard and really should have been in my glory. This divide we had come to was keeping both of us from enjoying the successes of the past few years and the early years of our marriage. I was saving Vermont's precious views but I was ignoring a pressing problem right in my own home.

All of this is written after a good deal of introspection and reflection, of course, but also with the benefit of all we've learned in the past thirty years about mood swings, chemical imbalances, alcohol as a depressive, and the negative impact of overmedication. When Liz and I were growing up and dating, alcohol—and cigarettes, I must add—were seen as sophisticated. In the movies, the most romantic stars spent their days and nights slugging down belts of alcohol and exhaling dreamily. I myself certainly indulged in serious alcohol consumption at times during my college and navy years. But I've not been tempted to use alcohol to dull my emotions. Liz did. She must have had some inkling that she was in trouble because she mentioned to her doctor that she sometimes overindulged in alcohol, particularly before her menstrual period when her mood swings were so dramatic. Sometimes she did so just to get some rest. The doctor told her not to worry because she wasn't drinking every day; she'd been through a lot and would just need to take time to heal. This was the same doctor who was prescribing Librium.

This was, of course, just prior to the women's movement and the strength that it gave to women like Liz, bright women who had put their own careers on hold to support their husbands and their families, who found the role of wife and mother less fulfilling than they had imagined. I came from a world where Mother questioned little, even her husband's announcement that Saturday night was his club night. Liz on the other hand had had a vibrant career before we married, one that took her to exciting places and provided the opportunity to meet all sorts of interesting people and stretch herself mentally. She had willingly given that up to advance my career and to be a mother. But she had done so with the understanding that she would be a partner in my career, yet now I was too busy most of the time to even have a half-hour chat with her. Was I a cad? I don't think so. Like so many men in America, I was playing a role and expecting my wife to play hers. The fact that Liz couldn't or wouldn't accept that this was to be her life was beyond me.

It wasn't that I was totally unaware of her distress. In fact, we moved to my mother's house in Rutland for the winter legislative session, hoping that would help. I even hired a neighbor's child, Melanie Gregory, as a mother's helper. Liz always loved Rutland; she had her own friends there and we thought Mother could also benefit from having the family close to her. Although pretty independent herself, she was aging. My sister, Mary, visited once a year but she had moved far away, to Brewer, Maine, where her husband, Brooks, was a forester. Between her two children, John and Hope, and her job as a primary school teacher, her trips home were infrequent.

To facilitate living arrangements and provide Mother with the privacy she needed, we made a little apartment for her in the back of the house, where the housekeeper had once lived, for when she wasn't in Florida. But Mother never really gave over her control of the house to Liz, and although they were fond of each other, there were sometimes conflicts. During the week I was often away from home for days on end, and quite frankly, I was not very adept at handling this sort of problem. I was becoming more like my father every day, except in one regard: The children were growing and I liked to spend as much time as possible with them. On weekends, when I wasn't busy at the office getting caught up on my cases, I was with them, often introducing them to the rudiments of various sporting activities. Liz sometimes complained that I was moving away from her, that I wasn't including her in the campaign and the decision-making part of my life, and, probably more important, that I wasn't interested in her life.

• • •

After the legislature went home, Liz and I took a long-awaited vacation, flying to Bermuda for a week alone in the sun. We walked the beaches and swam a lot, but to truly get away wasn't really possible. Every time we picked up a newspaper, something historic seemed to be happening back home. On March 31, President Johnson surprised the country by announcing that he would not seek reelection. Four days later, in Memphis, Tennessee, the Reverend Martin Luther King Jr. was assassinated. It seemed, at times, that the nation was coming apart.

These events made us aware again of the importance of public service and of our shared commitment to make the world a better place. In the Caribbean sunshine, Liz and I had a long talk about the future, and I told her that I wanted to run for attorney general. As on our little beach in Shrewsbury nearly two years before, she said that if it was what I really wanted, I should go for it. We didn't talk about Liz's problems and her loneliness, her frustrations with my overly busy schedule, her feeling of being shut out from my political life. Instead, glazing over our problems as was our optimistic natures, we came back to Vermont ready to hit the campaign trail again, and found out that another Republican had beat me out of the starting gate.

CHAPTER 7

Making Environmental History

MY OPPONENT in the primary race for attorney general was Joseph Palmisano, the short and feisty state's attorney from Washington County, seat of the Vermont capital of Montpelier. I knew Palmisano only slightly, and I didn't care much for him. He strutted around portraying himself as a law-and-order man. I knew he was fond of staking out Goddard College, a very liberal little school in Plainfield, ten miles east of Montpelier, looking for marijuana users. He also had a reputation among the state's legal community for being something less than honest. In his announcement for the office of Vermont attorney general, Palmisano criticized the U.S. Supreme Court and its chief justice, Earl Warren, saying that its civil libertarian decisions were hampering law enforcement officials. He said, "It is time we become more concerned with the victims of the crime and a little less concerned with the accused criminals." I couldn't have agreed less with the man, believing that the Warren court's decisions on the rights of the accused were long overdue.

I decided I'd better get my campaign up and running. Two days back from the Caribbean, I announced my candidacy, holding a party at our house in North Shrewsbury. About fifty neighbors and a handful of press showed up. To Liz and my surprise, just before I started to talk, in walked gubernatorial candidate Deane Davis.

We kept the announcement party informal. I made a brief statement in which I took a far different tack than Palmisano, emphasizing the need for environmental regulations at a time when few protections had been enacted here or elsewhere. I was responding to a growing concern among Vermonters about the impact of vacation homes and ski developments on the environment. I told the group, "We must have new laws to prevent the citizens of this state from being deprived of the potential and the benefit of our natural resources."

My other theme had to do with balancing a firm position against drug dealers with a compassionate view toward users and rehabilitation. My friend Attorney General Jim Oakes had recently said the Mafia might be involved in Vermont land speculation and other illegal activities, including drug dealing. I said, "There will be no mercy for those who would seek to profit from the violation of our laws by organized crime, especially through the sale of drugs. On the other hand, modern knowledge has taught us much about those who deviate from our laws through lack of normal necessities. My program will be aimed at the rehabilitation of these citizens."

The next day the *Rutland Herald* summarized my views, but the reporter seemed more interested with the informality of the event and the odd fact that Davis was at the party of an Oakes supporter.

The *Herald* reporter wrote,

Three-year-old Leonard Jeffords was wandering among the crowd in pajamas. Nobody chuckled or patted him on the head. He's just one of the neighborhood kids. The talk wasn't about politics. It was about things such as milk prices, the dry weather, and whether a certain stretch of road is going to be blacktopped.

Nobody had a martini or a scotch and soda. There was punch—the bowl on the right was "with"—and in the kitchen Ed Briggs would show you where the beer was stored (top of the refrigerator, hope you like Schlitz).

Someone in the kitchen had an Oakes petition. "Sign it," he said to a neighbor.

"Well, there's another man out in the front room who wants to be governor," he was told.

"Who's that?"

"Deane Davis"

"Never heard of him."

"Good man."

"So's Oakes."

"Give me the damned thing. I'll sign."

After the speech-making, the ties were loosened and the suit-coats came off. The speech was short and to the point. Jeffords was happy, and he and his wife wanted to share their happiness with their neighbors. That was about it.

Mrs. Jeffords said she always heard the Democrats throw good parties. "We wanted to have a good one, too," she said. Well, they did. Anybody in North Shrewsbury will tell you that.

Each weekend Liz and I packed the kids into the car and set out for somewhere in the state. Liz remembers that we seemed to be in the Northeast Kingdom all the time, referring to the three very rural counties that make up Vermont's northeastern section—Caledonia, Orleans, and Essex Counties. The place is as Republican as it is woodsy. For anyone running in a statewide Republican primary it was important to spend a lot of time up there.

I took careful note of a speech made a few days later in the southern part of the state by Al Moulton, the Republican state chair of elephant-riding fame. "I don't think you can any longer call Vermont a Republican state," Al told Republican women meeting in Windham County. "We need to recognize that fact and plan our campaign around it." Al clearly saw the need for the Republican Party in Vermont to broaden its political base, to reach out to the growing number of independent-minded voters in the state and to young people.

Despite those words of wisdom, I was receiving reports that a lot of old-time party regulars, including gubernatorial candidate Davis, were quietly backing Palmisano. The suspicion was strengthened one weekend when I ran into the Davis campaign at one of the county fairs that take place in Vermont nearly every weekend from mid-summer to late September. Davis was traveling with a camper that served as sort of portable campaign headquarters. Anywhere it stopped, people were welcomed in to pick up campaign literature, Republican political buttons, and such. I went inside and saw a lot of Palmisano's campaign stuff, but none of mine. I asked if I could leave my campaign material and was told that, of course, I could. A few days later we came on the camper again at another fair. Again, I saw plenty of Palmisano propaganda, but none of my own. I asked where my campaign material had gone and was told that it was so popular, the supply had run out. I was pretty sure the Jeffords-for-Attorney-General stuff had gone into the nearest trash can.

I knew Davis and Palmisano were of a like mind on the subject of get-tough law enforcement. I had nothing against tough law enforcement, but the whole matter of enforcing laws is a lot more complex than that, and I intended to talk to the voters about it. Looking back, the whole matter of the missing campaign materials seems a bit comic. But at the time, I took it as fair warning that, though I was much better known statewide than my opponent, with such in-party shenanigans, the outcome of the primary election was very much in doubt.

In late May I challenged Palmisano to a debate. He replied, "As soon as he gives me the courtesy of sending me a letter, I'd be glad to." I sent the letter but got no response.

World events often overshadowed Vermont politics. On June 5 the nation was again rocked by violence as Robert Kennedy, just after winning the Democratic presidential primary in California, was fatally shot in Los Angeles. In Vietnam, U.S. Marines were surrounded and under siege at Khe Sanh.

By late June, Palmisano still hadn't agreed to debate, so I told the press that he was evading me. Still no debate. Then Palmisano announced there would be no debate because of my "mudslinging."

I was getting fed up. I told a Rutland audience, "I will offer a platform which deals boldly and effectively with all the functions of the attorney general's office, not just drug abuse or some other single phase of its complex responsibilities." I added that while I certainly agreed that drug abuse was a problem in Vermont, "I also agree that the American flag is a very fine thing. I am in favor of motherhood, and I am a great lover of apple pie."

On July 20 the nation's hopes were lifted when an Apollo spacecraft landed on the moon and astronaut Neil Armstrong became the first human being to walk on the lunar surface. Liz and I and the children, like the rest of America, watched the whole thing on television that Sunday afternoon, absolutely spellbound.

In mid-campaign I made a financially costly little mistake. I'd had a brochure printed with my smiling picture on the front. We'd just begun to distribute them when a woman in Burlington took one, looked, and said, "It's too bad they shot that poor man." Then I realized that my picture looked alarmingly like Robert Kennedy. A Kennedy-looking brochure in a Republican primary wouldn't do. A lot of brochures went in the trash, and we had to have a new one designed. And finances were tight; we had to worry about every penny.

Joe and I finally came face-to-face on an August afternoon at a candidates' forum in Montpelier put on by the Republican State Committee. Candidates for all the state's attorney offices were on hand, so each was limited to a two-minute statement. We drew numbers, and Joe got number one, I number two. Just before Joe was to speak, a policeman hurried from the back of the room to the podium and whispered in Joe's ear. Joe immediately told the moderator that a police emergency had come up. He moved to the side of the stage for what appeared to be an important conversation with the officer.

As that distracting sideshow went on well in sight of the audience, the moderator called me up to speak. I dutifully followed the rules by talking for just two minutes. All the while Joe and the officer stood to the side of the stage, whispering and gesturing and holding the audience's curiosity. When I finished, Joe took the microphone and said he was dealing with an urgent criminal matter and couldn't stick around to answer questions. He begged the crowd's indulgence, went on to speak a full twenty minutes, then left the hall. He got the longest applause of the day.

Two days later, he and I were at a candidates' forum at Madeline Harwood's house in Manchester. Each candidate gave a speech. Joe said he couldn't stay because it was his wedding anniversary and he wanted to spend the night with his wife. Later that evening, Liz and I and the children went to the Vermont State Fair in Rutland. Something happened that night that we Jeffordses have never forgotten and still laugh about three and a half decades later. We saw the pressured prosecutor and devoted husband on his anniversary night campaigning alone and passing out balloons along the midway of the Vermont State Fair.

Leonard had strayed a few feet away and Joe handed him a balloon that said, "Palmisano for Attorney General." Leonard smiled and took it, then said, "Thank you, Mr. Palmisano. My daddy is Jim Jeffords." Joe snatched the balloon back and walked off in a huff.

As Election Day got close the campaigning was day-to-day, and tiring. I'd go down a street, or midway, shaking hands, usually saying, "I'm Jim Jeffords. Nice to see you." One day in Shelburne I shook a woman's hand and said, "Hi, I'm Jim Jeffords. Nice to see you." The woman said, "I know, I'm your wife." Liz told me I looked kind of glazed over and it was time to go home.

September 10 was primary day in Vermont. When the votes were counted, old George Aiken led the Republican ticket, brushing aside an archconservative Republican opponent to win the party's nomination for his sixth senate term. Davis easily beat my friend Jim Oakes to win the gubernatorial nomination. Tom Hayes won the lieutenant governor primary. Friend Ted Riehle lost to Dick Thomas in the race for the secretary of state nomination. And I beat Joe Palmisano by 32,000 to 22,000 votes. I believed my biggest hurdle on the way to the attorney general's office had been cleared. Palmisano went back to his hometown of Barre and practiced law. More than twenty years later he was charged with fraud for misuse of clients' funds, convicted, and sentenced in 1997 to at least seven years in prison.

To manage the Republicans' fall campaign, Roland Q. Seward had convinced Al Moulton to be the State Committee's first salaried full-time director. Roland Q couldn't have picked a better man. Al was a master promoter, having served in the Hoff administration as state commissioner of development. As Vermont's chief salesman, Al had come up with the very successful "Beckoning Country" advertising campaign that lured tourists and new business to the state. For the 1968 Republican campaign, he invented a new slogan, calling the Republican ticket "The Team for the Times."

That campaign was a very happy experience. My opponent, Democrat Peter Whalen, was a nice enough fellow but lacked firm ideas on how to manage the attorney general's office. Liz and I worked steadily, visiting all parts of the state, usually taking the kids along. What made it nice was that the sense of urgency I had felt in the Palmisano campaign was gone. We were able to relax a bit and enjoy our wanderings throughout Vermont at its most beautiful time of year. I was able to concentrate on substantive issues rather than react to Palmisano's jibes. That's the kind of campaigning I like.

On election night Liz and I got together with the Team for the Times and a few hundred other Republicans at the Tavern Motor Inn in Montpelier to watch the returns. Nixon carried Vermont in his near landslide victory in the presidential race. Davis won the governorship pretty handily over Jack Daley. I got 68,000 votes to Peter Whalen's 44,000. My total was 3,000 less than Davis's but 2,000 more than Nixon received in Vermont. So the Republican Party swept Vermont in 1968. I was the attor-

ney general–elect of the state. That night we stayed around and had a
few beers. This election night we had made sure we had a baby-sitter.

But winning the election meant that we would have to move to
Montpelier full-time. Liz and I had loved North Shrewsbury from the first
time we drove through there. I tried to put the best light on it I could.
We'd always had a hard time watching TV in Shrewsbury because the
mountain winds kept blowing the antenna off the roof. "Come to Montpelier, we'll watch TV without any problems," I said. Liz was not particularly impressed.

We settled on a white Colonial house in a quiet hillside neighborhood
near the schools and I quit another law firm in Rutland. I got busy right
off assembling a first-rate staff for the attorney general's office, and when
I was done, I think I had as fine a group of assistant attorneys general as
Vermont has ever seen. The first person I brought on board was John
Hansen, a young lawyer and old friend from Rutland. Bright and full of
fun, John would be the perfect person to handle the environmental issues
I wanted to tackle right away. Then I signed on young Fred Parker, very
serious and very smart, as deputy attorney general and gave him much of
the responsibility for running the legal aspects of the office. I found a very
experienced older lawyer to run the office's litigation division, which I
rightly expected would be very busy. Russell Morse was a retired major
general who had worked in the U.S. Army's Judge Advocate General, or
JAG, office. From Jim Oakes, I inherited the experienced Louis Peck who
proved to be very savvy politically. Louis later became an associate justice
of the Vermont Supreme Court.

Also joining my office was Martin Miller, who had a brilliant analyti-
cal mind and in future years would be chair of the Vermont Public Ser-
vice Board and president of a big electrical company. Round-faced John
Calhoun, with a diabolical wit and a cunning legal mind, was an old
Capitol Hill hand who'd spent years working for Senator Winston Prouty.
Other talented assistants included Edward Amidon, John Stahl, Layton
Klavana, Bill Gilbert, George Rice, Will Griffin, and Bill Keefe. Dick
Blum, as smart as he was liberal, became head of the Consumer Protec-
tion Division I started in the office. And I appointed the first woman
assistant attorney general Georgiana Miranda.

We were such a team that I never really needed to have staff meetings.
Instead, we met most days for lunch at the Miss Montpelier Diner, just

down the street from the State House. They had a blue plate special so, over meatloaf, or grilled cheese sandwiches, or hash and eggs, we talked business and laughed a lot.

My term as Vermont attorney general coincided with an era of momentous happenings in America. The years 1969 through 1972 saw extraordinary social change as the Vietnam War touched virtually every aspect of American life. It was really a time of revolution and many of the difficult problems that arose ended up in the legal system and profoundly influenced life even in remote little Vermont. The crime rate went up. There were protests against the war, riots over racial injustice, and a growing disgust with the political system. Young people were demanding a greater say in government. The U.S. Supreme Court decided *Rowe vs. Wade* and I found myself being sued to validate Vermont's antiabortion statute. This was no easy task. Because I was essentially the attorney representing Vermont, I had to defend an antiabortion statute that I strongly disagreed with. Pat Leahy, now a fellow U.S. Senator representing Vermont, was my legal opponent as state's attorney for Chittenden County. The court threw out the Vermont antiabortion statute. I won for losing.

A remarkable influx of young members of the counterculture moved to Vermont, bringing with them social change and an appreciation of nature. At the same time, ordinary citizens began to demand increased environmental protections. The people of my state seemed to realize en masse that the unspoiled beauty of Vermont could not be taken for granted, that it would not last unless strong actions were taken. Vermonters also awakened to the fact that their state had already been polluted to a surprising degree and that corrective action was needed. Those years were exciting, challenging, sometimes a bit scary, but taken as a whole I think they were wonderful. My little attorney general's office got right in the middle of most of the key issues that suddenly confronted Vermont.

These were the busiest years yet of my career; unfortunately, that meant I had little extra time for my wife. The problems she was already experiencing—a sense of isolation, distrust in the political system, the pressure to be a perfect political wife and mother, her own longing for creative fulfillment—took their toll on her. And she was adamantly opposed to the Vietnam War. I, too, was dismayed about the mounting deaths and felt it was time to get out. I kept those thoughts to myself, a stance Liz found increasingly hypocritical. Regretfully, I paid too little attention to the growing signs that she was in trouble. Mostly, I worked and worked and worked.

The big issue in the legislature in 1969 was Governor Davis's desire to enact a state sales tax for Vermont. Davis had a good head for business. He knew the state needed more revenue, and fast. Still, it was unusual for a Republican to even think about taxes. It was even more ironic because the governor also set about trying to make good on a campaign promise to cut government spending. Right off, he went after part of the attorney general's budget. By mid-March I'd had enough and went to a legislative committee to complain that the governor was breaking a campaign promise about maintaining law and order by trying to cut state law enforcement budgets. My office and the Department of Public Safety, which included the Vermont State Police, were "damned poor places to save money," I said. The governor was not pleased. In the end, the sales tax got passed but my budget wasn't cut and I didn't lose any staff.

In early spring, as soon as the snow melted, Governor Davis accepted an invitation from some people in the town of Stratton, along the southern part of the Green Mountains, to see firsthand the mess some vacation home developers had made. It proved to be a historic trip. On a mountainside next to a ski area, Deane Davis, a devout believer in unbridled free enterprise, had a life-changing experience that altered the course of Vermont's history forever. The governor was shown raw sewage bubbling out of the ground next to some quick-built ski chalets. He was so infuriated that when he got back to Montpelier he set about putting a stop to that kind of thing.

Within weeks, Davis appointed the Governor's Commission on Environmental Controls and instructed it to come up with legislation to protect Vermont from the kind of pollution he had just witnessed. He named a gentleman who had served with me in the senate, Arthur Gibb, as head of the commission. Gibb was a Yale graduate who had been an investment banker until, in middle age, he bought a farm in Addison County near Lake Champlain. Art was one of those Vermont newcomers who saw more clearly than a lot of natives that we needed to get a handle on the state's future. He became a stalwart of the environmental movement. Senator Gibb and his commission held meetings and hearings around the state, gathering testimony and ideas from Vermonters. The trouble was, there was nothing Gibb's group could get done until the next year, when the legislature came back to Montpelier to hopefully turn Gibb's recommendations into laws. The governor and I agreed that was too long to wait.

Part of the answer, I decided, was to rearrange the attorney general's office. I created a Division of Environmental Controls and Local Affairs and asked John Hansen to run it. Its main responsibility was to work on writing new land-use, pollution, and conservation legislation. But the first job I gave John was to find a legal way to stop the kind of reckless, polluting development the governor had witnessed. Nobody knew better than I how ridiculously easy it was to get a permit to develop Vermont land. After all, I'd done legal work for land developers around the Killington ski area and had discovered that Vermont really didn't have any land-use controls on the books. We were wide open to fast-buck developers.

John discovered that the Vermont State Board of Health had some amazing legal powers to protect public health, powers that had never been put to use. John and I set up a meeting with Robert Aiken, the health commissioner, to see if he would be willing to use these powers. Was he ever. Bob Aiken was ready to go to war.

I really liked Commissioner Aiken. He was a New York State native who had lived most of his life in Vermont. Bob was a distant cousin of Senator Aiken, and he'd been a practicing physician until he got into state government. He'd been the state health commissioner for a dozen years and was a savvy administrator who knew his way around state government and the legislature. Bob was crusty, bright, and had a dry sense of humor. In his spare time, he liked to fly fish the swift streams that come down off the Green Mountains. He liked a good fight, be it with a sizable rainbow trout or a bunch of developers. And one thing that incensed him was the idea of developers making money while raw sewage polluted Vermont's pristine rivers.

John Hansen went to work searching through the laws of other states to find existing regulations that Vermont could use as a model for its own. He quickly hit on a set of development regulations from Westchester County, just outside New York City. They were unbelievably tough laws, written for subdivisions planned for a very densely populated urban area.

John and I agreed that if Vermont had regulations like that, the kind of problems the governor had seen in southern Vermont would come to a quick halt.

One evening John, Fred Parker, and I sat down in my office to talk about the Westchester regulations. Somebody had a fifth of Scotch and we put it to good use. John warned us both, "You'd better understand what's coming. You'd better read them carefully." We had a frank talk, and a few laughs, and in the end we agreed to recommend the Westchester regulations to Commissioner Aiken and to the governor. As attorneys in private practice, all three of us had represented developers. The impact of the regulations was crystal clear. Developers were going to get hit hard and would fight back. If those regulations went into effect, we probably could never go back to private law practice. Certainly we'd get few of our old clients back. But we decided to go ahead. We took the regulations to Bob Aiken first; he didn't bat an eyelash. Aiken backed them 100 percent. "When you fly under the banner of health, they've got to prove you wrong," he said. Then Aiken sounded out the health board and got a prompt okay.

We weren't sure how the governor would react. He'd been talking tough about unregulated development since his visit to Stratton. Still, this was Deane Davis, the businessman's friend. Yet the governor told us to go ahead, too. "Start out tough," he said. "It's easier to tone 'em down than to strengthen 'em."

We changed the Westchester regulations to better fit a rural state. The health board adopted them on September 19, acting in response to what its members believed amounted to a statewide health emergency. The firestorm I expected hit almost immediately. The developers were up in arms and their anger came to focus on a hearing set for the State House on a November night. I had the job of presiding over the meeting. The governor couldn't be there, but he sent one of his top assistants, Fred Reed, to represent him. That memorable evening the house of representatives was packed to the rafters. It's understating things to say the conservationists were in a minority. Developers and their friends were out in force, as were many conservative Vermonters who were opposed to governmental control of any kind.

The tone of the meeting was established early on when a couple of speakers who said Vermont needed strong conservation laws were booed loudly. Pretty soon, the environmentalists stopped trying to talk at all. Hour after hour, speaker after speaker let me, the health commissioner, the board, and the governor's representative know they considered the regulations unnecessary and onerous. I was about to call on Fred Reed to give the governor's position when Fred appeared at my side. While still another speaker was venting his spleen, Fred said, "Well, Jim, I see you've got things well under control. Guess I'll go on back to the office." He walked out. I felt like General Custer at Big Horn. But we got through the hearing and the brave health board and its wonderful commissioner held to their tough subdivision regulations. Vermont was not going to be at the mercy of careless out-of-state developers. The regulations stayed on the books.

We knew, however, that we had only earned a reprieve. Broad land-use regulations needed to be written if Vermont was to find a way to balance needed development with protection of its natural resources. Gibb and Governor Davis recognized that as well. While the health regulations were being written and adopted, the Gibb Commission and John Hansen continued their work to prepare conservation legislation to present at the upcoming session. We soon realized it was too much work to meet the deadline. So we divided the tasks with me taking responsibility for land-use and development matters and John overseeing water-pollution regulations.

Meanwhile, Liz was doing her best to get used to being the wife of a high-ranking state official serving in the Republican administration of Governor Davis. The first lady, Marjorie Davis, was a woman fond of formality. Her politics were highly conservative, as was her lifestyle. She often hosted social gatherings for the wives of the men who served in her husband's cabinet. Liz would put on the white gloves, a nice dress, and a little hat; grit her teeth; and go to the event. She dreaded each gathering, but she went anyhow, finding the whole thing very difficult.

The house we bought in Montpelier was beautiful with its maple woodwork, hardwood floors, and four bedrooms, but it was way beyond our budget and way too much work for a politician's wife with two small children. Liz spent too many days at home, alone. Often, there were social and political events that she couldn't attend because we didn't have a baby-sitter. Or, if she went, sometimes she'd say something I wished she hadn't. Either way, the night might end in a fight.

And those luncheons hosted by Governor Davis's wife didn't help. Liz felt like a round peg in a square hole. She felt she couldn't trust anyone and couldn't speak her mind. At home Liz often vented her frustrations on me. I didn't listen very well. During my years as attorney general, I'd often come home for dinner, help put the kids to bed, and then go back to the office. Liz began hyperventilating, a physical sign of her emotional distress. She felt better after she became friends with the wife of one of the assistant AGs in my office. The woman really doted on Liz. She was very helpful, gave Liz a list of baby-sitters and places to shop, and invited us both over for dinner several times. I kept making excuses until, finally, on Liz's birthday in 1969, she confronted me over the fact that we had been invited to this couple's house five or six times and I'd made her decline every offer. Was I trying to keep her home all the time and deny her any friends?

I had to tell Liz I was about to fire the woman's husband. That hit Liz hard. She realized she, too, could be used for political purposes. She suspected that the woman had been nice to her in hopes of saving her husband's job, a realization that hurt. But Liz was also hurt that I could not or would not discuss the details of my work with her. I told her quite bluntly that she was not to associate with any of the assistant AGs' wives again. I wanted to keep my work life and my social life separate. One reason I wanted to do so was my concern about Liz's behavior, but I really didn't know how to address my concerns without starting another fight. Sometimes she'd have a few drinks too many, and when she did, heaven only knew what she might say. Ginny Hayes, lieutenant governor Tom Hayes's wife, once told Liz to keep her mouth shut after she'd expressed one of her famous opinions. "Your husband has political ambitions and you could damage his career," she warned. She was right of course, but Liz didn't want to hear it. And what about her opinions; didn't she have a right to express them?

It wasn't her fault and it wasn't mine. Ours was one of those relationships where both partners were right and both were wrong. We were doing the best we could but we had basic value clashes that we simply couldn't get around. It was wrong of me to expect her to keep her opinions to herself and wrong of her to expect me to think otherwise given the realities of political survival. And the fact that we truly loved each other only compounded these difficulties and made our arguments and the distance they placed between us even more painful.

I don't think it had to have turned out that way. The pressures of my growing political responsibilities and the emotional toll of the deaths of my father, Liz's father, and Harriet exacerbated whatever problems Liz and I had. I should have been more considerate. I didn't understand that Liz had given up a life she truly loved and all her friends in Shrewsbury, and now felt cut off from making new ones. But we did agree that there were serious problems and Liz began to see a psychiatrist—she was hyperventilating more and more—perhaps he could help.

If she could have had what she wanted, it would have been to return to our life in Shrewsbury, yet she knew that was impossible. She was in conflict. She believed in me and the concept of public service. She knew I had no choice but to stay with the Republican Party and to fight for the more moderate stances that many Vermonters supported. But she believed the Vietnam War was evil and she was opposed to almost everyone who was Republican. She was angry about so many things, personal and political, and the lieutenant governor's wife was telling her to shut up.

Meanwhile, through the summer and into the fall of 1969, momentous events continued to affect the state and nation. In August, a music festival was held near Woodstock, New York, and the lovers of peace and alternate lifestyles became known as "Woodstock Nation." Soon, my office was working on a statute to help Vermont towns regulate rock festivals. All the while the fighting raged on far away in Vietnam, though President Nixon was beginning to reduce troop strength there. Still, the heavy bombing didn't slacken and the war spread to Laos and Cambodia. Protests broke out across the country. Governor Davis was letting it be known that he was behind the war effort and President Nixon 100 percent. Meanwhile, I was convinced that the president's Southeast Asia policy was not working. At home, Liz wondered aloud and often why I didn't break with the party over my convictions. She was right of course, but I decided to concentrate on matters at home and do what I could here in Vermont.

I was busier that ever. In 1969 there arose, as expected, several legal challenges to the billboard law. One came from my old adversary Joe Palmisano, who went to court trying to stop the removal of a pair of big signs advertising a golf driving range he'd opened. He lost the case. Expecting a bigger legal battle about the sign law, I set to work researching and happened on a thirty-year-old legal opinion written by my father. Justice Jeffords had ruled years ago that the state did, indeed, have jurisdiction over billboards. Highwaymen might lurk behind them to rob innocent travelers along the state's highways, he had reasoned. So the state should have some authority over where they were placed.

Ted Riehle and I knew that sooner or later the outdoor advertising industry would take the law to court. And they'd hired some expensive lobbyists to fight it in the legislature. When the big test came, the sign people went to the federal courts with a clever strategy. They based their case on a well-known Vermont billboard along Interstate 91 in southeastern Vermont that advertised a business that was quite popular with kids and parents alike called Santa's Land. The test case went into the court dockets as *State of Vermont vs. Santa's Land.*

The case worried me for two reasons. First, Vermont could lose its right to control billboards. Second, if we lost, other states would find it impossible to regulate billboards. I was already beginning to think nationally although I hadn't articulated it. We prepared for trial, but within hours of going to court I got a call from Washington telling me that the outdoor advertising people had withdrawn. It turned out that somebody had taken a chain saw to the Santa's Land sign. It had disappeared in the night. Suddenly, there was no Santa's sign to base a legal case on. Of course, another sign could have been found. But the sign people never tried again. I guess they were more concerned than I was about losing in court.

It wasn't just environmental matters that kept the attorney general's office busy in the early months of my tenure. Governor Davis summarized the work ahead of us in his speech to the legislature when it convened on January 7, 1970. I was in the audience as he told the legislators, "Attorney General Jeffords has proposed legislation to speed up court procedures; to utilize more fully the well-trained deputy sheriffs throughout the state; to combat organized crime as it begins to find its way into Vermont; to permit wiretapping under strict, constitutionally approved conditions; to improve law enforcement training; and to grant immunity to witnesses in certain cases. I believe these matters should have our approval."

The centerpiece of the 1970 session was the major bill that resulted from the Gibb Commission's deliberations, a proposed law drafted by the attorney general's office. We hoped it would give the state firm control over development for a long time to come. The proposal we drafted was based on the idea that the impact of development projects ought to be fairly weighed to see if the community and environment could support the project without adverse impact. As the bill began its uncertain journey through the legislature, only those emergency rules of the health board were holding the line against unregulated development in Vermont.

The legislature was also reviewing a comprehensive water pollution control bill that had been promulgated by the Gibb Commission and written by John Hansen and the staff of the state Water Resources Board. Like the land-use act, it had received strong support from our conservative governor. Such a law was badly needed. The state's rivers and streams had become badly fouled over the years. People had this idyllic picture of Vermont as pure, but in truth many of our waterways had untreated sewage being discharged directly into them, not just from homes but from municipal sewage systems. Industrial and agricultural pollution of Vermont's rivers had also been rampant. Hansen and the state's water experts wrote a water pollution statute meant to be the nation's toughest. It would make it a crime to put *anything* into a body of water without a permit. And polluters would have to pay a fee while they were cleaning up their messes, forcing them to get the job done faster.

While we were promoting these environmental bills in early 1970, conservation battles seemed to be breaking out all over the state. Near the big Sugarbush and Mad River Glen ski areas, for instance, a company called Hemco Inc., planned to dam the Mad River and build 400 vacation units. The state Water Resources Board held a hearing and about 400 people turned out in the little riverside town of Waitsfield, most to oppose the project. Phones in state offices, including the attorney general's, rang off the wall when residents of the town of Dover, in far southern Vermont, learned that a developer wanted to put 2,800 vacation home units next to the big Mount Snow ski area. That would have increased Dover's population five times over. The only tool available at the time to make sure that such projects would not bring financial and environmental ruin on a community was the emergency health regulations.

Then there was the matter of Vermont's flood control dams. After major floods in 1927 and 1938 devastated parts of Vermont, the federal government built several large flood control dams on streams feeding Vermont's bigger rivers. Though Vermonters had once welcomed the dams, by 1970 people had started to wonder whether they were such a good idea. Among the concerns was the impact on native fish species. Especially strong opposition developed against the U.S. Army Corps of Engineers' plans to build a huge earth-and-stone dam on the Moose River in the remote little town of Victory in the Northeast Kingdom. About 3,000 woodland acres of prime deer and bear country would be flooded. The dam was a pet project of Senator Aiken, who thought his beloved Northeast Kingdom would get a big economic boost from the recreation lake the dam would create. But when new studies showed that the lake's waters would be the color of dark tea due to runoff and decaying vegetation, the locals began turning against the Victory Dam and so did Aiken. Soon, planned dams on the White River at Gaysville and the Saxtons River at Cambridgeport in southern Vermont were facing formidable opposition. Perhaps no issue more dramatically defined the growing support for conservation in Vermont than the state's sudden turn against the big dams. None of them were ever built and many dams have since been removed. But when my office had to deal with the legal issues surrounding these dams, there was little legal history for us to rely on. Here, as in many of the challenges our nation faced during these years, we were in unchartered waters.

As expected, development interests rose up to battle the Gibb Commission's proposals. While lobbyists usually prefer to work quietly, attracting as little attention as possible, those who fought the big environmental bills found that impossible. A former lieutenant governor, Ralph Foote of Middlebury, was hired to lead the fight. Somebody tipped off the press the day he arrived at the State House, and every reporter in town seemed to be waiting within the gaze of Lincoln's bust when Ralph walked in the door. The reporters were quite anxious to interview someone who might try to defend the dumping of human waste onto Vermont's mountainsides and into the rivers. He never had a chance after that.

What the Gibb Commission wanted was a law that would set up a state system for controlling development based on criteria that would assess a project's impact on a host of measurable concerns such as water, air, soil, local government, schools, highways, agricultural land, natural habitat—and much more. A housing project that would destroy a deer-wintering yard, for example, would have a hard time getting approval, as would a ski development that would negatively impact a bear-feeding area. If schools and roads could not sustain a particular development, it couldn't be built.

The law my staff developed established district environmental commissions made up of ordinary citizens who would decide whether development proposals met these criteria. Appeals of district decisions would go to a state environmental board. At the same time, the law would have required the state to adopt a land-use plan, creating a set of maps to guide the district commissions and environmental board in determining where development should take place. Public interest in the legislation was so intense that the *Rutland Herald* sent a reporter to baby-sit the bill, staying with it every day to make certain no major changes went unreported.

From the beginning, the idea of the environmental board, district commissions, and development criteria seemed to sit well with most senators and representatives. After all, their constituents were screaming for development controls. The land-use plan was another story. Many Vermonters saw it as going too far in telling individual property owners what they could, and could not, do with their land. That aspect of the plan was defeated, although it was reincarnated in still-controversial regional planning legislation passed twenty years later.

John and I had made a bet: I'd have to buy him a bottle of Scotch if the water bill was signed into law first; he'd have to buy one for me if the land-use act got the governor's signature first. The Cedar Creek Room of the State House was packed with conservationists, legislators, and state officials as the governor walked in to put his signature on several bills, including ours.

The governor had gotten wind that a bottle of Scotch was at stake. Davis sat down, took out his pen, then said he understood that an illegal wager was afoot. He took out a coin, flipped it, and the land-use bill won. On his signing, the bill officially became Act 250 of the Vermont General Assembly. It remains the most stringent and important conservation law ever enacted by any one of the fifty states. Then the governor signed the water bill, and it was known as Act 252. John bought me a bottle of Chivas Regal. One evening we raised our glasses to what we thought had been two jobs pretty well done.

And so the 1970 session of the Vermont Legislature came to an end. It had been as hectic as it was historic. I learned that when you're in public office with a two-year term, time goes by very quickly. Just as you're finally settling into the job, you're facing another election.

Early in 1970, I'd started thinking about the next campaign. Liz and I talked and, while she wasn't fond of Montpelier and continued to have problems of her own, she agreed that I should seek a second term as attorney general. I really wanted to. I loved the job. Nobody was showing any interest in running against me in a Republican primary. But who would the Democrats run? It began to look like a well-known member of the house, Thomas Salmon from Rockingham, would go after my job.

Tom had chaired the important House Judiciary Committee, and he'd been a member of my committee that investigated the highway department. I liked him, and knew he was a good legislator and lawyer. Tom was also a first-rate speaker with a good Irish wit and gift of gab. To tell the truth, he reminded me of the gentleman I'd beaten four years back to win a senate seat, Joe O'Neill. I also knew that Tom would come into a statewide race carrying some heavy political baggage. He'd fought in the legislature against Act 250.

By the time spring came in 1970, cracks were appearing in the Republican Team for the Times. Lieutenant Governor Hayes was criticizing the governor for supporting the Vietnam War and President Nixon. Davis snapped, "Tom Hayes is not a Republican." Hayes said, "Dean Davis has supported every reactionary candidate in the last twenty years." Now Nixon had American soldiers in Cambodia and Vermont's two U.S. Senators, Republicans Aiken and Prouty, were expressing concern.

Then, on May 4, the Ohio National Guard opened fire on Kent State University students who were demonstrating against the war. At the time, Davis was attending a governors' meeting in New Mexico and planned to fly from there with some of his fellow governors to a meeting in Switzerland. Back in Vermont, with Davis out of the state, Tom Hayes was acting governor. Tom held a rally at the State House to mourn the Kent State students. Then he ordered U.S. flags in Vermont brought to half-staff and the flag at the State House lowered. Forget the trip to Switzerland, Davis was on the first plane home.

My office got calls from postmasters all over Vermont saying the U.S. President was the only person who could order the flag down. I did some research and found they were right. I quickly issued a legal opinion that said, in effect, the lieutenant governor had no legal right to do what he had done. Up went the State House flag, and when I walked home from work that evening, people came out of their homes to thank me. I wasn't sure how to react. I was emotionally torn because I was now pretty certain that the war was a big mistake. I was a military man, but I believed those national guardsmen had been placed in a terrible position. How had we come to this—young Americans shooting other young Americans? I understood the emotion behind the desire to lower those flags. I felt grief at the terrible thing that had happened to those students and to the country, and I personally would have preferred to leave the flags down.

But I had a job to do, and it was my responsibility to follow the law, much as I personally disagreed with it. A few days later, moderate Vermont congressman Bob Stafford, a Republican, gave the commencement address at the University of Vermont and called the Vietnam War "the worst thing that has happened to America in modern times." I didn't disagree.

On May 22 I announced that I'd run for another term as attorney general. Tom Salmon had already said he'd probably run. I was pretty sure I could use his opposition to Act 250 against him, but I never relished the times I had to defend myself over the flag issue.

I won the election easily. Salmon told me years later that he ran a lousy campaign for attorney general. It's probably a good thing he did. In the summer of 1970 I had my hands full with two important conservation matters. Time for campaigning was pretty limited. My office was getting ready to take one of America's biggest corporations to court, all the way to the U.S. Supreme Court. And we were preparing to take a stab at regulating a nuclear power plant.

CHAPTER 8

David and Goliath

LAKE CHAMPLAIN is Vermont's west coast—an ancient body of water that marks our western border with New York and our northern border with Canada. It's considered the sixth Great Lake despite its diminutive size of 435 square miles of surface compared to, for example, Lake Superior with 31,700 square miles. From the time of the Abenaki Indians, through its discovery by Samuel de Champlain, to its current status as a recreational mecca, Vermonters have been justly proud of this natural treasure.

Unfortunately, both in Vermont and across the lake in New York, farmers, homeowners, and industrialists have too often used the lake as a dumping ground. One of the worst of these polluters was the International Paper Company located across Lake Champlain not far from Fort Ticonderoga. For decades, the company had deposited sludge from its paper-making process into the lake. The problem was that the sludge bed was high in mercury and other residues that posed particular health problems for animals and humans alike. On top of that, IPC's old mill stunk. Under certain conditions, the plant gave off the smell of rotten eggs. It would waft across the lake onto Vermont's shores. I wanted to force IPC to clean up its operation.

Simultaneously, I needed to apply myself and the staff to the upcoming licensing of the Vermont Yankee plant, the state's only nuclear facility in southern Vermont. Here again, we were in nearly unchartered territory with too little precedent to know how to proceed.

These two issues took up the bulk of my second term as attorney general.

A book could be written on the IPC case, and maybe someday somebody will write it. Suffice it to say that in taking on the paper company, the State of Vermont was just like David going after Goliath.

In the early going, Vermont had a strong ally in Walter Hickel,

Nixon's interior secretary. Right after the election, Hickel said his department would support Vermont in the sludge bed case. A week later I announced that I would include the State of New York in any legal action I brought against IPC because New York environmental officials had failed to take action against IPC on their own. Whether Hickel's support of Vermont in the case had anything to do with it or not, I never knew for sure. But two weeks after the interior secretary said he would support Vermont against IPC, Nixon fired him, axed him the day before Thanksgiving. Walter Hickel was a great friend of the environment, and I knew Vermont had lost a powerful ally. His firing marked an antienvironment turn in the Nixon administration, and soon my office found itself not just up against IPC and New York in the courts but also the Nixon administration.

In December, John Hansen suffered a serious heart attack. His recovery was slow and I had to replace him with Fred Parker as lead attorney in the IPC case. Before we could even get to court, we had to convince the Supreme Court that we had a case. The key to our argument was that IPC, by creating sludge beds in the lake, was changing the boundary between Vermont and New York. The Supreme Court adjudicates boundary disputes between states. We argued that, because the sludge beds were filling up the lake, our boundary was being encroached upon. The dividing point was the deepest point of the lake's channel and that deep point was getting filled with sludge, thus moving the boundary eastward.

A hearing was set for the Supreme Court building in Washington. Fred Parker and I went down. The morning of the hearing, Fred carried his documents in a shirt box under his arm. We glanced into a side room and got our first look at the legal team representing the paper company. They had nine lawyers from the law firm Davis, Polk & Wardwell, the largest in the country, and file box after file box filled with documents.

The next morning, we appeared before the Supreme Court and Chief Justice Warren Burger. Fred put our case on and he was extremely nervous. But Burger got him to relax, and it quickly became apparent from the questions the judges asked that two of the justices were on our side, Justices William Brennan and William O. Douglas, who was one of America's noted conservationists. IPC's chief lawyer was Taggert Whipple, a veteran of many important courtroom fights. At one point,

Whipple tried to make light of the sludge's impact on the lake. Douglas asked him incredulously, "Are you trying to suggest the lake needs this pollution?"

The Supreme Court bought our arguments and we were off on an awesome legal adventure. Their decision simply to take the case was a major legal victory for Vermont.

The court appointed R. Ammi Cutter, a retired Massachusetts Supreme Court justice, to hold hearings in the case. Cutter proved to be tough and demanding but completely fair. He forced both sides to work day and night in prefiling testimony. Even during Christmas week, we often had to work all day and into the wee hours of the next morning.

The IPC case lasted throughout my remaining time as attorney general and then dragged on into the term of my successor. Hearings took place in the federal courthouse on Foley Square in lower Manhattan. Before the case was very old, I began to wonder whether we had taken on too big a task—our little legal staff faced the biggest law firm in America. We had $50,000 appropriated to hire expert witnesses. The paper industry had come up with a defense fund that was reported to be at least $2 million. We also faced the big New York State attorney general's office. And the federal government was behind the paper company.

Then we discovered we were being attacked behind our backs. Back in Vermont, IPC had hired Vermont's most able lobbyist, attorney Henry Black, to convince the legislature to cut off state funding for the case. I had to go to the legislature to fight for our money, and finally won the argument to keep the Supreme Court case ongoing. Davis was signaling that he was less than pleased with the scope this case was taking and how it was being viewed in Washington.

To keep down expenses, as many as eight members of my staff often shared one Manhattan hotel room. Our wits had to make up for lack of funds. One day Fred had a huge map of the Ticonderoga area that he planned to bring to the hearing room as an exhibit. When he arrived just a few minutes before the day's court session was to begin, he found several big trucks blocking the courthouse loading dock. One of my assistants hustled around the city until he found a shop that sold Vermont maple syrup. When he gave the loading dock foreman a gallon, the man moved the trucks so we could unload our map.

As the case went on, some friends of mine had bumper stickers made up that said, "Jeffords Won't Let 'Em Do It in the Lake." Those bumper stickers came in handy in my next campaign.

By the time the hearings started, the old IPC mill at Ticonderoga had been shut down and the company's new mill north of town was up and running. We asked the Supreme Court to broaden the scope of our case to include the new mill, and again it agreed with us and ruled against IPC. Early on, one of our experts visited the new plant and found, to his astonishment, that IPC was bypassing its new pollution control equipment and discharging paper-making wastes directly into the lake. We brought that to the court's attention and got an immediate remedy. The hearings went on for months. Judge Cutter drove us unmercifully, holding court five days a week, seven hours a day. It was not until sometime in 1974 that the case was settled, a bit after I'd left office, though I stayed on the case as a consultant. In the end, at Cutter's urging, a settlement was finally reached. We conceded that dredging the sludge beds could do more harm than good. In truth, we worried that IPC would be unable to keep the sludge contained while removing it. Given the technology, we feared that toxins in the sludge might leach into the lake more readily if the material was dislodged.

In return, IPC agreed to abide by the toughest pollution standards ever set for a plant discharging into a freshwater lake. And we won $750,000 from IPC that set up a fund to monitor the new plant's operation and prevent further pollution of the lake. I counted it a considerable victory. Though the sludge beds remain, Addison County people no longer complain of odors from the mill. And apparently the new mill has not deposited any new sludge in Lake Champlain.

But that's getting ahead of the story. The year 1971 began as Governor Davis opened the legislative session by talking about the need for regulation. "The answer is in regulation—regulation built upon choice—regulation designed to use our land and water sensibly, reasonably, and fairly consistent with the interests of all," the governor said. He didn't mention his attorney general, who had been doing a lot of the regulating in Vermont. A week later the governor dropped a bombshell in another speech to the legislature. Davis said the state's constitution should be changed so that the governor and other high-ranking state officials would serve four-year terms. I thought that was a good idea, but then he said that the offices of treasurer, secretary of state, and attorney general should no longer be elective, but appointed by the governor. Quite obviously, Davis was sick and tired of having an attorney general who went his own way. The old company president thought that the chief attorney of any corporation ought to be appointed by, and take his orders from, the CEO. Nothing doing, I said, and took my case to the legislature.

I won that battle, but from then on I seemed to have one disagreement after another with Davis. Soon the governor set out to reduce the power of the health board. I disagreed. Then the man he'd appointed chair of the Water Resources Board wanted to allow Vermont Yankee to heat the Connecticut River as much as ten degrees with discharges from its nuclear plant. I said no. The governor proposed a sweeping reorganization of state government. I said, "The governor wants to go too far toward putting all the power in his own lap." Then I said my office would oppose a 19 percent rate increase awarded to the state's second largest power company, the Central Vermont Public Service Corporation. That company also happened to be the biggest shareholder in Vermont Yankee. Davis was a friend of Albert A. Cree, who was president of both CVPS and Vermont Yankee. I heard the governor was not pleased with my opposition to the rate hike.

Then Davis really moved against me. He had his administrative commissioner ask the general assembly to take several of the assistant attorneys general out of my office and assign them to various state departments, to report not to me but to the departments. I was so mad I told a reporter that I might resign. Again, after a fight, I was able to protect my office from being gutted by the governor.

In a state with two-year terms, political speculation never ceases, and early in 1971 there was considerable talk about the next governor's race. If Davis didn't run, many thought Mallary would. It seemed that Davis chose every opportunity to praise him. There was also considerable speculation about a Jeffords candidacy for governor. I didn't discourage it, nor did I get any praise from the governor. Late in the legislative session, it appeared the Davis administration had rethought its position on the water-pollution control law and was trying to weaken what we had worked so long and hard on. My response was to say, "Polluters are being made heroes and those who seek to reinforce environmental laws are being made villains in Vermont." Davis really bristled at that.

But the 1971 legislative session was by no means all trouble for me. I strongly backed the bottle bill I'd helped write. If passed, it would make Vermont only the second state, after Oregon, to outlaw the sale of non-returnable bottles and cans. The beverage industry put up a tough fight, turning its lobbyists loose in the State House. We also had many Vermont owners of "mom and pop" groceries complaining to their legislators that the result would be extra work and piles of empty bottles. I stuck by the bill and discovered another helpful legal precedent written by my father when he was on the Vermont Supreme Court. Justice Jeffords had held that the state did, indeed, have the right to control beverage containers because if people were allowed to throw bottles into the fields, cows might cut their udders on broken glass. My argument was a bit more practical. As I've said repeatedly, the best way to get people to recycle bottles is to put a deposit on them. Most people want their nickel back.

The bottle bill passed, and before long I was invited to California, Connecticut, Massachusetts, and several other states to give speeches about the Vermont law. I recall a story that went around soon after the law went into effect that got at its effectiveness. It seems that a fellow came into a country store one day with a huge bag of bottles and cans. He set them on the counter, asked for his nickel apiece, and said, "That damn law ain't working. Look at all this stuff I picked up along the road." The truth of the matter is that Vermont's roads are not littered with bottles and it's for two reasons: most people don't throw them out of their cars like they used to because they've paid a deposit on the bottle, and enterprising people patrol highways, making a profit from the thoughtless ones who do throw them away.

Press speculation was high about who would get the Republican nomination. Governor Davis told a reporter that news stories about him favoring Dick Mallary for governor were merely "speculative twaddle." I didn't believe it. Then Mallary got in a shot at me by denying my request to the state emergency board, which he chaired, for money to expand my new Consumer Protection Division's services. I went out and got a federal grant to pay for opening a consumer protection office in the southern part of Vermont. Mallary's emergency board said I couldn't accept it. "This is the consumer's loss," I told the press.

Later that month a Mallary for Governor Committee was organized with several important legislators including Speaker of the House Walter "Peanut" Kennedy and Luther F. Hackett, a Burlington insurance man and legislator who chaired the powerful House Appropriations Committee. Mallary's committee had Davis's fingerprints all over it. Then the conservative Republican state's attorney of Windsor County, Frank Mahady, said he might run against me for attorney general in a Republican primary. I was getting the political squeeze from the governor's people. An anti-Jeffords strategy seemed to be emerging from the Davis camp that I interpreted this way: The Republicans would keep Mahady out of the attorney general's race if I would stay out of the governor's race against Mallary.

Nationally, Nixon's war policy was even more unpopular, especially when the *New York Times* published the documents taken from the Pentagon by Daniel Ellsberg. Though Nixon was cutting troop strength in Southeast Asia, protests were being staged everywhere. Then Nixon shocked the world by traveling to China to meet with Chou En-Lai.

The state political scene changed radically on September 10, 1971, when Senator Prouty died in Washington after a long bout with cancer. The governor said he would appoint Congressman Bob Stafford to Prouty's Senate seat. President Nixon sent Bob home from Washington on an air force plane. Stafford voted that morning in the U.S. House of Representatives, flew to Montpelier where he was sworn in as senator at the State House, then flew straight back to Washington to vote in the Senate on a key Nixon war-related bill. Bob believes he is the only person ever to vote in both houses of Congress on the same day. Mallary quickly announced that he would be a candidate for Stafford's U.S. House seat and a special election was scheduled for January 7 to fill the House and Senate seats. Speculation then began to focus on whether I would run for Congress. I was tempted.

I should inject here that since the big water pollution bill had become law, my office had spent no small amount of time enforcing it. It could be a tough job. One night I went to the famous ski town of Stowe, which then touted itself as the ski capital of the East Coast, for a meeting with town officials. The town had refused to comply with Act 252, which required the municipality to build a new sewage treatment plant. The situation symbolized small-town politics at its worst. Within the town of

Stowe was the Village of Stowe, and the town and village were at odds. The village owned the Stowe electric plant and the town thought it was being charged exorbitant electric rates. Thus the town had no desire to build the new sewage treatment plant it knew it needed but that would mostly take care of the village's sewage.

The Stowe selectmen told me they weren't going to put in any treatment plant, and that their lawyers had said they didn't have to. I told them the law said they must. What would I do if they didn't, they asked? I said that, if necessary, I'd get a contempt of court order that could be enforced by jail time. One frail-looking elderly gentleman asked, "You mean you would throw me in jail?" I said, "Yes, sir." I realized that would probably not be a very productive thing to do so I took another tack. I held a press conference and said, "Stowe may claim to be the ski capital of the East. But as far as I'm concerned they're the sewage capital of the East." The *New York Times* and other national newspapers picked up the story and the quote. The sewer plant got built with no more hesitation, although some folks in Stowe still weren't speaking to me twenty years later.

Then there was the matter of a beer joint in southern Vermont. People downstream were complaining that the establishment was polluting the Battenkill River. That'll tell you something about Vermont—even the flushing of a toilet at a small-town bar can come to the attention of the attorney general, particularly when it impacts a prized trout stream. As a result of all these complaints, the Water Resources Department sent inspectors down time and again to take water samples. They all came back showing that the water downstream from the bar was fine. Finally, John Hansen suggested they stop going down during the daytime and try sampling at night when the bar was open. They did. The bar was cited and quickly came into compliance. That was how we waged the environmental battle in Vermont—in large cases and in small. In truth, it was just as much a matter of educating people about the problem as it was enforcement.

It was impossible to know ahead of time the amount of work we would encounter once the water law took effect. Within months, the state received hundreds and hundreds of reports of violations occurring everywhere in the state. The new law didn't just impact obvious sources of pollution like wastewater treatment plants; it also impacted industries that had traditionally been considered clean—dairy farms and milk processors.

I got some shocking news when I called Roland Q. Seward to test the political waters. "What would you think," I asked, "if I ran for Congress." There was a long pause before he said, "Jeffords, I worked hard to get you elected attorney general, and about the first thing you did was pass a law that costs me over $100,000. Not only will I not support you, but I will do everything I can to see you never get elected to anything again." Slam went the phone. I learned that Roland Q had been forced to install some rather expensive equipment at his creamery to keep the whey from his cheese-making operation from polluting a nearby stream.

Well, at least I knew where my enemies were. Still, I gave a lot of thought to taking on Mallary in a primary for the House seat. In the end I decided not to. The press thought I was going to run, and they all showed up at my office on October 6 to hear what they thought would be my announcement. I stayed up late the night before mulling the whole situation over. The *Rutland Herald* described me as "rumpled and displeased" when I told the reporters I wouldn't run for Congress. I also said a telephone poll some of my friends had taken in ten of the state's fourteen counties showed that I would probably beat Mallary. But I had to confess, "Though I turned up strong among Republicans polled, my major strength was with independent voters." I still wonder whether I should have gone ahead and run for Congress. But beating Mallary in a Republican primary, with Davis and his friends unofficially supporting him, and Seward working against me, would have been a tough task.

So I kept to the job of attorney general, spending much of my time on the nuclear power plant regulations. My office focused on setting strict limits on radiation that would be released into the air and on making sure the plant didn't overheat the Connecticut River. The Yankee plant came along at a time when a great deal of concern had developed nationwide about the safety of nuclear plants, and about the effects of radiation on human health, particularly the type of low-level radiation plants like this one released.

My predecessor Jim Oakes had hammered out an agreement from Vermont Yankee to abide by rather tough limits on the amount of heated water the plant could release into the Connecticut River. Yankee was balking about also building cooling towers and installing an expensive thing called an "off-gas holding system." But they would need these to meet the state limits I'd recommended on radiation levels.

Yankee argued that only the Atomic Energy Commission should set limits for nuclear plants, not the states. We thought that the federal standards were so inadequate that Vermont had to develop its own. We held hearings that included testimony from experts from around the country and even some foreign countries. We'd almost given up on the off-gas system when John Hansen found a way to get Vermont Yankee to do it. The company had had trouble raising money to build the plant and was just getting ready to issue $80 million in bonds. Vermont Yankee's big sponsor company, the Central Vermont Public Service Corporation, had recently raised its rates twice, over the objections of my office. I strongly suspected that the strain of paying for the nuclear plant was the main reason that CVPS needed more income. We also knew Yankee faced a deadline of September 29 with Wall Street for putting out its bonds. They'd already gotten the necessary approval of the Vermont Public Service Board for the bonds. But John Hansen learned that the attorney general's office had the legal right to appeal the board's approval of those bonds to the Vermont Supreme Court. Vermont Yankee needed to put those bonds out without delay. So we told Yankee we would appeal the bond issue to the supreme court, unless they agreed to the off-gas system.

Yankee flatly refused; the days went by until we came down to the last day they could issue their bonds. On September 29 we met with Vermont Yankee's lawyers at a restaurant in South Burlington called the Old Board, the very same place where Liz and I had had our wedding reception. The talks went into the night. Put in the off-gas system, we said. They said no way. The clock ticked on. I'd called the postmaster in South Burlington that day and said I might need to postmark an important piece of mail just before midnight. He agreed to stay open. We had the appeal of the financing all typed and ready to go and we had it out on the table, right in front of the Yankee people. We told them the post office was staying open late in case we needed to mail the document. The clock ticked on. I could see their lawyers getting more and more nervous. About eleven-thirty, I got up as if to go to the post office. The Yankee officials finally gave in and Vermont Yankee agreed to install the off-gas system. In return, I let the deadline pass without an appeal. I called the post office and told the postmaster he could go home.

Hearings on licensing the atomic plant were held in Brattleboro, a few miles from the plant, and they went on for months. Because the state was a party to the hearings, I kept somebody from my staff there at all times. When key issues came up, we often sided with the many conservation groups who were involved while the governor supported the Vermont Yankee side and its CEO, Albert Cree. Davis and I had several contentious meetings about Vermont Yankee. The governor made it clear he wanted the plant to start producing electricity as soon as possible and he argued that my office was holding things up. He said I was costing Vermont electric customers millions of dollars. But we checked with the construction superintendent at the plant and he told us they couldn't possibly get the plant ready for operation for months. Davis didn't like the fact that I'd questioned him and looked into the schedule. And when I publicized the response, he liked that even less.

One afternoon the governor marched into the hearings unannounced and took the witness stand. The governor said that Vermont Yankee "has met all the safety requirements it needs" and he urged a quick ruling. The hearings went on despite his pronouncement.

John Hansen and John Calhoun handled most of the Vermont Yankee work. I went to Brattleboro as often as I could. One afternoon I drove down from Montpelier, walked into the hearing, and went to the table where all the attorneys were seated at the front of the room. I asked the assistant if they needed anything. They said a cup of coffee would taste good. So I went out, got them coffee, and brought it to the table. The Commonwealth of Massachusetts was also a party in the licensing procedures, since the Yankee plant was close to its border. After I left that day, an assistant attorney general from Massachusetts asked John Hansen who had brought in the coffee. "The attorney general," John said. The Massachusetts man couldn't believe it—either that the AG would be hand-delivering coffee or that I was the attorney general, I'm not sure.

During that time I worked closely with the governor of Minnesota, John Love. A nuclear plant was also being built in his state and he shared my concerns about atomic power. He and I felt that the Atomic Energy Commission standards for nuclear plants were so lax that our states had no choice but to intervene in the licensing proceedings. Governor Love and I received invitations from Congress to testify about our state's views on federal nuclear power plant regulation. Needless to say, neither one of us was the darling of the atomic energy industry. Our testimony was

before the joint House-Senate Committee on Atomic Energy. Senator
Aiken was a member of that committee and he warmly welcomed us both
to the Capitol. The committee room was packed; dozens of reporters and
cameras were present, showing how interested the whole country was in
nuclear energy.

Governor Love testified first and the committee, which generally
favored atomic energy, was defensive to the point of being obnoxious.
When it was my turn, I was very nervous. It was my first time testifying in
Congress. Just as I was to take the stand, the committee chair passed over
me and called several witnesses to defend the current AEC radiation
standards. Senator Aiken finally intervened and got me to the witness
table. Just as I sat down, every committee member except one got up and
left the room. I guess they already knew what I had to say.

In the 1960s and 1970s, Catholic schools throughout the country were
closing as the church was forced to hire more and more laypeople to keep
them running. Very Catholic St. Albans, in northwestern Vermont, was
the hardest hit of all Vermont communities when two schools operated
by the Diocese of Vermont shut down. Time and again, St. Albans voters
refused to vote funds to expand their public schools to take care of the
Catholic students suddenly needing education. Finally my office was
asked to intervene. I studied the situation and decided that if the town
did not pass an adequate school budget, then the state could take over
the schools.

A public hearing was held in St. Albans. Half the town was there. I
told them what I'd decided and added that, even if the state took over
the schools, the town's residents would still have to pay to run them.
When one rather aggressive fellow challenged me, bellowing "How ya'
gonna make me pay?" I told him that if necessary we'd repossess the residents' cars and other personal property. I got loudly booed, but the school
budget passed on the next vote.

Mary and Jim on Christmas Eve 1939, at the family home on Kingsley Avenue, Rutland, Vermont, on the night Jim, age five, had an emergency appendectomy.

Jim was a high school football champion for the Rutland Red Raiders, pictured here in 1951.

Jim (right) was a member of the high school marching band and played the euphonium and the trumpet at this Vermont music festival in 1951.

Justice Olin Merrill Jeffords, Mary, Marion Hausman Jeffords, and Jim at Mary's graduation from Wheelock College, Massachusetts, 1954.

Ensign Jeffords, NROTC graduate from Yale University, 1956.

Jim and Liz's wedding day, August 26, 1961, at the Old Board Restaurant in South Burlington, Vermont. Left to right: Louise Laird Daley, John J. Daley, Elizabeth Cecile Daley Jeffords, Jim, Marion Hausman Jeffords, Laura Smith Hausman, and Chief Justice Jeffords.

Trout fishing with children Laura and Leonard at the Waterbury Dam, Vermont, 1970.

The Jeffords family (with Rasputin) on Christmas 1985, in back of the Shrewsbury house.

Jim and Liz's second wedding took place on the same date as the first one, twenty-five years later: August 26, 1986.

President Jimmy Carter signs the Dairy Bill in the Oval Office, 1976. Jim is second from left.

President Ronald Reagan speaks about the Agriculture Lands Protection Act in 1986. Jim is second from right.

President George Bush swears Jim in as U.S. senator for Vermont in the Old Senate Chamber of the United States Capitol, January 3, 1988.

Jim with President Bill Clinton at the opening of the new FDR memorial in 1998.

The Singing Senators perform at the PGA Tour–sponsored literacy charity event in Union Station, Washington, D.C., 1998. Left to right: Trent Lott (R., Miss.), Larry Craig (R., Idaho), John Ashcroft (R., Mo.), and Jim.

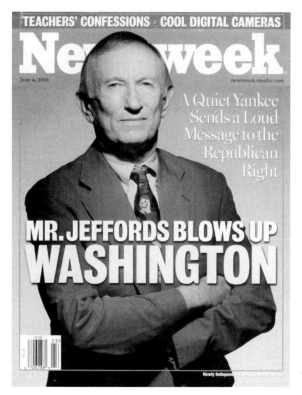

After the switch, June 4, 2001.

Jim logs firewood at the family home in Shrewsbury, Vermont, getting ready for winter.

CHAPTER 9

The Realities of Power

THE YEAR 1972 was a political one in Vermont and it's still talked about. It was wild. Nixon was up for reelection and about to face the liberal George McGovern, the senator from South Dakota. In Vermont, in January, Bob Stafford was elected to a full term in the Senate and Dick Mallary won Vermont's U.S. House seat. When the legislature returned to Montpelier, all political talk focused on Deane Davis and whether he would run for a third term. Four Republicans had said they might run if Davis retired. They were Lieutenant Governor John "Jack" Burgess, a political moderate from Brattleboro; Richard Snelling, a conservative multimillionaire businessman from Shelburne; Luther "Fred" Hackett, chairman of the Vermont House's Appropriations Committee; and me.

In early February I let it be known how serious I was about running for governor by telling a reporter that it was "highly unlikely" that I'd run for another term as attorney general. Five Vermont lawyers quickly said they were interested in my job. Then Dick Snelling said he'd taken a poll that showed he would win a primary election over Jack Burgess and me. I doubted that, but it gave me pause. I was much more troubled when the *Rutland Herald* polled the Republican State Committee and found that twenty-two of them favored Fred Hackett for governor. Not one committee member supported me.

In early March a reporter looked on the governor's desk and saw a document marked "Voter Reaction to Potential Gubernatorial Candidates." The document had "very confidential" stamped on it. I didn't even know a poll had been taken, but I eventually found out that the Republican State Committee had paid for it and that it showed I had the highest recognition factor among the potential candidates for governor. I didn't like the state committee conducting a poll behind my back, but even more I resented their not sharing the results with me. I guessed, correctly, that the governor was passing the numbers to his friends, especially Hackett.

I stayed out of politics throughout the legislative session, tending to the job of attorney general. That was a mistake. Hackett's people had been busy getting commitments from Republicans in the house and senate. When I started calling people after the legislature went home, a lot of them had already committed themselves to Hackett. Some said that they wished I'd asked earlier—an easy out, perhaps.

On April 3, Davis announced he would not run again for governor. "I have done what I set out to do. Vermont's financial house has been set in order," he said. I announced my candidacy for governor two days later in Enosburg Falls, where the Jeffords family had lived for generations. I stood by a monument to my grandmother on the village green commemorating her service to the town. I said, "I sincerely believe that the most difficult challenge we face today is to reassure the nation and the state that the political systems under which we live can meet the needs of the people." And I was careful to say, "I have nothing but admiration for Governor Davis as a Vermonter, and as a Republican. I am proud of his accomplishments." In the middle of the speech, an elderly woman started heckling me. It wasn't a good sign.

Three days later I had an opponent for the Republican nomination in Luther Hackett. The announcement was cleverly staged in the same room at the Tavern Motor Inn in Montpelier where Davis had launched his campaign for a second term. Hackett praised Davis to the skies and promised to continue his work. He was a successful investment banker in Burlington, a quiet, studious, politically conservative, crew-cut man. A reporter once wrote that Hackett's idea of a good time was balancing a budget. But he was an able legislator who had been majority leader in the Vermont House. He preferred to be called Fred, and most of his friends did, but all through the coming campaign I called him Luther. As childish as it may seem, it was years before I called him Fred. In the years since we ran against each other, we've become friends and he was a strong supporter of me, at least before I left the Republican Party.

Because of the heavy workload on the attorney general's office, especially the Vermont Yankee and IPC cases, I wasn't able to campaign full time until the middle of the summer. Also, I'd gotten the state into another big legal fight. I'd joined attorneys general in several other states in a class action lawsuit against several big drug companies, charging them with price fixing. Among the AGs who joined me were Slade Gorton of Oregon, Jack Danforth from Missouri, and Warren Rudman of New Hampshire. All three became good friends and I would later serve with them in the U.S. Senate. We eventually got a settlement out of the companies; Vermont got a check for $8 million. In another case ongoing that summer, my office joined with the Massachusetts and Maine AG offices to sue the state of New Hampshire over the income tax they were taking out of the paychecks of Vermonters who crossed the border to work there. New Hampshire has never had its own income tax, and it still doesn't. But it saw nothing wrong in dipping into out-of-staters' paychecks. This time I was opposing Warren Rudman. The tax case, too, wound up in the U.S. Supreme Court. We eventually won, and saved Vermonters millions of tax dollars.

Though I couldn't do a lot of campaigning straight off, I was on the phone trying to raise money. I didn't have a whole lot of luck. Liz and I reluctantly decided to sell the house and barn in Shrewsbury to pay for the campaign; we kept 150 acres. Still, it was going to be a low-budget campaign. To cut expenses, I bought a travel home into which Liz and I found we could squeeze seven or eight people. Among those I hired for the campaign was six-foot-four Tim Soule, and he really was too big for the camper. When the weather was good, he'd put a sleeping bag out on the ground. Another regular day traveler was Bernice Murray, whom Liz had met through her work with the League of Woman Voters. Bernice was smart, politically savvy, and a tireless worker who, it seemed to me, could do five jobs at once and live on four hours' sleep a night. From 1972 on, she always worked for me in some capacity—that is, until President George Walker Bush appointed her director of the Farmers Home Administration. She died at far too young an age in May of 1992. During the years Bernice worked with me she was indefatigable. Over the weekend she might sew new curtains for the campaign office, bake three lasagnas for the staff, and make cookies for her four children's bake sale—and that was before she really got busy. Liz's nieces Annie and Kathleen McGreevy were with us as they had been during the state senate and AG races. Kathleen would often bring her best friend, Susan Boardman. Thirty years later, Susan Boardman Russ is now—and has been for more than twenty years—my top aide. Another teenager, Lisa Butler, was with us the whole summer. She helped Liz with the kids and we were so close we called her our adopted niece. Did I forget to mention the dog? Thumper was with us, too. We were crowded and stepping all over one another, but we made that camper do, living on fast food and sandwiches as we hit the campaign trail.

I set out across Vermont, full of enthusiasm, about the first of July, believing that the voters had liked the job I'd done as attorney general and would give me enough votes in the primary. It was Liz who first began to see the problems. She noticed that a lot of people we thought were our friends wouldn't make any commitment to support our campaign. Some, she found, would walk away or just turn their heads when she walked up to them on the street or at some event. We picked up reports that a lot of Republicans were saying that I was too young to be governor, that I didn't have enough experience. Jack Burgess, the lieutenant governor, saw it, too. When he decided in late May that he wouldn't run for governor, he said: "Jim Jeffords is opposing the people currently in control of the Republican Party apparatus." Jack, like myself, was a political moderate. When Dick Snelling also said he wasn't running for governor, that left Hackett and me in a head-to-head race.

The Republican state convention was held in May; Roland Q. Seward was elected to represent Vermont on the Republican National Committee, replacing my friend and former senate colleague Ed Janeway. Now Roland Q was in a position of even greater power within the party. Hackett and I were introduced to the convention and we both got good ovations, though one newspaper said it was the younger people in the crowd who cheered for me.

A few days later the *Rutland Herald* broke an exclusive story that a private organization called Common Sense Associates had been organized in Vermont. It was made up of prominent Vermont businessmen and its president was none other than the just elected Republican national committeeman, Roland Q. What they were after, he explained, was "balance between economic growth and environmental controls." What they really wanted, it soon became clear, was to weaken the state's tough new conservation laws.

So wasn't this wonderful? The Republican Party had a national committeeman running an antienvironmental organization. I guessed the cost of installing the water pollution control equipment at Roland Q's cheese factory probably had something to do with it. One thing was clear to me: Roland Q's position was going to hurt the Republican Party's chances in the general election in November. And it was going to hurt mine in the primary.

The news wasn't good nationally either. Alabama governor George Wallace, running for the presidency, had barely survived an assassination attempt that left him paralyzed. Nixon was continuing the heavy bombing of North Vietnam, even hitting the capital city of Hanoi. American troops and their Vietnamese allies were losing the ground war in the south. In May the press reported that five burglars had been arrested in the offices of the Democratic National Committee in Washington's Watergate Complex.

In July the Democratic Party held its national convention in Miami and nominated George McGovern. Tom Salmon, whom I had beaten for Vermont Attorney General, was one of the convention delegates. He told me years later that he and other Vermont delegates went out on the beach with some beers the night before the nomination and talked politics. Out of that very informal meeting came Tom's decision to run for governor of Vermont. Until that time, the Democrats didn't have a candidate.

By late August it seemed that there was a story in some paper every day that Davis was secretly supporting Hackett against me. Luther was picking up Davis's endorsement without the governor actually making an announcement. It was a frustrating situation for me. I knew the governor and Hackett were close, and I knew that Davis very much wanted him to win. Years later, Davis wrote in his autobiography, "The press was right . . . I came to believe that Hackett fitted the times and the current needs of the state admirably and that he would make a good governor if elected."

Hackett really got under my skin when he said that I had gotten Vermont into the International Paper case for political gain and that I'd done it over the wishes of the governor. I shot back that the governor's office had also tried to stop me, as attorney general, from suing a New Hampshire contractor for damages after a roof collapsed at the state mental hospital in Waterbury. I'd gone ahead with that case over the governor's objections and won a $50,000 settlement for the state.

We had so little money in our campaign chest that we could only run still pictures on our ads; Luther could afford moving pictures and more sophisticated ads. I didn't put a lot of stock in these, hoping my accomplishments would speak for themselves. But I took it hard when the state's largest newspaper, the *Burlington Free Press*, endorsed him. A couple of days later the *Rutland Herald* endorsed me. It said, "In the belief that the Republican organization should stay out of the primary, we urge the ordinary voter who has no organizational ties to give his support to Jeffords."

As in my other statewide primary, I spent a good deal of time in the Northeast Kingdom. The last week in August I went to the Caledonia County Fair in St. Johnsbury, the biggest fair in the kingdom. I got a chance to speak, right there in the heart of farm country, and I said that Hackett had killed a land-use taxation bill in the last days of the 1970 legislative session. That bill would have given a tax break to the owners of agricultural land. I added for good measure, "The closest my opponent has ever been to a farm is a glass of milk."

We were in the last week of August and, particularly in the kingdom, the nights were getting a little cold. Tim Soule gave up trying to sleep outdoors and crowded himself into the camper with the rest of us. Here and there, especially in the north country, we began to see leaves changing color. Some mornings the high hills were white with frost. The last week in August, I asked for a meeting with the governor. He invited me to his home in Montpelier. I wanted to do what I could to keep him out of the race. We talked things over and I let him know that I wasn't pleased with his siding with Hackett. He said that he hadn't endorsed anybody and didn't intend to. But as for him saying anything to help, he certainly wasn't going to do that.

The campaign was wearing on me. I was tired and a little discouraged and the long-brewing problems between Liz and me came to a head. The travel home might have sounded like a good idea, but the close quarters made everyone tense. There was a lot of stress on the children to behave and a lot of stress on Liz to make sure they did. Sometimes she felt treated like part of the campaign and sometimes as just the wife of the campaigner. So there we would be, smiling by day and fighting by night.

A lot of the fights were over the Republican Party leadership. Long before I would admit it, Liz was convinced they were working hard against me. Why didn't I stand up to them? Until that meeting with Davis, I hadn't let myself believe it. So for too many nights Liz would berate me with her analysis that Hackett had been anointed as the chosen one and I just didn't get it. And for too many nights I told her she didn't know what she was talking about.

Of course she was right. The governor wasn't remaining neutral as he claimed, and neither was the party leadership. Bernice Murray discovered that some anti-Jeffords material put out by the Hackett campaign had been mimeographed on a machine in the governor's office. We also noticed that the state committee wasn't inviting us to a lot of Republican events. Hackett would show up and I was nowhere to be seen, with no explanation to the crowd.

On August 27, Hackett and I had a live televised debate at which I decided to make Vermont's Republican national committeeman an issue in the campaign. I didn't have much to lose. I said, "Seward used to be a supporter of mine. But he told me that if I didn't change my stand on water pollution, it would cost him some money. . . . I didn't change. I'm an independent guy."

I asked for and got a second meeting with Davis. It did more harm than good. After I left, the governor told a reporter that my accusation about the state hospital roofing matter "is making it difficult for me to maintain my neutrality."

Roland Q hit me again by claiming that "supporters of Senator McGovern are working and organizing to help the Jeffords campaign." The inference that some of my people were aligned with the liberal Democratic presidential candidate was a shot I didn't need to take in a Republican primary. The only person I knew closely who was aligned to the McGovern campaign was my wife, and she was keeping her McGovern button hidden on the underside of her lapel.

As the campaign went into its last two weeks, Ed Janeway told a reporter that my treatment by the party leadership was "shameful." Appearing on a radio station in Springfield, in southern Vermont, I said that I couldn't be faulted, under the circumstances, for seeking Democratic and independent votes. "They're trying to force me out of the party," I said.

Still they came at me. On September 5 the Republican state's attorneys in five of Vermont's fourteen counties backed Hackett. The next day, eight prominent environmentalists, including Arthur Gibb, chair of the Gibb Commission that I had worked so closely with, said they were backing Luther. That devastated me. I told a reporter, "I'm tired. I've been campaign manager, strategist, and candidate." In truth, many of our campaign staffers were student volunteers. The colleges were opening for the fall semester. Liz, Bernice, Tim, and I would soon be doing most of the work ourselves.

About that time Tom Salmon put a toe in the Republican race. He denied that he had been urging supporters to vote for Hackett, thinking he would be the easier opponent in the general election. The message was thus delivered. A vote for Hackett in the Republican primary would, in a way, be a vote for Salmon. It was a prophetic remark.

The last days of the campaign were surprisingly quiet. Hackett's wife, Sally, suffered a miscarriage and Luther canceled a lot of his appearances to stay close to her. I kept on campaigning full time, but it became clear that I wasn't too likely to win the primary. Now I was really tired.

Election day, September 12, Liz and I voted in the morning at the Montpelier fire station. I worked the rest of the day in the attorney general's office. Liz and I had decided that I couldn't face spending election night at Republican headquarters in Montpelier. I felt betrayed by the people with whom and for whom I had worked for so long.

We rented a little tavern some friends of ours owned a few miles south of Montpelier, The Little Valley House, for the evening. About 150 people gathered there to watch the returns. They had a pretty good party going early in the evening, with all our young campaign workers and some old friends. But by the time I walked in, about nine, it was clear that I wasn't going to be the Republican nominee for governor. As more and more results came in from more and more counties, Hackett's lead got bigger and bigger.

As the outcome became sadly clear, a small group of people in the crowd asked me to step aside for a moment. They wanted to talk about the upcoming election. It turned out they had a check for $5,000 that they wanted to give me to help fund a Jeffords candidacy in the general election. They wanted me to run as an independent. The idea was somewhat tempting. I knew my personal popularity with voters was high, though it hadn't carried me through a Republican primary.

But I was a Republican, always had been, and always meant to be. I knew that a run as an independent would destroy my future in the party. And I knew that if Salmon won, I'd be blamed by the party. So despite the mistreatment by the party regulars and the frustrations of the long campaign, I said no thanks.

But I've thought back to that moment many times. And in other future elections when I wasn't seeing eye to eye with the party and the future looked in doubt, I always knew that an independent run was a real option.

About eleven, I stepped up on a wooden chair to concede defeat. The room got very quiet. The papers the next day said I had tears in my eyes, though I don't remember it. First, I thanked all the people who had worked for me and said, "I hope next time we can do better." I said that I would not run in the general election as an independent candidate for governor, as some people had speculated.

Then I said, "I love you all. Liz and I will have a fine life back in Rutland." There was applause and quite a lot of tears. When it quieted down, Liz shouted, "We'll beat the bastards yet."

That night in Burlington, Tom Salmon went on statewide television and talked about the primary and the coming election. He was about to run against Hackett for governor, but he barely mentioned his opponent. Tom instead praised the courageous campaign I had run against the Republican machine and said that his views were much more in keeping with mine. It was a sharp political move, making a pitch for my supporters on primary night.

As for Liz and me, we said good-bye to the party a little before midnight and drove through the mild September night south toward Rutland. About eight miles short of the city we pulled into the Pico Ski Area and drove to the mountainside chalet owned by John Hansen. John had let me have the use of it for a few days after the election, win or lose. I was tired out and slept pretty well that night. I woke up the next morning feeling very depressed and not a little angry. Losing an election is bad enough, but I also felt that I'd gotten a raw deal from the party. I'd been forced to run, really, not against a little-known state legislator named Hackett, but against the incumbent governor of Vermont. I was also convinced that I was the strongest candidate for governor the Republicans could have put up. I thought they were going to lose the upcoming election.

I got up pretty early, had coffee, then walked out into the misty and cool morning. The air was moist and fresh as I walked to the base of Pico Mountain and started walking up the chairlift line. I kept on going, climbing higher and higher, walking up and up, into clouds that had built up along the entire Coolidge Range of the Green Mountains. After perhaps two hours of steady hiking, I had climbed above the overcast skies and into sunlight. The summit was still well above me and I sat down on a rock to catch my breath. I could see all the way across western Vermont to the Adirondacks in New York State. I got up and kept on going, and in another hour I was on top of Pico, about 4,000 feet up. The valleys of Vermont below were filled with fog, the mountain ridges and peaks in sunlight. I stood for many minutes and I began to feel better about things. Then I walked back down the long mountainside, not getting back to the chalet until late afternoon. When I got there, I picked up an ax and split a good-sized pile of wood. I split a lot of wood in the next few days, and Liz remembers that I didn't talk very much. I guess I was depressed. Liz has always said that losing that election to Hackett was the best thing that ever happened to me, politically, that I built a career on that loss. Maybe it was, but it sure hurt.

If Tom Salmon ran a lousy campaign against me in 1970, he ran a masterful campaign against Luther Hackett in 1972. Though Tom hadn't been much of a friend of the environment in his legislative days, by late September of 1972 he was sounding like a hair-shirt naturalist. "Vermont is not for sale," he declared in one of his first speeches, and that phrase became a key part of his campaign for governor right up until the November election.

A week after the primary election Roland Q gave a speech in Springfield to the Rotary Club. The president of the new antienvironment group Common Sense Associates made a statement that got picked up by the media throughout the state: "What are we preserving the environment for? The animals?" he asked. The next day, Hackett said Vermont should repeal the bottle bill that I had worked so hard to pass. He called the ban on nonreturnable containers too cumbersome. Salmon immediately jumped on the issue, calling Luther anticonservation. Then two days later, Wall Street cut Vermont's credit rating from an excellent triple A to a much less satisfactory double A. Now it would be more expensive for Vermont to borrow money, and it raised questions about the Davis administration's fiscal record, which Hackett had been so quick to praise.

Hackett and friends were clearly worried about the split in the party that the primary had caused. They feared a lot of my supporters would vote for Salmon. On September 24 the Republican State Convention was held in Montpelier and I was given something of a peace offering. I was chosen one of Vermont's three presidential electors. Hackett told the convention, "Mr. Jeffords has worked very hard for the Republican Party and for the State of Vermont, and has earned our respect and dedication. He will join in the Republican effort this fall." But when a reporter asked me to comment, I said I would not be campaigning for Hackett because I would be "too busy as attorney general."

Certainly, a major cause for the Hackett folks' concern lay in the polling numbers they were getting from their professional pollster John Becker from Boston. Becker later told me that my popularity had continued to increase after I lost the primary. I felt I could have given Tom Salmon a much better race than Hackett. After all, I'd already beaten him once.

Even Governor Davis, during the last week in October, admitted that the gubernatorial election was a horse race. On November 1, a poll showed it too close to call. Davis said, "I know some significant Republicans who were Jeffords supporters who are now Salmon supporters, and some who are less than enthusiastic about Hackett." That same day, a television crew from WCAX-TV came to my office and asked whether I was supporting Hackett. I knew that the station owner, Stuart Martin, was a Republican candidate for the state senate and had given money to Hackett's campaign. I said I was supporting the Republican ticket, and got no more specific.

One day not long before the election I was walking down the street in Rutland when a big car pulled up to the curb. Out stepped Tom Salmon. We shook hands and chatted for a few minutes. Neither Tom nor I can remember, more than thirty years later, what we said. I know we had a pleasant talk. I've always liked Tom. Then he went on his way. Though there's been a lot of talk about other meetings between the two of us that fall, that was the only one.

On November 6 I got a call from an old friend, William Franke of Rutland, who had been Dwight Eisenhower's secretary of the navy. He had helped extend my tour of duty so many years previously and was now asking me for a favor. Would I put out a statement of support for Hackett? I couldn't say no. So on election eve I released a brief, terse statement to the press saying that I supported Hackett. That was all. I knew it was too late to have much of any effect on the outcome.

Election day 1972 fell on November 8; Richard Nixon won a second term in a landslide over McGovern, carrying Vermont 92,000 to 53,000. But not even the president's long coattails could save Hackett. He lost to Tom Salmon 83,000 to 65,000.

Liz and I voted in Montpelier. The thought was much with me that day that I could have been elected governor but for that Republican primary. Now, after the Davis years, the GOP had lost the governorship again. Maybe it was just what the party deserved. As for me, I knew that another election was just two years away.

The last two months of my four years as attorney general were extremely busy as the International Paper case was going full tilt. Judge Cutter held a hearing at the county courthouse in Middlebury to hear from local residents. We lined up about fifty people to describe how IPC was fouling Lake Champlain's waters and the Vermont air. John Calhoun and I planned to lead the witnesses through their testimony. Our office was so busy that we had almost no time to prepare for the hearings, so we agreed that while one of us was in court, the other would be outside the courtroom preparing the next witness.

The morning of the hearings, John arrived at the courthouse and mouthed to me, "I can't talk." He had a horrible case of laryngitis. So I had to question all those people by myself, with no preparation whatsoever. Yet somehow it all went fine, and Judge Cutter heard a lot of Vermonters talk about rotten-egg smells from the IPC plant and chunks of sludge washing up on the Vermont shore.

About the only politics I got into between the election and the year's end was to get on the phone and try to help a friend, Connie Johnson, who was campaigning to be chair of the Republican State Committee. In a final shot at me, the party instead chose a friend of Roland Q's, Stewart Smith, a car dealer from Rutland. I knew Stewart well and I liked him. I thought Stewart would prove to be a very good chair. And soon enough, he and Roland Q were having serious disagreements of their own.

My term as attorney general ended in early January when Republican Kimberly Cheney from Montpelier was sworn in to succeed me. He promptly hired me as a consultant to work on the International Paper case. On my last official day as AG I had some of my closest staff members into my office for a farewell chat. We agreed that the years had been fun and, we thought, important. Looking back, I don't think any Vermont attorney general ever had a more eventful time in office. And when you look back at the environmental laws we passed, in particular, and the Yankee and IPC cases, I think we got an awful lot done.

CHAPTER 10

After Nixon

THE EARLY MONTHS of 1973 were momentous times in America and the world. A cease-fire began in Vietnam, though it didn't last very long. The North Vietnamese released the first American prisoners of war. America was still rocked by protests, and not all were about the war. In South Dakota federal marshals opened fire at the Wounded Knee Battlefield on Native Americans protesting the treatment of their race by the government. The Watergate break-in had become a national scandal as the press, then Congress, pressed investigations.

I kept very busy. I joined a fellow Montpelier lawyer, George Rice, in his downtown Montpelier office and resumed practicing law. I also accepted an offer from Johnson State College to teach a course on environmental law. My son, Leonard, had taken up hockey and I coached his bantam league team. I worked on remodeling the house in Montpelier. Liz and I put in a new kitchen and built a playroom for the kids in the cellar. Liz says we never talked about politics, and I guess she's right. But I certainly was thinking politics.

Politics was the last thing on Liz's mind. The Shrewsbury house had funded the governor's race. One doesn't mind giving up something precious for a victory, but it's tough to swallow when you have little to show for that sacrifice but more debts. That race for governor had done serious damage to our marriage.

But Liz heard a warning in the words of my mother, who called to tell her there had been rumors about her drinking. And she began doing things for herself, including taking courses and volunteering at the nursing home across the street from our house.

Meanwhile Bernice Murray set to work on my political recuperation. Bernice and the League of Women Voters came up with a project to educate young voters on the responsibilities of citizenship, and she recruited my help in doing so. Eighteen-year-olds had just gotten the right to vote. Frankly, if truth be known, Bernice's motivation was to keep my name in the public eye. It was very clever. It's important for a defeated candidate, if he's thinking about running again, to keep his name before the public. The work with the League of Women Voters most certainly did that. Bernice and the league set up a speakers' bureau and arranged for us to travel around the state talking about citizenship.

I also got appointed to a committee overseeing the reapportionment of the legislature. And I put out press releases, from time to time, commenting on state matters.

By the early summer of 1973, the Watergate scandal was closing in on President Nixon. Congressional hearings were under way and it became clear that people high in the White House, including Attorney General John Mitchell, had been involved in the illegal bugging of the Democratic Party's national headquarters. The Republican State Committee met on June 11 and was given a resolution critical of the Watergate mess written by my successor as attorney general, Kim Cheney. The committee voted it down, then passed its own resolution praising Nixon's "matchless record of accomplishment." The Vermont GOP pattern of head in the sand was in full display.

In July, Vermont was hit by two days of heavy rain that brought flooding to much of the state. Damage was in the many millions of dollars, though no lives were lost. A few days later I broke a political silence by charging that Governor Salmon was mishandling flood relief. The press said I might have just fired the opening salvo of the 1974 campaign.

But the big question dominating Vermont politics in 1973 concerned whether George Aiken would run for another term in the Senate. At eighty-one, Aiken was in good health and he was keeping his intentions to himself. If he retired, a whole lot of political possibilities would open up. Most candidates like myself were waiting out of respect before making our intentions known.

In August, while Congress was in recess, Aiken and his wife, Lola, came home for a leisurely tour around Vermont. Media speculation began immediately that Aiken might be on a campaign tour for another term after all. The *Rutland Herald* caught up with him at Addison County Field Days and put the question to him. "Oh, no. None of that politics," the senator said. "That's why it's nice to get away from Washington. Just havin' a good time."

After eating supper at the fair, Aiken waited for a convertible with the top down that would drive him around the racetrack. Davis was supposed to be parade marshal, riding one of his prize Morgan horses. But Davis telephoned to say he'd been called away to South Carolina on a legal matter. The *Herald* said, "Just before the parade, Aiken remarked, in apparent relation to nothing at all, 'Who would want to be in South Carolina on a nice day like this?'"

A few days later Aiken attended the dedication of a flood control dam in Ludlow for which he'd helped get funding. Somebody asked Lola about her husband's age and politics. "Because of Watergate," she said, "age isn't so important anymore. What people want are honest men." Old George was keeping us all guessing.

The fall of 1973 was a bad one for Republicans. Federal Judge John Sirica ordered the president to hand over the Watergate tapes, recordings made secretly by Nixon in the Oval Office. In October, Vice President Spiro Agnew resigned, cutting a deal with the Justice Department after he was charged with income tax evasion. Nixon chose Michigan congressman Gerald Ford to succeed Agnew as vice president. Vermont's congressional delegation continued to be loyal to the president.

In September, Roland Q took another shot at me. He said I would not run for governor in 1974 "because he's scared of Salmon." Roland Q told a reporter that the Republican State Committee's fall fund-raising dinner had been canceled because he couldn't get a major Republican figure to speak. The real problem was that he couldn't sell any tickets. Party morale was that low.

October brought the "Saturday Night Massacre" as Nixon fired Attorney General Elliott Richardson, Watergate Special Prosecutor Archibald Cox, and others. Aiken supported firing Cox, which caused the chair of the Democratic State Committee to say that his party "must consider strong opposition to Senator Aiken's reelection bid next year." It had been a long time since talk like that had been heard about Senator Aiken in Vermont. As a testament to Aiken's continuing popularity, the Democratic chair was soon voted out of office and replaced by former governor Phil Hoff.

As November began, Vermont congressman Dick Mallary finally broke with Nixon and said the president should resign from office. Mallary said calls to his office were running ten to one against the president.

State Committee chairman Stewart Smith told the papers that committee members were mad at Mallary because he'd abandoned Nixon.

By December the national energy crisis had caused gasoline prices to reach the unheard-of level of fifty cents a gallon. It was another big problem confronting the White House. As the year ended, the State Committee mailed petitions around Vermont seeking support for the president, planning to mail them to the White House. Less than 1,000 Vermont Republicans signed, and the whole thing was given up.

The year 1974 began with Vermonters still wondering what Senator Aiken would decide. In Chittenden County, State's Attorney Patrick Leahy was saying he would probably run for the Senate regardless of what Aiken did. Phil Hoff said Aiken should retire because of his age. The *Rutland Herald* set the stage for the political year when it editorialized: "Vermonters in 1974 will elect one U.S. Senator, one U.S. House member, one governor, and the remainder of a full slate of constitutional officers."

I went to the Barre Auditorium the night of January 20 for a Republican dinner honoring Connie Bailey, who was retiring from the job of Republican national committeewoman. California governor Ronald Reagan, a friend of Deane Davis's, was the keynote speaker. More than a hundred protestors showed up to greet Reagan and his wife, Nancy. Inside, the party faithful heard Reagan say, "Let there be no question in the minds of any of you. My loyalty to Richard Nixon is 100 percent, God Bless America and President Nixon." Reagan said Nixon "has been the victim of machine politics in cities where tombstones, warehouses, and empty lots have regularly been turned into votes against us. For America's sake, let's get on with the business of government."

I left the dinner shaking my head. I thought Nixon had become a national disgrace and a liability to the party. But he sure got loud applause in Barre that night. It seemed to me that getting elected as a Republican in 1974 might be a tough job. Bernice Murray and some of my friends did a phone poll in early February that showed that the president's popularity was way down in Vermont, but my popularity looked fine.

On Valentine's Day, George Aiken said in Washington, "I want to come home and take care of some unfinished business." He would not run for another term in the Senate. Aiken thus ended fifty-three years of wonderful public service to Vermont. When the media called, I said I'd probably run for Congress. Five days later Vermont's only seat in the U.S.

House opened up when Dick Mallary announced he would run for Aiken's Senate seat. The next day, February 20, I made an informal announcement that I intended to run for Congress.

I felt ready to campaign again in part because Liz had stopped drinking and was working hard to get off prescription drugs. She was even trying to give up cigarettes, perhaps the hardest addiction of all. And she began to set her own rules on which Republican events she would attend and which she would not. She remained active in my run for the U.S. Congress, but on her terms.

Democrat Pat Leahy, a liberal man with strong values, entered the Senate race on March 1. Unfortunately, he had to share the headlines with three top members of the Nixon administration who were indicted the same day in the Watergate cover-up. A week later, Republican National Committeewoman Madeline Harwood said she would probably run for the Republican nomination for Congress as well.

On March 25, Lieutenant Governor Burgess said he, too, was running for Congress. Now it looked like I had a three-way race for the Republican nomination. Several Democrats had also jumped into their House primary, although the clear favorite appeared to be fifty-two-year-old Frank Cain, a former mayor of Burlington.

I hit the campaign trail in late March even though I hadn't officially announced my candidacy. I traveled in the same old camper, moving through a Vermont countryside that was beginning to show signs of spring. The three Republican candidates—Burgess, Harwood, and I— were pretty much going our separate ways. Then Jack made a speech in which he said I should get out of the race because he and I were both political moderates and might cancel each other out. He predicted that Mrs. Harwood was likely to win because she'd have the conservative vote all to herself. Jack said about me, "His overall political career might be improved by not suffering a second defeat in a Republican primary."

When I heard that, I was in bed in Montpelier with a miserable case of the flu. I managed to tell a reporter who called, "I don't intend to have another defeat. I have no intentions of getting out of this race." I was still under the weather on April 19 when I made my formal announcement for Congress. My throat was so sore that I canceled a press conference and instead gave the press a two-paragraph statement. Then I went home and got back in bed.

• • •

Madeline Harwood was a veteran politician who knew full well that conservatives usually win Republican primaries. She announced for Congress on May 16 wearing a red, white, and blue dress. "I wish to state that I am known as a conservative," she said, "and I expect to run a conservative campaign." But she was careful to put some distance between herself and Nixon. She said, "I feel the Watergate affair is a shocking and disgraceful situation."

Through the summer of 1974, the Nixon administration continued to unravel. In June the president himself was indicted as a coconspirator in the Watergate break-in. Al Moulton tried to put the best light on things when he spoke at a Republican dinner held in Burlington.

"I'm sick and tired of hearing the Republican Party maligned for something that most Republicans had nothing to do with," Al said. "I'm sick and tired of having good Republicans turned out of office because of the actions of some staff people."

Madeline, because she was national committeewoman, and Burgess, as lieutenant governor, were at the head table. I went around the room shaking hands from my table down on the floor. Two weeks later, Republican National Committee chairman George Bush spoke in Vermont and echoed Moulton's words. He said the Republican Party as a whole should not be blamed for "the way a handful of people conducted themselves in the last campaign."

While I didn't actually express my disdain for the party for sticking so long with Nixon, I didn't defend the Republicans either. Instead, I put my attentions to the issues, which included restoring the public's trust in government. I thought I had shown that I was my own man and that I was not afraid to take on unpopular causes. I didn't take it upon myself to castigate the party, but neither did I defend it.

Near the backstretch of the campaign, Jack was running in third place and I was pretty sure I had a good lead on Mrs. Harwood. I was getting a good reception from the voters everywhere I went, from the Northeast Kingdom to the Massachusetts border. It was good to be a front-runner again. But still, a Republican primary was an unpredictable thing, especially for a political moderate in a three-way race. When a respected poll showed me with a good lead in the Republican House primary, I was on cloud nine.

The noose tightened on Nixon late in July. In a unanimous decision the Supreme Court ordered him to hand over the Watergate tapes to the Justice Department. Then the House Judiciary Committee passed its second impeachment resolution. Everybody was talking about the president resigning. On August 6, Congressman Mallary finally announced he would vote for impeachment. He had probably waited too long. The next day Nixon said that his impeachment was "a foregone conclusion." His official resignation was given on August 8, 1974. As I traveled around Vermont, it was getting hard to find anybody who would admit to having voted for the president in the last election. Vermont newspapers reported that Vermont Republican leaders had given up on Nixon and were concentrating on who would be selected as vice president when Nixon left office. Nixon quit on August 8, and Gerald Ford became president. Ford chose New York governor Nelson Rockefeller as his vice president.

September came in warm and mild, good campaigning weather, I thought. Everyone turned out at the Rutland Fairgrounds on Labor Day for George Aiken Day. Lieutenant Governor Burgess gave the speech and said quite aptly of the retiring senator, "He never rose so high that he forgot a neighbor in trouble. That is the measure of the man."

On September 8, President Ford pardoned Richard Nixon. That same day the *Bennington Banner*, the paper of record in Mrs. Harwood's home county, endorsed me for Congress. The publisher was Kelton Miller, my old friend who had gotten Act 250 through the Vermont House. Miller was upset because Madeline had said draft resistors should be sent to jail. "She would be out of her league in Congress," the paper said. The *Banner* endorsement wasn't entirely glowing. It said some people considered me "a fence straddler" and "a political lightweight." Oh well, an endorsement was an endorsement.

Nixon's resignation was greeted with relief among Republicans in Vermont, and in the final days of the campaign, Mrs. Harwood's numbers began to go up. It was good news for conservatives. I was still confident, but the sooner the election was over, the better. The voters went to the polls September 11. That night I went to election central in Montpelier, where a big crowd watched the vote count. I was in good spirits, but the early returns showed the race was very close. It was a long night and a tense one. Madeline conceded to me about midnight in a gracious statement in which she wished me well and promised her support in the general election. We've been friends ever since. The final totals showed me with 16,579 votes to her 14,894. Jack Burgess got a little more than 10,000. It had, indeed, been a close race. Mayor Frank Cain won the Democratic nomination. I would have to beat him in November to win a seat in Congress.

I went to a Republican meeting in Montpelier arranged by Stewart Smith the morning after the election. Congressman Mallary, who had easily won his primary over Charley Ross, was there as were lieutenant governor nominee T. Gary Buckley, House Speaker "Peanut" Kennedy, who was now running against Tom Salmon, and the pollster John Becker. It seemed strange at best—all that Republican unity and I was a part of it. I got a lot of congratulations. Smith said the State Committee would give me campaign money, about $25,000. I was grateful, but cautious.

President Ford seemed to calm the country, getting things back to normal as quickly as anyone could have. I thought I could beat Frank Cain, mainly because I had statewide experience and name recognition. But Frank had been mayor of Burlington for two terms and had done a good job in the state's largest city. He was a good-looking, soft-spoken fellow who tended to be quite conservative for a Democrat. I didn't take a win for granted.

The general election for Congress was actually a three-way race because Michael Parenti was running on the liberal Liberty Union Party ticket. A university professor who strongly opposed the Vietnam War, Parenti was a very good speaker and debater. Cain and I often found ourselves on common ground on issues, so when the three of us were on stage together, Parenti was often taking us both on. I started calling the three of us Tweedle-dee, Tweedle-dum, and the Wild One. I found the campaign sort of boring. I didn't miss the dirty tricks but I was used to a tougher political fight. Still, I wasn't complaining.

The campaign was going exceedingly well when, in mid-September, my luck changed. I was driving a car in Rutland City when I got rear-ended at a stoplight. I suffered a serious whiplash injury to my back and neck. In a few days the doctor put me in a surgical collar that I had to wear for the rest of the campaign.

President Ford came to Burlington on October 7 for a Republican dinner at the University of Vermont to honor George Aiken. More than eighteen hundred Republicans paid $50 for a ticket, putting a nice piece of change in the Republican State Committee's coffers. I sat at the head table near the president, ate roast beef, and heard Ford endorse my candidacy. I got a big cheer when I was introduced as "the next congressman from Vermont."

I worked hard despite my sore back and neck, shaking hands and hitting the chicken pie suppers. While I made my biggest effort in Cain's home territory of Chittenden County, I didn't neglect the rest of Vermont. I was surprised to find that in many of the places I went, Cain hadn't been there at all. It began to seem he wasn't campaigning all that hard. He certainly wasn't raising many issues.

After a breakdown, the camper was fixed and back on the road on October 24. I told a reporter I planned to "keep cool" the next two weeks. That day Cain finally got aggressive and said that I'd spent too much money while attorney general. I stayed cool.

Four days later Cain and his wife, Mary, were driving in Williston, near Burlington. Frank was at the wheel when there was an accident. Their car rolled over and was demolished. Frank escaped with bruises, but Mary ended up in the hospital with a cracked sternum. Frank canceled his appearances that afternoon, and I did the same out of deference to him. It seemed that our campaigns might be jinxed.

Election day came on November 5, a rainy day all around Vermont. I voted in Montpelier in the morning, then went home and went to bed. It wasn't just my neck; I'd come down with a bad cold. That night I went to election central at the Tavern Motor Inn to watch the results wearing my white neck brace. My race was over early, as the returns showed me winning throughout the state, even in Chittenden County. Cain called at nine-fifteen to concede and very graciously said, "Jim, the best man won."

For Republicans generally, however, the night was a long one. Tom Salmon got reelected, easily beating "Peanut" Kennedy. But the real shocker was Pat Leahy's upset of Dick Mallary. Vermont Democrats had themselves a U.S. Senate seat for the first time since before the Civil War. That race was decided late, and by the time all the votes were counted, I was home in bed.

I had beaten Cain 74,000 to 56,000 votes, pretty close to a landslide while Mallary lost to Leahy by 4,000 votes. I had a cold and my neck hurt but, for somebody in that shape, I felt pretty good. Leaving election central that chilly, wet Montpelier night alone, I stopped for a minute on the sidewalk. A touch of winter was in the air. Across the street was the building where I'd spent four years as attorney general. Beyond it was the supreme court where my father had worked many years before. I wished he could have been with me. I was the congressman-elect from the state of Vermont, the pick of the voters to fill the only seat our little state held in the U.S. House of Representatives. In January, Jim Jeffords, Republican of Vermont, would be in Congress. I think I was about as happy at that moment as I have ever been. There are some nights we remember all of our lives. And that is one of mine.

It was good to have that feeling. It sustained me as the problems at home became more pressing in the weeks and months ahead.

CHAPTER 11

The Walking Wounded

AT THE START of each new legislative session, the press holds a welcoming social for the new members of Congress so everyone can get to know one another. I arrived with my neck in a brace, still walking gingerly from the injuries I'd sustained in my car accident. Chuck Grassley from Iowa, another freshman Republican, had broken his ankle and arrived at the event on crutches. The post-Watergate election had been a disaster for Republicans. Of the ninety-two new members only seventeen were Republican. The Republicans were down to 144 out of 435 members. When Chuck and I hobbled in, someone in the crowd—a Democrat no doubt—shouted, "There's two we almost got." I didn't point out that Chuck had broken his ankle playing Ping-Pong while I had received my injuries while campaigning in my hometown. It soon became clear that, as far as political power and particularly legislative clout were concerned, I was about as far down the pecking order as I could get. Not only was I in a very distinct minority in the House, where the majority holds almost all of the procedural cards, but I was a moderate within that minority.

My first day in office as Vermont's lone U.S. congressman, January 15, 1975, began unceremoniously enough when I was dislodged from my preferred Agricultural Committee seat by seniority. What happened was that the Agriculture Committee, which had long been the quiet resting place of aging former farmers, had suddenly become a popular committee due to the growing national interest in food production and food prices. When I had arrived in Washington the previous day, I had been assured of an assignment on the Agriculture Committee. But by the next afternoon, Margaret Heckler, (R., Mass.) had exercised her seniority rights to transfer from the Banking Committee to Agriculture, bumping the most junior member, which happened to be me. I figured I ranked 435 in the 435-member House. Despite my first lesson in humility, I was still able to tell a *Rutland Herald* reporter, "As I took the oath of office, I had a feeling of awe, and I realized I was participating in something meaningful, that this was a very critical time in the history of this country."

Fortunately, at my request, Republican leaders were able to convince the Democrats to add seats to the Agriculture Committee by raising hell about the broken promise. I wonder why that doesn't work anymore. As it turned out, fortune remained with me. When I drew for rank on that committee, I drew number one of the four freshman congressman, making me the ranking member on the subcommittee on dairy. My luck stayed with me. I had offered to draw for fellow Republican Ben Gilman of New York for his seat on the House Foreign Affairs Committee because he couldn't be there. I reached into the box and pulled number one for him, giving him the ranking seat on that committee. Then it came time for me to pull for my other seat on the Education and Labor Committee, which was a very important issue for me. Five other freshman had also picked that committee. I was told I had to pick last. I couldn't complain. I expected a high number but, as luck would have it, the piece of paper left for me held the number one. The groans in the room that day were very loud. This meant that, as long as I was in the U.S. House of Representatives, I would rank higher than the other freshman legislators on two important committees and I could pick the subcommittees I wanted to be on, which were dairy and select education, which handled the Individuals with Disabilities Education Act. Dairy and IDEA have been the areas I've most committed myself to from those earliest days in Washington until now.

The most astounding event of my first months in office began while I was reading the history of 504 regulations dealing with removing architectural barriers so people with disabilities would have access to buildings open to the public. I was astounded when I realized that an assistant attorney general in Nixon's administration had ruled that the 504 law did not apply to federal property. Didn't people in wheelchairs have the right to use the post office or visit their national parks? I brought this loophole to the attention of John Brademus, a Democrat from New York and a most able legislator who later became president of New York University. He was chairman of my subcommittee on select education. John listened to me, then said, "Jim, you're absolutely right. We should fix that problem. We have what is called the suspension calendar for noncontroversial amendments. I'll put an amendment on for you to overrule the attorney general's ruling on the suspension of the calendar. Later on, you'll understand what you did."

About a month later, an office staffer called to say the office was full of important people from the department of federal buildings, the parks department, and the like—and they were all mad as hell. My staffer told me I'd best get there right away. At that time, we had a tiny office at the top of the Cannon Building. When I arrived, I was greeted by the head of federal buildings yelling "Do you know what you've done?" I said, "I'm not sure but it must have been important." He said, thanks to you all federal buildings have to be made accessible to people with handicaps and that's going to cost America $20 billion. It took a minute but I finally realized he was talking about the so-called noncontroversial amendment to make federal buildings comply with the accessibility codes. I told him I thought it was terrific that people with disabilities would finally be able to avail themselves of these resources.

He was dumbfounded with my remark. "Who's going to pay for it?" he asked. "That's your problem," I said, turned, and left.

Now when I walk into the post office or even upon entering the Capitol through a handicapped accessible door, I have that rare experience of seeing a concrete example of an accomplishment. And, looking back, getting approval of a $20 billion expenditure to make the country a little more democratic was a pretty good feat for my first six months in office.

I had gone to Washington alone and broke. Liz had decided to stay home in Montpelier rather than join me, which was a mixed blessing given the strain in our relationship. I missed her and the children very much, but in reality I don't know how I could have afforded a home for all of us. I took the train to D.C. and I still remember Laura saying, "Papa, every time I close my eyes I see you waving from the back of the train." I had $44,000 in campaign and personal debts, not much by today's standards but overwhelming for me at the time. I wanted to keep the family in the style they had become accustomed to or as close to it as I could manage. It was a lot easier to do that in Vermont's capital than the nation's. In 1975 my salary as a U.S. congressman was just $600 more than my debts, $44,600. After the Vermont expenses, I figured I had $58 a month to live on in D.C.

I learned that I could rent a site at the travel park behind the Holiday Inn in College Park, Maryland, for about $25 a month plus utilities and live in my travel home. If I was careful with my money and took advantage of free lunches and breakfast get-togethers, I might not starve to death. And my family could continue to live in our Montpelier home.

News somehow got out that I was going to live in the travel home. Thus, when I drove it from Montpelier to D.C., I did so in glorious style and with lots of press coverage. Bob Hager of NBC News accompanied me to New York City, where I appeared on "Good Morning America" in my first national news event. The mother of Martin Luther King Jr. was on the show at the same time, which made it particularly special for me.

Once in D.C., I decided to do without a car. I took the bus to work every morning and evening, again to save money. Finally, a staff member loaned me a car so I could drive back and forth to work. I was definitely the epitome of the post-Watergate Republican Party—limping along and barely making it financially. I called our party the Walking Wounded.

Right off the bat I got to be friends with Millicent Fenwick, a Republican member of Congress from New Jersey and an editor of *Vogue* magazine in Garry Trudeau's "Doonesbury." She was a celebrity because she was a survivor of Watergate, not to mention a rare woman in Washington politics. She was the real item, smart and witty, and we really hit it off. Not long after I moved into my palatial environs behind the Holiday Inn, Millicent and I were invited to appear on the District's Channel 9 talk show. The host asked Millicent how she found life as a member of Congress. She said quite grandly, "I get up in the morning and I throw open the drapes of my apartment and I see the Capitol and I say how lucky I am." Then they asked me, and I said, "I go to the front of my travel home and throw open the door and look out onto the Dumpsters outside the Holiday Inn and wonder what the heck am I doing here."

Another time Millicent invited me to the grand opening of the movie *All the President's Men*. We showed up to the event with more than the usual hoopla surrounding the previewing of a movie. How exciting it was to rush through the throng of reporters with their bright lights and shouted questions. The next day when the newspapers featured Millicent's photo, I was identified with the ignoble identification "and escort."

Living in the motor home so far from the capital was less than ideal for obvious reasons. So in July 1975 I decided to sell the house in Montpelier and the camper to pay off my debts. I was able to do so because the minister of a local church who had read about my problems came to my rescue. His church had two guest houses and he offered me one. It was located in Suitland, Maryland, in a fairly low-income district that was a bit out of town. But living in an actual building would be a vast improvement and I gratefully accepted the offer, especially as the house had a telephone, which the camper did not. I still needed to live closer to Washington but I decided to stay there through the summer, in part because the rent was free but also because I wanted to have a small garden to help reduce my expenses. I bought a dozen tomato plants but I only got around to planting six of them before nightfall. During the night, those six plants disappeared. I figured I'd better plant the other six. I did, but the next night, three were gone. Someone must have decided that three was the appropriate number of plants for a man living alone because they left me with those.

I was able to sell the camper because Liz had returned to Rutland and took up residency in the Jeffords homestead on Kingsley Avenue. She was glad to be back in Rutland, back among her friends and people she felt she could trust. She enjoyed having the children in school in Rutland and being involved in community activities such as the Rutland Crossroads Arts Council and the Girl Scouts, but we had little married life. I was away all week and busy with work or the children on weekends. I loved going to the kids' sporting events. I had decided not to take honorariums or throw parties so I could continue to reduce my debts; meanwhile, Liz was shopping for herself and the children at the Not-New Shop. Perhaps hardest of all for Liz was the adjustment to living back with my mother, who was something of a neatnik. Despite the fact that Mother had her own apartment, she still couldn't relinquish control of the house. Liz felt she had to keep the house spotless and that the kids had to be perfect—not for her but for Nana.

Meanwhile, as Liz liked to say, I was so busy I could barely catch my breath. Almost right out of the gate, I introduced a proposal for a bottle ban based on Vermont's law, essentially banning nonrecyclable bottles and placing a deposit on most beverage containers, exempting milk and water. At the time, the EPA estimated that the bill could lead to energy savings equal to 92,000 barrels of oil a day. That bottle bill effort died, as did each subsequent one I introduced in each new legislative session over the next twelve years and at the start of every two years during my two terms in the Senate. But I do not view this as a failure. My persistence drew more state legislatures into the mix and caused some to pass their own bottle deposit and recycling laws, whereas when I arrived in the District, only Vermont and Oregon had passed such a law. Now, ten states—California, Connecticut, Delaware, Iowa, Maine, Massachusetts, Michigan, New York, Oregon, and Vermont—and the city of Columbia, Missouri, have bottle bills.

I also began my long and arduous effort to gain greater and more consistent support for dairy farmers, almost from day one, going so far as to accuse the U.S. Department of Agriculture during my fourth month in office of lying about the cost to consumers of increasing federal milk supports. Today, as I struggle to reinstate a dairy compact that has helped to keep small family farms in Vermont and other New England states in business, I could be frustrated by the fact that the fight for so many commonsense proposals I've made to improve our nation's educational system, environment, energy independence, and dairy industry have been defeated by those who respond to special interest, greed, short-sightedness, and, frankly, a lack of concern for the average person and the natural world.

But I learned in my first years in Congress that success in the legislature should not always be measured by final enactment of a law, even though that is our main concern. Success can also come from making a cause more visible or more coherent and in building public sentiment, understanding, and a database for the future. Sometimes one uses public office to help or promote causes that eventually assume legitimacy simply through education and familiarity. In that way, even failed legislation can succeed in enhancing an issue and lead to gaining support in ways not at first contemplated.

Certainly this was the purpose of many of my earliest efforts, such as studies I had sponsored in farmland preservation, the creation of solar energy and wood energy caucuses, in promoting U.S. relations with Indonesia, in helping to improve human dignity and human rights for

Soviet citizens and dissidents, and in championing the rights of people with disabilities. To be an implement of change, one must be patient. I will speak more of some of these efforts later, but I want to say at the out-set that, even though more than 75 percent of the 350 bills, amend-ments, and other initiatives that I sponsored from 1975 to 1988 passed the House and more than 50 percent became law, I do not view the 50 percent that did not pass as failures.

Of course, when I arrived in Washington I was fresh from all the suc-cesses and changes that we had brought to Vermont. I knew that Wash-ington was not Montpelier, but I didn't expect it to be so difficult to get things done. The first thing I did was to find out how the system worked. The first obvious fact was that no one was going to hand you anything that you had not earned on your own. Without seniority, my ideas would be listened to only if they were fresh, good ideas that more senior people had not already thought of or were putting their energies into. Second, however, the House, although run by a seniority system and rules of pro-cedure that stacked the odds against someone new like me, was not the sharp-edged partisan body in the mean sense that would come later, especially during and after the rise of Speaker Newt Gingrich (R., Ga.).

In 1975 the Republican minority leader of the House was the affable John Rhodes of Arizona, who, while conservative, wished all his mem-bers well. Tolerance of different opinions and of eager freshmen with new ideas existed. Perhaps because of the Republican minority as well as my natural inclination, I worked hard to build coalitions across the aisle. I soon discovered that other members were willing to cosponsor my bills and amendments, but like an eager salesmen, I had to gain their support one by one, which required considerable shoe leather in order to make a dent in 435 members. It also required a bit of analysis to figure out which key cosponsors would want to sign on to the bills in which I was inter-ested. Thus, one of the most important lessons I learned early on was to be inclusive and share the limelight, to the extent that I could find it.

It was also crucial to get the attention of senior members on the right committees of jurisdiction, so that the legislation might get a hearing, which was difficult enough given the large number of bills that are intro-duced. One of the problems with the two-year term for the U.S. Congress is that a freshman legislator spends his first year learning the ropes and making contacts and then has to get ready to run again. Turnovers and change in leadership mean that each session requires a certain amount of renegotiating the territory for even the most senior members. All this is particularly frustrating for a freshman legislator. Even after months of work on garnering support across the aisle for a measure, the work could be easily wiped out with a presidential veto.

For example, my freshman term was characterized by a conflict with President Ford over price supports for dairy. My very first bill, which would have raised the price support for milk to 85 percent of parity, got rolled into the 1975 Omnibus Emergency Farm Bill. The federal price support got reduced to 80 percent in floor debate. I tried—and failed—to get it up to 82 percent. Using the coalitions I had been building, I was able to gain passage for the bill in both the House and the Senate, but Ford vetoed the measure on May 1. I knew this could devastate Vermont farmers so I led the fight for a free-standing dairy support increase, which passed both houses at 85 percent parity, the amount I had initially asked for. Ford vetoed that, too. Fortunately, we were able to pass a law that allowed farmers to consolidate loans and get a better interest rate, help-ing to slow down the loss of small family farms for a bit.

These efforts in my first term of office led the dairy industry to ask me to resign from Congress to become their national lobbyist at a salary three times what I was being paid. Along with the pay, they offered some substantial perks that included a new black Cadillac limousine. That limo was the worst thing they could have offered me. How can you iden-tify with the Vermont diary farmer and get them to trust you when you're being driven around in a big, black limousine? I've never regretted turn-ing down the offer, but I sure wish the fight for small dairy farmers was not such a difficult one.

I must have been doing something right because in 1976—and again in 1978—I was virtually unopposed in the GOP primary. John A. Burgess, a lawyer like me, was my Democratic opponent in 1976. I got my old friend Stewart Smith to run my campaign. He had been ousted from party chair after a bitter fight with Roland Q and I was anxious not only for Stewart Smith's expertise but to restore credibility to moderate Republicans.

I didn't want to abuse the taxpayers and voters by spending my last six months in office campaigning, so I stayed in Washington, except for weekends, until about October 15, when Congress recessed. I placed my future on my record. One of the things that endeared me to the voters, I believe, was my commonsense approach to problems. As part of my investigation of the food stamp program, for example, I actually went to the social service agency in Rutland and went through the application process. I saw how demoralizing it could be. Partly as a result of my efforts, in 1976 the government changed its food stamp regulations so the elderly could get cash instead of food stamps. This was part of my overall effort to ensure adequate nutrition for needy Americans. I fought hard for passage of a food stamp reform bill, an effort that didn't pay off until the next session. But in my freshman term, not only did we gain access for the handicapped to federal buildings and parks but we were also able to strengthen civil rights protections for the elderly by barring discrimination on the basis of age. I think it was efforts like these, and my work for the state's dairy industry, that sent me back to Washington.

Back at home, however, my relationship with Liz had not improved. I had hoped it would but Liz and I seemed at a standoff. We argued a good deal during the campaign and afterward, sometimes about substantive issues, sometimes about nothing at all. She was feeling the strain of my mother's everyday presence in her life and things that would seem small or inconsequential to me were big issues to her. Once I arrived home with a broken finger, an injury sustained in a softball game. Liz had been looking forward to my help on some much-needed home repairs. During the weeks and months alone in Vermont, she had begun drinking again and was again taking prescription tranquilizers. From her viewpoint, I think, she was simply having a hard time getting her life back on track and felt I wasn't of much help. Our marriage had not turned out the way she had hoped. From mine, I wanted those minutes in Vermont to be peaceful and productive and I resented what seemed like constant conflict awaiting me at my doorstep. I had tried not to be like my father, but in this way—the desire not to be bothered but rather allowed to relax from work—I was very much like him. Liz was not a stoic like my mother had been. Her role models were her gregarious parents who talked, and sometimes argued, things out.

In November 1976, shortly after the election, Liz accompanied me on a trip to Indonesia, hoping that, as our previous sojourn to Bermuda had done, the time together without children, my mother, or the constant pressures of work and the scrutiny of the press would help get our relationship back on track.

It was, however, a working trip. My key foreign policy aide, Dick D'Amato, now a member of the Maryland House of Representatives, had, while in the navy, been assigned as an adviser to the Indonesian navy in Java. He had introduced me to the mysterious and magical land of Indonesia and its politicians and made me aware of that country's unrecognized importance in the world as the largest Muslim nation and the fifth largest country in the world. He had helped arrange my hosting of key members of the Indonesian cabinet to the U.S. Congress, which resulted in an invitation from the Indonesian president to visit that country to deliver a series of lectures and meet with academic and government leaders. The trip was sponsored by the Center for Strategic and International Studies in Jakarta, a nonprofit organization that explored international food sharing, energy, and U.S.-Indonesian relations. It also coincided with another long interest of mine as a member of the Food for Peace project, the U.S. Agency for International Development's program to improve agriculture, health, nutrition, and education worldwide.

While so far from home, I also visited New Zealand to examine dairy operations in that country. I was interested because I'd learned that New Zealand was the only nation producing unsubsidized dairy products at a lower cost than that achieved by U.S. farmers. They were also successful in exporting dairy products and meat over most of the world.

Everywhere we went, we toured farms and talked to agriculture experts, trying to glean as much information as possible that might help Vermont farmers and dairy operators as well as solve international problems with food shortages and distribution while exchanging ideas on innovative programs that could benefit people at home and abroad.

The trip had other positive outcomes. The CIA had done an extensive, but classified, study of a brutal series of events in 1965 involving widespread massacres and violence against members of the Indonesian Communist Party, many of whom were ethnic Chinese. Charges had been leveled that the Indonesian military leadership had acted wrongly and racially against the Chinese people in the country. But the CIA study revealed, on the contrary, that the events were precipitated by a planned attack on the Indonesia general staff by the PKI, the Indonesian Communist Party. This attempted coup d'état had apparently been undertaken with the knowledge of Chinese authorities in Beijing. The CIA found that the Indonesian authorities had reacted to a clear attack on their existence. This response had escalated into an uncontrolled nationwide orgy of violence by ethnic Indonesians against the Communist Party, which lasted most of a year and effectively extinguished the Indonesian Communist Party from power. I was successful in convincing the CIA to declassify and release the text of its analysis, which put to rest a nasty debate on the matter. For this, naturally, the Indonesian government was grateful, as were historians of the age.

My trip allowed me not only to meet the Indonesian president and his advisers but also to convince them to release a number of human rights dissidents imprisoned since the 1965 coup. All in all, it was an educational and fascinating visit to one of the least understood nations of Asia, one which has proven to be a steadfast ally of the United States. As events in the Muslim world have unfolded over the past few months, coupled with the problems experienced in Indonesia in the past few years, I have concluded that it's unfortunate that more of our political leaders haven't educated themselves about cultures far and wide. Our parochialism, I believe, contributes to our misunderstanding of people whose ethnic, religious, and/or cultural orientation is different from ours and it contributes to their misunderstanding of us.

But while the trip was useful to me in terms of broadening my agricultural and foreign policy understanding, it did little to improve my relationship with Liz. Years later she told me that she had fallen back in love with me during that trip, that she saw again a person who wanted to change the world, and that she had promised herself that she would try harder to be a part of that mission. But I had just about had it. Although she did not drink on that trip, I was discouraged that she had gone back to alcohol. One of her doctors had told me that she would have to come out of it herself and that some people did not stop drinking until they reached rock bottom. For Liz and the children's sake, I did not want that to happen. I really did not know what to do.

Not too long afterward, during a visit home, we were fighting again. Liz was gilding some picture frames, doing her darndest to place her signature on this house that had been the Jeffordses' home since before I was born. Neither one of us can remember exactly what we were arguing about, only that we were arguing, when she turned to me and yelled, "Jim, what do you want? A divorce?"

I said yes.

CHAPTER 12

Leo Ryan, Baby Seals, Solzhenitsyn, and Energy Wars

IF PEOPLE HADN'T yet gotten the point that I was not your typical Republican, my friendship with Leo Ryan, my intervention on the part of Soviet dissident Aleksandr Solzhenitsyn, and my efforts to decrease our dependence on foreign oil made it perfectly clear. In the arena of successes and failures, the next few years had some of both.

Ryan and I had been freshmen congressmen together in 1975. He was a Democrat from San Francisco, about as wacky as they come, a born challenger who wanted to build a coalition to save the world. Frankly, I found some of his ideas quite interesting if not persuasive, and during the years I knew him, he got me involved in one adventure after another. I was chair of the Congressional Environmental Study Conference, an informal group of House and Senate members we had created to learn about and monitor environmental issues here in the United States and around the world. Leo had become obsessed with the killing of baby seals and, as he told us about how the hunters killed these animals, I decided I wanted to see for myself whether what he was saying was true. Leo told us the seals were brutally killed during the first days of their lives because after that their snow-white pelts started to turn brown. He explained that the hunters bopped the baby seals on the head rather than shoot them because they didn't want to get blood on the pelts or put holes in the skins. He said the seals were so defenseless that the hunters could walk right up to them on the ice and kill them with a single blow. Coming from Vermont, a place where people still hunted for food, I was interested in learning whether seal-hunting contributed either to the natives' food supply or their income. While I was beginning to develop some sympathy for animal rights, I also believed there was a place for hunting—for food and clothing or to control overpopulation of species.

On March 12, 1978, Leo and I, accompanied by the actress Pamela Sue Martin, then the star of the Nancy Drew series, and my niece Kathleen McGreevy, traveled to Newfoundland at the expense of Greenpeace to monitor the harvest of Canadian harp seals on ice floes located two hundred miles north of the northwestern port of St. Anthony. It turned into a full-fledged drama. I thought Leo was obnoxious, attracting the attention of the press by getting right in the face of the hunters, some of whom were native people who had had little exposure to Hollywood or TV cameras. While Leo was busy with the media, I talked to the native people.

It didn't take long to conclude that they had few resources and that this hunt was their main source of income. I felt there were two sides to the story and I was trying to sort through them. On the one hand, I learned, the hunt might make the difference between whether or not a family made it through the year. Some families told me they got a quarter of their yearly income—roughly $2,500—from the annual hunt.

On the other hand, I thought the clubbing of baby seals was barbaric.

We had left the mainland in a raging blizzard, flying in a really small plane and landing against the orders of the Canadian government. As soon as we touched down, the mounted police arrested the pilot. The day the hunt was scheduled to start, we were delayed from witnessing it when a huge ice pack separated the hunters from the seal herd. We learned that six Canadian and four Norwegian sealing vessels had been stalled because of the ice jam. The Canadians brought in an icebreaker to clear a path to the herding grounds while the protesters waited for the Canadian government to rule on whether they would let us observe the kill.

Canadian law bans anyone without the proper permit from going within half a mile of a seal and we had no permits. Meanwhile, Greenpeace had hired helicopters to take the protesters and our small congressional delegation to the site, creating a standoff between the congressional delegation and the Canadian government. While we negotiated with the authorities, there were lots of unpleasant exchanges between the two groups. I felt these exchanges accomplished little. Finally, the government conceded and allowed us onto the hunting grounds. It was a brutal scene. I saw about a hundred hunters working the ice pack; the ice was literally littered with the carcasses of baby seals they had simply walked up to and clubbed to death. It really bothered me that these newborn animals were slaughtered—not for food but for fur coats and trinkets.

When I talked to the press, I expressed my understanding of the two sides of the issue and the reliance of the native people on the hunt. Yet, I said, I had to come down on the side of the defenseless baby seals.

I learned some valuable lessons from this trip. Much as Leo's tactics turned me off, the whole outing was a textbook example of how advocacy groups can use the press to advance their causes, take on industries, and, in some cases, even government. Eventually, based on our testimony and the negative press, Congress banned the import of baby seal skins and products made from them. Overseas, the market dried up so much, partly because it became politically incorrect to wear animal fur, that the hunt became economically unproductive.

Because of my work to save the baby seals in Newfoundland, Friends of the Animals invited me, in May 1979, to join their protest of the seal fur hunt in the Aleutian Islands. Vermonters had participated in the defense of the Aleutians against the Japanese in World War II, so I was particularly interested in that part of the world. I went by myself, flew up there, met the environmentalists, fell in love with the Aleutians, and came away with a far different opinion than I had in Newfoundland. The natives told me they didn't kill baby seals or even female seals but rather killed only the "excess males." Those words went through me; there are no excess males. That's a pretty horrible term. But despite my visceral response to the phrase, I got their point. I refused to take part in the confrontation and did not offer my help to raise attention to the cause of the fur seals. I felt this hunt did not threaten the species and that these native people's livelihood depended on it. Needless to say, Friends of the Animals were not very pleased with me.

My long relationship with Aleksandr Solzhenitsyn, his wife, Natalia, and other Soviet dissidents began in 1976 after I read a news story that said Solzhenitsyn wanted to emigrate to the United States and liked what he had heard about the state of Vermont. How to get hold of him? Certainly the Soviet government wasn't going to help me get highly visible dissidents out of their country.

We found a Soviet émigré who was working on the staff of Senator Strom Thurmond (R., S.C.). Over coffee one morning Dick D'Amato struck up a conversation with him and asked if he could get a letter from me translated and somehow delivered to Solzhenitsyn. The letter would be one of welcome and an offer of assistance to find Solzhenitsyn a suitable place, safe and appropriate in Vermont where he could live when and if he departed from his homeland. The letter was translated and disappeared. I was assured it would get to him through the "right channel." We heard nothing for some months.

Then one day our contact called to say he had a letter for me—the answer was yes, Solzhenitsyn wanted to take up my offer and meet me immediately at a location of my choosing when he got to the United States. I contacted Norman Campbell, the president of the Vermont Life Insurance Company, who immediately offered the company's guest house in a rural area outside the Vermont capital of Montpelier. Solzhenitsyn also asked me to provide him with a gun—an odd request that we said we'd help him with later, if he thought it still necessary. When he immigrated to the United States, we whisked him to Vermont, settled him in, and spent most of the first night finishing off a bottle of excellent Russian vodka.

The Solzhenitsyns settled into the rugged mountain town of Cavendish. It was my assistant and right-hand person in Vermont, Bernice Murray, who helped them with the mundane but confounding tasks of everyday living—how to enroll the children in school, how to get a driver's license, how to shop, how to avoid the swarms of press that sometimes camped outside Solzhenitsyn's compound. In this, the wonderful residents of Cavendish were the Solzhenitsyns' biggest allies. When reporters asked for directions, they were told to go home and leave the Soviet writer alone. The sign in the general store said it all: "No shoes—no service. And no directions to Solzhenitsyn's."

Aleksandr was all work and very little play. After years in the gulag, he was interested in restoring his health and dedicating himself to his writing. He woke early, took a swim in the pond on his property, even in frigid weather, and spent most of the day in his studio, writing. We helped arrange the few press interviews he accepted. He eschewed political events and declined public speaking offers. Natalia, however, testified frequently before congressional committees and was a leader in her own right of the Soviet dissident movement. Her efforts and those of others led to the release of another famous dissident, Alexander Ginzburg, from the gulag into the United States. It was the incredibly emotional human side of these events that drove home to me how important American policy was in holding out beacons of hope to these courageous adversaries of a brutal dictatorship. It was a rare privilege to play a bit part in this drama and help make real the workings of our values in ways one can hardly foresee. It was also a rare privilege to bring the beauty and serenity of Vermont into the lives of those who have championed, often alone and under oppression, the values we take for granted.

When we got Ginzburg out along with four other political prisoners in 1979, it was driven home to me the success we had as a country, particularly through the persistence of men like Scoop Jackson, to pressure the Soviet regime to free these intellectual writers and dissidents. Ginzburg had been jailed some forty times for his activities and beliefs, and he would surely have died in prison were it not for American pressure. When we drove him from the airport to a meeting in the U.S. Senate in the office of Senator Abraham Ribicoff (D., Conn.), Ginzburg was so nervous that we had to sit him in the corner of Ribicoff's office in such a way that he could see all the doors coming into the room. He could not psychologically stand to be seated with his back to a door—just a hint of the frightful experiences he had been put through.

It was a time when hawk and dove worked together on an issue without the contentiousness that I find so distasteful now. Henry "Scoop" Jackson (D., Wash.), a man who had been talked of as John F. Kennedy's running mate and who later became Democratic Party chairman, a hawk if there ever was one, worked together with Senator Ribicoff on the mutual goal of helping these Russian dissidents.

Most of my efforts were focused on helping dairy farmers, promoting sound energy policies, and improving conditions for the elderly. As the 1978 campaign approached, my third for Vermont's lone congressional seat, a *Rutland Herald* article said I was "now generally regarded as the most popular politician and potent voter-getter in Vermont." I not only stood little opposition from the GOP but by June I had no opponent from the Democrats, and people were urging me to consider running against

Patrick Leahy for the U.S. Senate. I felt that would be wrong. I've always admired Leahy and felt that he has done outstanding work for Vermont and the country. I decided to run again for the House of Representatives.

As it turned out, I had two opponents that year: S. Marie Dietz, a Democrat and antiabortionist, and Peter Diamondstone, a colorful Liberty Union candidate. Those years on Rutland's football field came in handy when the *Herald* endorsed me, saying, "As a football player in high school, Jeffords was not a particularly graceful runner. But he covered a lot of territory for Dido Flaitz and he didn't go down easily after the tackle. . . . Rep. Jeffords has carried over into his political method some of the mannerisms of his high school football strategy: he doesn't try to be a spellbinder on the stump, but he nevertheless is effective as a candidate and as a congressman."

I won the election, as did Leo, and we continued to work on a wide (and sometimes wild) variety of issues together. With Leo, there was always a sense of possibility. He had that California optimism, that why-not attitude. One of his ongoing concerns was the People's Church of Jim Jones. During the mid-1970s, Jones had lured many of his parishioners, primarily African Americans from San Francisco, to a church compound in the jungles of Guyana. Ryan had become more and more convinced that some of these people were being held against their will and that some were being abused. He got me involved in the inquiry—I must have looked like a sucker, a person willing to take on lost causes, but Leo was hard to refuse. We spent one long day, sitting in the back of the congressional chamber, talking about the situation and he convinced me to go with him, bringing my skills as an attorney to help him sort through the legal issues. He thought I might prove particularly useful in helping him determine whether people were being kept at Jonestown against their will and figure out a way to get them out if the situation turned dicey.

When I told my staff about the plan to join Leo on the trip, however, they said it was one of the stupidest things I'd ever considered. Baby seals was one thing but what did this situation in Guyana have to do with Vermont and our Vermont constituents? I eventually came to agree and, at the last minute, told Leo I wasn't going with him.

On November 19, 1978, while trying to fly some of those dissident church members back to the States, Leo was assassinated by Jones's followers. Subsequently, more than nine hundred members of Jones's group committed suicide by drinking cyanide-laced Kool-Aid. Leo was a complex character. He could drive you crazy with his shenanigans, but he had a big heart and was willing to take big risks for causes he believed in. He died doing so and his death haunts me to this day. Could I have done something to deescalate the situation or would I, too, have died had I been along? I'll never know.

The Carter years represent a time when government really began to lose its effectiveness because of the growing partisan nature of Congress and the administration. President Carter was a wonderful man, perhaps in some ways too trusting to be president. We shared one quality that, unfortunately, some others see as a flaw. We both like to believe our fellow humans will do the right thing if given the opportunity. But in the end, I think his training as a governor of a midsize southern state had not adequately prepared him for the job at hand.

President Carter often asked me to the White House for a breakfast chat and to get a gauge of how the moderate Republicans stood on an issue. One morning, when yet another invitation to breakfast was issued, I jokingly said to my staffer, "Find out what they're having to eat." I was so embarrassed when I found out she took me seriously and actually called the White House to inquire. Their response was, "Whatever Congressman Jeffords wants."

Jimmy Carter and I agreed on the rightness of the Equal Rights Amendment and the need for a national health plan. But we had very strong and difficult disagreements over energy and the hostage situation in Iran.

The late 1970s and early 1980s were times of crisis in the energy arena. For much of that time I was a member of a small but active coalition of congressmen who forced debate on utility rate reform, financial enticements for conservation efforts, and development of what we now call renewable energy.

I often debated these issues with President Carter but it remains a mystery to me why he failed to promote sound energy policies and neglected to do more to protect our precious agricultural lands. These seemed like natural issues for the man. But my bills that would have accomplished these two goals got the cold shoulder from Carter's White

House in the spring of 1979. On the dairy issue, we had passed a bill that would keep federal milk support prices in place. Bob Bergland, the secretary of agriculture, favored the measure and the Dairy Subcommittee unanimously approved it. But the administration rejected the milk support program in favor of legislation that would have reduced support prices, another blow for the small dairy farmer of the north. Small dairy farms of the Northeast have a difficult time competing with large factory farms. It's not just a matter of scale but of the higher costs of fuel in the Northeast. In Vermont, many farms are located far from interstates; transportation can be costly. On top of that, the small family farmer rarely gets time off from work and can only afford a skeleton crew of farmhands. Federal supports make the difference between bankruptcy and holding their heads above water.

At the same time that the Carter administration was killing the support program, it had refused to endorse my Agricultural Lands Protection Bill, which was designed to help state and local governments assist farmers in staving off pressures from developers. Carter did increase protections of federal lands, especially in Alaska, where I had joined in the lobbying effort to protect the calving ground of the nation's largest caribou herd. But I felt that, either through ineptitude or design, the Carter administration did everything in its power to hasten the demise of rural America, especially in my neck of the woods.

I also thought his record on energy issues was deeply flawed. In June 1979, for example, I introduced a proposal that won the support of the House Education and Labor Subcommittee on Employment Opportunities to set up a quasi-government corporation, capable of issuing up to $200 billion in bonds to promote the production of synthetic fuels. I unveiled this proposal as an alternative to President Carter's oil price decontrol program. My bill required the phasing in of substitute fuels, beginning in 1981, with quantities increasing to 10 percent of the total gasoline production by 1987 and 20 percent by 1990. Obviously, the bill didn't make it. How sad to read now my prediction that "25 percent of New England's energy needs could be met by alternative fuels by the year 2000."

Nothing upset me more than the calls from poor Vermonters, especially the elderly, who were telling me they had to choose between food and fuel each month. Few people were more greatly affected by the escalating costs of fuels. Vermont has a very long winter season, no natural sources of fuel other than wood, and no pipeline for gas. For this reason and also because of its availability, Vermonters use more wood for home heating per capita than any state in the union, and so it was natural that I championed the idea of a tax credit for the purchase of energy-efficient wood-burning stoves as an oil-saving alternative for home heating.

The idea came from my state office director, Tim Hayward. He phoned Dick D'Amato in Washington early one morning to ask if we could devise a way to give a tax break to the nearly 70 percent of state residents who used wood-burning stoves for some of their heat. That call was the start of a long, multifaceted effort, legislatively and in the executive branch, and eventually triggered the creation of the Congressional Wood Energy Caucus and a variety of related legislative efforts to use wood and other biomass fuels as alternative energy.

The Wood-Burning Stove Credit was introduced as bills in both 1977 and 1979. I testified on the matter before the conservative Ways and Means tax-writing committee, which ironically enough was controlled by the Democrats. Unlike my other initiatives, this one was endorsed by President Carter twice in televised speeches. However, the credit did not survive the final conference committee. We did get one concession—the secretary of the treasury was given the authority to include woodstoves as an eligible tax break item, an authority he never used.

Nonetheless, we used the Wood Energy Caucus as a vehicle to prod the administration into providing more information nationwide on the vast potential of wood as an energy source. It was little known that wood actually surpassed hydroelectric and nuclear in end-use consumption. We were anxious to get news out on the newest line of stoves with catalytic converters that lessened the pollutants from wood and pellet stoves, making them much more environmentally sound than fireplaces—not to mention more energy efficient.

I certainly wasn't the only one working on the issue. A small but active group of legislators from both parties banded together in the late 1970s and early 1980s to try to solve our mutual energy problems. We presented scores of successful legislative initiatives and created bipartisan caucuses, coalitions, and other nontraditional legislative devices in an effort to shift the nation's gluttonous consumption of oil and coal to renewable, domestic sources.

At the same time, representatives from the Northeast—Democrat and Republican alike—joined together to fight those who wanted to drive up heating oil prices by taxing imported oil coming into East Coast ports. Under the direction of Tip O'Neill, the wily congressman from Boston and Speaker of the House, the New England Energy Caucus tackled this and other fuel-related problems. We used all the power that our meager numbers would allow and the clout of our senior members, especially those of the Speaker, to thwart nearly annual efforts to tax imported oil. Until we could find alternative sources of fuel, the last thing consumers in the Northeast needed was higher fuel costs.

During this time our fuel-oil dealers worked closely with caucus members to assure adequate supplies. Their leader, Charlie Burkhardt from Massachusetts, led them in a seamless web of lobbying, together with the congressional delegation, to hold the line on prices. Those dealers had a human face, too, and often made sure supplies got through first, knowing that payment would come sooner or later.

We also banded together to provide fuel assistance and weatherization subsidies for low-income people through my Education and Labor Committee, which had jurisdiction over the matter. This is the kind of program I can really get behind, unlike so many of my Republican colleagues. It just makes sense: make a house more energy efficient and the owner's fuel needs and expenses will go down. It's good for the family and good for the country. I've always thought concepts like these are perfect for the Republican Party—they save money.

I understood that the real solution to the energy problem lay in reducing our reliance on foreign oil and increasing our sources of clean, sustainable energy. During the Carter years, we also formed a solar caucus that supported an amendment to the Energy Appropriations Bill for $80 million to jump-start the photovoltaic research industry.

This was an idea whose time had come and we had a substantial number of cosponsors for our amendment. However, we had never discussed the amendment with the appropriations subcommittee chairman, Tom Bevill (D., Ala.). It had seemed unlikely that an Alabama politician would support the measure.

When the appropriations bill came to the floor, Bevill put his arm around me and said in his slow, southern drawl, "Son, I understand you have an amendment. I don't think you understand you don't offer amendments without speaking to me first. Why don't you come with me and talk it over and I'll see if I can't find you a couple million to get you started."

I said, "Sir, I can't do that. I have to offer my amendment."

He looked at me with total disbelief, then repeated, "You don't understand; that's not the way we do things here."

I said, "It's not just me; there are a lot of members who want this amendment."

"Well, who are they?" he asked.

I told him I had eighty cosponsors. He repeated my statement in disbelief. He said, "Well, I guess we'll just have to fight it out."

The amendment passed, with only slight modifications. It was the beginning of serious research into the photovoltaic and solar energy–generating technologies. We still have a long ways to go, of course. Just imagine where we would be today if we had made that sort of commitment to researching sustainable energies consistently over the last twenty years.

One of my favorite moments of this era came on May 4, 1978, when I led the nation's celebration of the first Sun Day, beginning with a predawn trek up Maine's Mount Cadillac to catch the first glimpse of the sun rising over the United States. The day ended with an evening address before an estimated 10,000 people thronged around the Washington Monument in the nation's capital. I really used the occasion to prod the Carter administration into making a greater commitment to solar energy and alternative fuels. I had hoped that this celebration would become an annual event to raise awareness about the potential that solar energy holds for safe energy that costs almost nothing and could free us from our dependence on foreign oil.

Of course, I am a Vermonter at heart, and many of these issues, while national, have a special import for the folks at home. At one point I almost succeeded in convincing the Energy Department to support a photovoltaic pilot project in Burlington, Vermont, to be hooked up to the city's electric plant. While the idea was supported by enthusiastic utility officials in our largest Vermont city, it was finally shelved because Burlington is one of the most cloud-covered cities in the United States. I argued that this was a great place for the pilot project; if it could work here, it could work nearly anywhere. Energy Department officials, however, were afraid of failure, and the project died, though it did publicize the need to support small-scale photovoltaic entrepreneurs to help get the costs down and to spur new research in more efficient photovoltaic-generating chips. I had to concede that, as far as cloudy Vermont was concerned, it was an idea a little ahead of the technology curve!

Three of us started the wind energy caucus together—Senators John Blanchard (D., Mich.), Norm Mannetta (D., Calif.), and I. We wanted to capitalize on the substantial national potential for wind-generating facilities and small-scale hydro projects that could be used in free-flowing streams and rivers without the need for dams.

Our bill to establish federal subsidies for development of projects like these was finally passed into law after a lot of lobbying. President Carter signed the bill on September 8, 1980. It authorized $100 million to accelerate the development of wind energy systems. Its goal was to have 800 megawatts of electricity come from windmills by 1988, with 1.7 quads of energy from this source by 2000. In fact, this modest goal was exceeded before 1988; installed capacity from wind energy sources reached 1,150 megawatts by 1986. This program proved to quite be a success. Thanks to the research that came out of this program, wind energy is being generated across the nation from the large wind farms near Stockton, California, to a pilot program currently being developed for Killington, Vermont. Much more can be done, and further federal help should reap additional national long-term dividends on at least three fronts: economic, environmental, and in terms of national security.

In the late 1970s I teamed up with a diminutive fireball of a legislator from California named John Moss, the chairman of an investigative subcommittee of the House Armed Services Committee. I had detected what I felt was a practice of raiding our Elk Hills Petroleum Storage facility in California for local energy markets on the West Coast. The purpose of the storage facility was to provide the navy with fuel in the event of war, but unless we took action, it looked like the reserve would be lost to commercial purposes. After I raised the issue in the House, Moss, a well-known crusader against government abuse and shady practices, joined me in a vigorous effort to not only save the storage facility but to also incorporate it into the national strategic energy reserve.

In 1977 I joined forces with an aggressive and liberal Democratic representative from Westchester County, New York, Dick Ottinger, to form what became probably the most effective caucus in modern House history, the Environmental Study Conference. It eventually was composed of more than 240 House members, more than a majority. It spread its wings to the Senate and eventually 70 senators signed on. The study conference became one of the most respected sources of information on environmental and energy issues for members of Congress and the general public. We received monthly contributions from all participating offices, established staff spaces in a House building, hired a professional and young but knowledgeable staff, and created a widely read weekly newsletter that provided information on legislative actions on environment and energy issues for news organizations across the country.

Because the newsletter was published on environmentally sound green paper, it became widely known as the weekly greensheet. We established workshops, conferences, and became an increasingly influential body on a continuing series of issues. I took a personal interest in the conference, and many of its staff members became influential members of various administrations. Mike McCabe, formerly a key staffer for Senator Gary Hart, for example, was one of its first directors and went on to be regional administrator for EPA on the East Coast. Its existence and success is a real testimony to the forward leaning actions that were taken for many years at the national legislative level on behalf of environmental issues.

It's hard to judge President Carter's overall effectiveness. He signed the Salt II Treaty with the Soviet Union in 1979, which I backed, only to have the treaty defeated by Senate conservatives. He was a critic of the violent regime of Idi Amin in Uganda and a leader in human rights around the world. Carter not only denounced the treatment of the Soviet dissidents but he spoke out for the rights of Eastern Europeans and condemned Soviet atrocities in Afghanistan. Indeed, Carter worked hard to build a global coalition to protest the 1979 invasion of Afghanistan and, in 1980, suspended all high-technology and grain shipments to the Soviet Union in protest of human rights violations.

Perhaps his greatest success was the Camp David Accords in 1978, which would lead to a peace treaty that formally ended the thirty-one-year war between Israel and Egypt. After Carter's defeat to Reagan, it took the United States another ten years to pick up where the Carter administration had left off.

Carter also helped the United States lessen its hostile relationship with China. Following Nixon's lead, Carter fortified positive relations with China in 1979 and the United States formally recognized Beijing as the legitimate government. Deputy Premier Teng Hsiao-ping became the first Chinese Communist leader to visit the United States. I don't believe Carter has received the credit he deserves for these accomplishments.

Yet there were many areas where his administration was a failure in my opinion—policies about food stamps, education, and training for the unemployed and, finally, the handling of the Iranian crisis, which came to a head during the hostage situation.

On November 4, 1979, 3,000 Iranian students and militants seized the U.S. embassy in Teheran, capturing 54 embassy staff members and demanding that the exiled shah be extradited from the United States to Iran to stand trial. Carter had granted sanctuary to Shah Mohammad Reza Pahlavi so he could receive medical treatment. The move, while recognizing the long-standing relationship between the United States and the more secular elements of Iran, was a great insult to many Iranian people, especially the country's fundamentalist religious leaders. The shah had greatly modernized Iran and established many social reforms, but these were considered heretical by the fundamentalists who, led by Ayatollah Ruholla Khomeini, had driven the shah into exile.

At the time of the hostage crisis, the Carter administration lacked significant contacts with the Islamic clerics in Iran—in many ways similar to our lack of communication with the leaders of today's Islamic hardliners—because it had continued to do business with the secularist government of Mehdi Bazargan. Carter was really in a pinch when, shortly after the storming of the embassy, the Bazargan government resigned. Things quickly got worse—for both the hostages and Carter. In mid-November, Iran's acting foreign minister, Abolhassan Bani-Sadr, proposed the creation of an international commission to investigate Iranian grievances against the United States and to establish a procedure for returning the shah's assets to Iran. Under the proposal, the U.N. Security Council would have overseen the investigation. U.N. Secretary General Kurt Waldheim formally requested that the Security Council form the commission whereupon Carter announced that the United States would seek economic sanctions against Iran by the Security Council, a move the council summarily rejected. Rather than achieve his goal, Carter had further antagonized the Iranian leadership and also damaged our standing in the world arena.

The U.N. commission was finally constituted and arrived in Teheran on February 23, 1980, to hear grievances relative to the shah's reign and the support he had received from the United States. On the same day, the Ayatollah Khomeini announced that the Majles, essentially the Iranian parliament, would decide on the release of the hostages. Khomeini said the U.N. commission would not be able to meet with the hostages until after the Majles had issued its report. None of this moved along quickly. Frustrated, the Carter administration began planning a military rescue of the hostages, a move Secretary of State Cyrus Vance was so opposed to that he subsequently quit the office. As Vance had warned, the mission went badly. Eight helicopters took off from an aircraft carrier headed for Iranian territory on April 24, 1980. Several helicopters developed mechanical problems and the mission encountered a fierce dust cloud in the Iranian desert. The commander on the scene abandoned the mission. During the evacuation from the desert, a helicopter collided with a refueling aircraft and eight Americans died. Meanwhile, we often didn't even know where the hostages were being held.

As the hostage situation continued and the upcoming election between Carter and Ronald Reagan neared, Carter's State Department persisted in negotiating through private intermediaries for the hostages' release. A breakthrough occurred in early September when Iran indicated it would talk directly with a U.S. official if the United States agreed to four conditions: a pledge of nonintervention in Iranian affairs, the return of the shah's assets, unfreezing of Iranian assets in the United States, and cancellation of all U.S. claims against Iran. Deputy Secretary of State Warren Christopher was assigned to lead the U.S. negotiating team and met with Iranian officials for the next several weeks, until September 22, 1980, when Iraq invaded Iran, introducing a new problem into the negotiations. Prior to the shah's overthrow, Iran had purchased arms and spare parts from the United States. We had refused to release the arms. Now the Iranian government was demanding the release of the weapons as yet another condition for the release of the hostages. Because of the war with Iraq, the Majles was extremely busy and negotiations for the release of the hostages often took a back seat.

As the situation continued, I joined fifty-four bipartisan congressmen who were urging Carter to give Iran an ultimatum: free the fifty-two American hostages or face what we called "selected, deliberate, sustained, and increasingly severe military operations." Carter refused the idea of setting a deadline, believing it could result in the harm or death of some of the hostages. And after the failure of the rescue mission, he feared another military action.

There was renewed hope in October that the hostages would soon be released but, for no apparent reason, the Iranians quite suddenly broke off all contact with the Carter administration. Every day that the hostages remained in Iran, Carter's hope of reelection fell. The hostages were not released until January 20, 1981, a half-hour after Reagan was inaugurated president of the United States and 444 days after they had been taken.

For more than a decade afterward, some Democrats believed that the Republicans—in particular William Casey, Ronald Reagan's 1980 campaign director, and George Bush, Reagan's VP who had been head of the CIA—had developed an elaborate intelligence operation to influence and perhaps even slow the release of the hostages until after the 1980 election. Ten years later, it fell upon me and a handful of others to try to learn the truth.

CHAPTER 13

Musical Homes

Liz and I tried our best to be civilized, at least where the children were concerned. We had a saying, "We weren't divorcing the children, just each other." We didn't divorce right away, although, I guess, we both thought we were heading that way. All through 1977, we struggled on. Death took Mother in April. She had been going to Florida for the winter for many years, ever since the doctors had recommended the southern climate for Father's health. Mother's younger sister Doris lived nearby in Daytona Beach and visited Mother often. That winter Mother had been tired and said she didn't feel like herself, but we had little warning how sick she really was.

When I got a call from Doris telling me to come down immediately because Mother had become quite frail, I should have realized how serious her condition was. Mother was not one to ask for help. I rushed to Florida and brought her home by plane—she had told me she wanted to die in Rutland. I didn't really think she was dying. She had lost weight and was weak but she was certainly clear of mind. I delivered her to the hospital, spent a few more hours with her, then went home for the evening. She wasn't one to go to the doctor so we had no idea what was wrong with her; I hoped they'd figure that out in the next few days.

Mother died a few hours later of a stroke. She really had come home to die. Later the doctors told us that she had had breast cancer. We never knew until then.

They say that you're not really a man, a full-fledged grown-up that is, until you've lost your parents. Both Liz and I took Mother's death hard. We felt so bad that we'd had no inkling of how ill she had become and that we'd had no time to say good-bye. I came to understand that that was how she wanted it. She had cared for Father through a long and arduous illness and, I believe, did not want to go through the same with us. Mother was a strong woman and we believe she chose her own way to die.

After Mother's death, Liz and I went to marriage counseling for a while. But as Liz often pointed out to me, she did all the talking. Liz and I formally separated on May 25, 1978; we divorced legally the following June, just two months shy of our seventeenth wedding anniversary. It must have been hard on the children, who were young teens at the time, but the arguing hadn't been doing them any good either.

Initially, Liz lived in the Rutland house during the week to be with the kids and moved out for the weekend so I could have my time with them. I had the children three weekends a month. Thus, on top of our already strapped financial situation, we both had to juggle the cost of a small apartment. Mine was a one-bedroom flat in Rutland; Liz's was a small place on the road up the mountain.

I had found a relatively cheap apartment in Washington closer to the office so I could walk to work. It was not, however, a very acceptable situation. I don't know which were larger, the cockroaches in that building or the rats. It was called the Capitol Hill Hole by my staff. I was only there a few months before I moved into a better apartment quite close to the office at 110 D Street. The building was filled with young people and a few young lawyers, and I liked it just fine.

But this was the era of condominiums, and the building's owner, Beau Bogen, realized he could make more money by converting the units to condominiums than by renting. He hired a top Washington law firm to help him with the changes. Their plan was to create a corporation that would buy the apartments and then sell the condos at a profit while also taking advantage of capital gains laws. I panicked when I realized my monthly housing expense was about to go from $280 to $900.

What the building owner and his lawyers had overlooked were recent District of Columbia laws that had been passed to protect tenants from just such a thing. Under the law, the seller first had to offer the apartments to the tenants at the lower price. They'd also overlooked the fact that so many of their tenants were lawyers who were aware of the new D.C. law. We got together and said we would buy the building, which we really had little intention or ability to do. We were calling the landlord's bluff and it worked. The landlord paid us $10,000 each to move out. I took that $10,000 and put it away for future use and moved into my office in the Longworth House Office Building. I felt this would allow me the opportunity to save for a down payment on a house in D.C. But I also saw my situation as a way of bringing national attention to the thousands of people nationwide who were being forced out of their apartments through condominium conversions.

The press, particularly in Vermont, was curious about what I was up to and where I was going to live. On the day in March 1981 when I moved into my office, Lee Shields, a staff member, pushed a big wheelbarrow full of my stuff in front of him while he pulled a small appliance by its cord behind him. The reporters thought he was me and asked, "Is that your dog?" He sarcastically replied, "No, it's my cat." Thus, I got more publicity—this time for being the congressman from Vermont who was either so poor or so frugal that he had to sleep on the pull-out couch in his office.

While the press thought I'd totally lost my mind—and some of my staffers agreed—I thought of it as a practical solution to a problem. I'm not poor. I have assets. But I had the choice of living with a negative cash flow or finding a more affordable solution. The reality was that I had just been through a divorce at the age of forty-six. Finances were tough at home. I figured it would be better for me to install a couch that could be converted into a bed in my private office than spend money my family needed on another expensive apartment in Washington. When I was living in my apartment, half of my $60,662 salary had gotten eaten up by taxes and the expenses of city living. I had little hope of finding another $300 apartment. The office had closet space, a refrigerator and hot plate, and I had joined a gym where I could shower or use the adjacent House office building, which also had a shower.

Quite frankly, with the expense of an apartment in Rutland plus the maintenance of the family and the Rutland house, that $10,000 could have disappeared rather quickly. My idea was to invest it, let it grow for a little, then buy my own house so I wouldn't be throwing money down the drain on a rental every month.

You would have thought I had dyed my hair purple and was advocating the end of the Cuban embargo—or something equally extreme or newsworthy. As many as a dozen news crews came by my office every day for weeks, asking the same dumb questions. Meanwhile, I couldn't draw much interest in my efforts to save dairy price supports.

Unfortunately, I failed to mention to the reporters that I was paid to move out of the apartment in the out-of-court settlement with the owner of the complex. The press thought that was a really big story, as if I had been obliged to tell them about the settlement. I thought it was no big deal and, quite frankly, nobody's business. My main motivation was that I had made up my mind that my next dwelling place would be my own. I'd had enough of paying rent. Nonetheless, some of the stories were far from flattering.

One of the things I enjoyed most about these years was the freedom I felt coming home to be with the children, to watch their games or otherwise spend time with them without the pressure of other demands. I dated, as did Liz, but whatever spare time I had was primarily devoted to my children.

One time an obnoxious high school student who was a member of a group visiting Washington from Vermont challenged me on why I had missed what he had called an "important vote." I don't remember what the vote was for but I remembered why I'd missed work that day. My son was playing in the high school hockey championship—the vote wasn't going to be one where I could make a difference—so I skipped it and instead saw Leonard score the winning goal of the championship game. To me, that was far more important.

When I told my young interrogator that, all the other kids stood up and cheered. That kid slumped down in his seat and kept his mouth shut after that.

Laura was very involved in basketball and tennis and I liked playing with her, even though she was so much better than I. In high school it could be excruciating to watch a match because she would often have several stellar days followed by a bad one. There was no predicting why. When she was in the state tennis championships, Laura made it clear she didn't want me to watch her in the semifinals. My nervousness made her nervous.

The night before the match I was scheduled to fly via Philly to Vermont, but weather grounded the planes. Instead, I rented a car and drove all the way to the site of the tournament. When I arrived, I found a hedgerow sufficiently close so I could see her play but sufficiently dense so she couldn't see me. I crawled in on my hands and knees and watched her play. She won that game but lost in the finals.

A few weeks later we went to visit the College of Boca Raton, to which she was thinking of applying. One afternoon we went outside and hit the ball around. The next day the tennis coach took her aside and said, "Notwithstanding how terrible the guy was that you were playing with, you have some real talent and we would like to offer you a scholarship."

I also tried my hand at cooking, especially as I was living alone in Washington and cooking for the children on my weekends with them. One night I made a stir-fry, a very ambitious project for me. Leonard started eating and then said, "Hey, Pops. This is almost not bad." They hadn't complained, but I got the message that I was no substitute for their mother, who had become quite the culinary expert since her blue spaghetti days.

During these unsettling years I spent some of my free time in Washington at the House members' gym, where I particularly liked playing half-court basketball. But sometime in the early 1980s the members decided to return to full-court play; I thought it was time to retire from the game.

Around this time I'd seen people involved in tai kwan do and introduced myself to Joon Rhee, a master with his own martial arts institute. He became my instructor. I found the discipline very interesting and useful. I eventually earned a black belt after about ten years of practice. I still do a daily exercise routine, especially the stretching exercises that Joon Rhee taught me. I'd hate to think how tight my muscles and joints would be without them. But the last time I broke a board was more than ten years ago, although I worked with some young kids at a tai kwan do meet during the last campaign in Burlington. I mention all this because I think it's important to stretch yourself mentally and physically and try something challenging, especially when you are going through difficult times. Those years of moving around Washington and the problems with my wife were difficult ones, and while I have often been accused of not being in touch with my feelings, that doesn't preclude me from having suffered from a lot of stress myself in those years—from several car accidents in which I was injured, from the deaths of loved ones, from the family duress, and, much as I loved it, from the trials and tribulations of my congressional work. I am not complaining; I'm simply saying that those years of martial arts practice have served me well.

In February 1982 the Hide-a-Bed was gone—I found another home. I'd been given the dubious achievement award of 1981 by *Esquire* magazine, which laughingly wrote that I had to share my bathroom and shower with 434 other representatives. Shame on *Esquire;* they forgot about the handful of women representatives who didn't use the men's shower.

My good luck at finding a home came from the bad luck of others. I'd found a place that two months previously had been listed for sale for about $160,000. But a person who lived across the street had been tortured and murdered, which caused the owner to lower the price by more than $20,000. It's the house I live in now. Back then, it was not a very secure neighborhood. My daughter Laura was living at that time in the back apartment with her eighty-pound Rhodesian Ridgeback, Gossamer. Maura Blue, my soon-to-be daughter-in-law, was living there, too. I came home one night to find the front door had been jimmied with a crowbar and was hanging by the hinges.

When I entered the house with the police, the laptop computer and TV were stacked together by the front door. We thought this was unusual. The two front bedrooms had been ransacked. Then we saw the door to the back apartment ajar and Gossamer, sitting there, looking quite pleased with himself. The police and I figured the robbers had opened the door, saw Gossamer and raced out the front door. The story was written up in the *Hill* paper and Goss was the hero.

The house has taken many years of work and still needs more. I didn't realize how bad it was until one day a few years ago when I came home and found the dishwasher had fallen through the floor into the basement. Until then I didn't even know I had a basement. Laura was studying to be an architect at the time. She has spent many long hours working on my home and has helped make it into a quite lovely abode.

It's a redbrick, two-story Colonial with an apartment in back that Leonard and Maura now live in with their dogs Calvin (Coolidge) and Montgomery—the granddogs. It's in a quiet, residential neighborhood not far from several wonderful ethnic restaurants. The house has a nice yard and fireplace; a bright, big kitchen that Maura updated; and a roomy living room.

While I was researching the history of the house, I learned that the neighborhood had been a dairy center at the beginning of our country's history. The house predated 1850 and had been the home of a dairy magnet. I figure that's a perfect abode for a man who, during his years as the lone congressman from Vermont, earned the title Mister Dairy.

CHAPTER 14

Trickle-Down Economy, the Contras, and the Evil Empire

RONALD REAGAN HAD good reason to be wary of me. In February 1980 I supported John Anderson in the upcoming presidential primary election. Anderson, a longtime Republican, had formed the National Unity Party to promote grassroots citizen action. He was the first serious third-party candidate in more than thirty years. I supported him because I agreed with his platform that negotiation was a more productive resolution to tension than war-mongering, particularly in the Middle East and Central America. I believed many of the problems we were encountering in these regions, as well as elsewhere, were exacerbated by our willingness to supply arms and other military aid to less than reliable foreign leaders. Doing so, I thought, should be a last resort after other efforts, such as improving the very conditions that lead to terrorism and unrest, were fully explored.

Anderson and I had other values in common. We were old friends and allies in the successful effort to gain support for the Alaska Land Bill, which conserved natural areas in that state. At the beginning of the primary campaign, I brought Anderson to Vermont to talk to Middlebury students and reporters in Rutland, a move that did little to improve my popularity with some members of my party. Anderson didn't fare very well in the primary but went on to have a distinguished career as a professor of political science and promoter of world peace through his organizations, which include the World Federalist Association and the Center for Voting and Democracy.

After the Vermont primary in March, I made it clear that I was more interested in supporting George Bush for the Republican nomination than Reagan. Although I disagreed with Bush on many issues, I felt he had a more worldly view of our political situation and was better equipped for the job than Reagan. Besides, I felt that Reagan had done a disservice to education in California while he was the governor. Since improving education was a top priority for me, I feared that Reagan would gut many of the programs my colleagues and I had worked so hard to improve or create, and I doubted he'd be much of a supporter in the work I expected to continue.

In May the Reagan campaign devised a hard-line strategy to keep me from the GOP convention slated for July in Detroit. Based on the Reagan plan, Vermont Republican leaders proposed sending seventeen committed Reagan delegates and two uncommitted delegates to the national convention. The slate certainly had no room for anyone supporting George Bush, and I was effectively told I wouldn't be invited. This was a break from tradition, which was to offer major officeholders a national delegate slot if they wanted one, and part of a growing trend in the Republican Party to stifle debate and the free flow of ideas.

Eventually, after receiving complaints from me and other moderate Republicans, the state committee offered me a place at the expense of a college student who had become active in the party, Susan Williams-Sweetser. It was a bit unfair to Sweetser because she represented the future of the party loyal. But I left for Detroit with the hope that I might bring some moderation both to the Vermont delegation and to the national platform.

It didn't turn out that way. That convention brought other breaks with the GOP establishment. I took part in a demonstration denouncing the convention's plans to withdraw Republican support for the proposed Equal Rights Amendment to the U.S. Constitution. When it became apparent that there was simply no room for my views, I left Detroit for a two-day fishing trip with my son. John McClaughry, a conservative from Kirby, Vermont, and Reagan loyalist, who became a senior White House adviser after the election, and other Vermont Republicans were offended. They were right to be, of course. They had made room for me and I had left the convention before the business was completed. I did so because I could not embrace many of the platforms the party was endorsing that year. I felt it was better to have quality time with my son than to continue to fight with them.

•   •   •

My first big conflict with President Reagan came over his budget and proposed tax cuts. Republicans do great things and support many important causes as long as they don't cost a lot of money—unless it's the defense budget.

Reagan had very cleverly approached the conservative Democrats, recognizing that he didn't have enough votes in the House among the Republicans to get his policies passed. This group of conservative Democrats who supported Reagan's budget and especially his plan to cut what I considered important programs in education and the arts came to be known as the Boll Weevils. Charlie Stenholm from Texas was their leader.

One day, as I was sitting in the chamber, I did a little math and figured out that we had enough moderate Republicans to neutralize the Boll Weevils. If we formed our own group, we could countermand their votes and use our coalition as a bargaining tool with the administration. As I left the Capitol that day I approached Bill Green, a moderate Republican from New York City, with my idea. He and I started going through the people who would support us: Carl Pursell of Michigan; Olympia Snowe of Maine; Larry DeNardis of Connecticut, now president of New Haven University; and others. We called ourselves the Gypsy Moths, taking on the name of a northern insect pest as an ironic parody of the Boll Weevils. That was Larry's idea.

One day in the heat of these discussions, Bob Michel, the Republican leader from Illinois, got word to me that there would be a meeting between the moderate Republican Gypsy Moths and President Reagan the next morning. I never got an invitation directly from the president to attend, but didn't think much about it. I showed up the next day, driving my little blue Jeep to the White House. When I got to the gate, a marine guard greeted me as usual, asked my name, and went to the booth to check my status. I could see him going up and down the list. Finally, after making a phone call, he said, "Yes, you can go in."

At the door to the White House, however, I was met by White House liaison Ken Duberstein, who told me that I had not been invited to the meeting. "I'd like to spend some time with you instead," he said. I was in no mood for a scolding and got right to the question at hand.

"Well, why wasn't I invited to the meeting?" I asked.

"Well, your name's not on the list. The White House doesn't think too highly of you setting up this countercoup," he said.

I said, "Well, this is going to be embarrassing. I just went by a covey of reporters who know about this meeting. What am I going to say to them on the way out?"

He said, "Don't worry, I'll take care of it," and he later sent me out through a secret route that allowed me to avoid the reporters. We then spent an hour on how we might be able to work together.

A few days later I went back to Vermont to explain to my constituency where I stood on the Reagan budget and the Reagan tax cuts. When it became clear that I might be opposing Reagan on these issues, David Broder of the *Washington Post* came to Vermont to travel with me and report the response of my constituents. One day Mr. Broder and I were in Brattleboro at my late friend Larry Cooks's real estate office when the phone rang.

Minutes after the receptionist answered, her eyes got as big as saucers. "Congressman Jeffords, it's for you," she said nervously. "It's the president."

Reagan had tracked me down through my scheduler. He wanted to talk about how I was going to vote on the budget. He started giving me the pitch on the budget, saying, "We've made these changes and I think you'll like them." The changes were even more conservative than his first version.

I was thinking, "You had your chance to convince me of your ideas and you didn't even let me into that meeting." But instead, I said, "Mr. President, you're going the wrong way for me. I don't agree with what you're doing."

Reagan hung up.

I later heard that when he got off the phone Reagan shouted at Duberstein, "Why did I call him? Don't you know what you're doing?" Max Friedersdorf, the liaison between the administration and Congress, immediately canceled my visitor's passes to the White House. This did not punish me so much as all Vermonters who visited Washington and wanted to see the White House. It showed how petty some people can be—even the powerful—and was fair warning that there would be repercussions if I went against the party leadership.

I refused to support the first budget proposal submitted by the Reagan administration, as did most of the Gypsy Moths. We spent many hours directly confronting Reagan's budget director David Stockman, causing him to make significant and substantial concessions equaling about $2 billion for programs that the Northeast moderates really wanted. After much negotiation and despite my reservations about the defense budget and other items, in July of 1981 I voted for Reagan's revised budget. I thought we had achieved about as much as we could.

One concession that the Gypsy Moths had caused was a 7.5 percent increase in Medicaid payments for 1982 rather than the 6 percent Stockman originally proposed. The administration also dropped its plan to cap Medicaid growth and to merge twenty-four health programs into three block grants. And we got the administration to restore $400 million for elementary and secondary education, including an increase of funding for the Title 1 program that oversaw the education of disadvantaged students. Other concessions included restoration of $110 million for the guaranteed student loan program; $259 million for youth-training programs; $500 million in low-income energy assistance, including funding for home weatherization; $126 million for the food stamp program; and $1.2 million for Amtrak, assuring funding through 1982 for the Montrealer train that ran through Vermont.

At the same time, however, my more moderate colleagues and I were concerned that the New Federalism, or Trickle-Down Economics, as the pundits liked to call Reagan's economic plan, would shift the economic burden back to the states. This would have a devastating impact on a place like Vermont, where so many people were already struggling to make ends meet. Thus, I also began to express a theme that I continue to espouse today: that the conservative upsurge in Congress with its bent toward supporting business interests at the expense of social programs could severely harm the nation and the state I so dearly love.

In truth, Vermont ranks near the bottom in average adjusted per capita income but near the top in percentage of income dedicated to taxes. Changes in the dairy price support system already had me worried about the sustainability of this industry and the impact its losses would have on the overall financial health of Vermont. In addition, our energy needs, because of our long winters, make our state even more vulnerable than most to the vagaries of oil prices.

So I began to fight Reagan's proposals, especially his tax cuts. Vermonters pay state taxes based on a percent of their federal taxes. Less federal tax would equal less state tax revenues. On the national level, I worried that decreased tax revenues, combined with increased defense spending, would result in even greater federal deficits that, in turn, could lead to even more drastic cuts in domestic programs.

A month later I was the only Republican to vote against Reagan's three-year tax cut. It passed easily, despite my vote, and, I believe, sent this country into an economic plunge and resulted in massive deficit spending. I would have considered the basic thrust of the Reagan economic recovery program—lower tax rates and improve capital recovery provisions—had the administration not also given special treatment to wealthy individuals and industries, including a $13 billion tax break to the big oil companies.

After the tax vote I had to hide in Sergeant of Arms Jack Russ's office because the Republicans were trying to get me to change my vote. They wanted the GOP to be united with the president. Although the tax cuts passed, the GOP members were very bitter toward me. After losing my White House passes, I knew I'd pay big for this one. But I was unwilling to cut essential programs and threaten social security insurance in the vain hope of giving the economy a boost through tax cuts. As it turned out, that idea didn't work anyhow; the economy continued to be sluggish. I thought the answer was simply to make the overall budget leaner without affecting programs that benefit the most needy and that enrich our lives on so many levels. All my suggestions for a stoic Yankee approach to the problem fell on deaf ears.

I also got a lot of grief at home from conservative Republicans. John McClaughry had called me before the final vote to ask for my support. I told him, "If the president needs me, I'll consider giving my support." He took that to mean I was going to vote for the tax cut, but I knew my vote wasn't going to make a difference when I made the statement. McClaughry never forgave me; he thought I'd lied to him, but technically I hadn't. I may have misled him but I didn't lie. Reagan hadn't needed my vote.

By then I'd gotten used to being snubbed by the hard-line GOP. I knew my constituency and I felt this was no time to abandon the independents, independent-minded Republicans, moderates, liberals, and Democrats who had long supported me and who would be hurt by the Reagan proposal. I simply could not go back to Vermont and tell an elderly widow that we had to cut her social security so that we can afford new multibillion-dollar welfare programs for the oil companies. GOP National Committee chair Richard Richards told me a few months later that I'd been forgiven for voting against the tax cuts but I never felt forgiven.

It does little good to say that my fears were quickly borne out: The federal deficit went from less than $58 billion in fiscal year 1981 to more than $207 billion just two years later.

During this time I became good friends with a Democratic congressman from New York City named Frederick "Freddie" Richmond. He was as concerned as I was about the proposed cuts to the National Endowment for the Arts that Reagan had been threatening and was seemingly now trying to make. We vowed to protect the endowment and formed the Congressional Arts Caucus with members from both sides of the aisle. Among our many efforts, we set up a national arts competition for high school students wherein each state winner's work would be displayed along the tunnel from the House buildings to the Capitol building. The architect of the Capitol liked our idea and he helped make the walls ready for this informal art gallery by installing lighting and preparing display areas.

The program has been a huge success that continues to this day. However, in 1995, Newt Gingrich, while allowing the contest to continue, eliminated the Congressional Arts Caucus. The various legislators who belonged to this and other caucuses funded them from their office budgets; Gingrich ruled that this was an improper use of funds.

During this period I also broke with the administration in two important areas—nuclear arms control and military intervention in Central America.

On the first issue, in August 1986 I strongly lobbied for a one-year nuclear testing pause, providing the Soviets would agree to the same thing. We had made some progress since Gorbachev had become president of the Soviet Union. I felt that we should build on his more moderate approach and receptivity to western ideas rather than revert to name-calling, such as Reagan's referral to the Soviet Union as "the Evil Empire," a reference that comes to mind in recent days as Bush bandies about the word *evil* on an almost daily basis. During the Reagan years, I also supported the House bill to continue a moratorium on tests of anti-satellite weapons, adhering to the Salt II Treaty and banning chemical weapons production.

When Reagan announced he would meet with Gorbachev in Iceland in October 1986, the House agreed to modify its arms control amendments to provide the president with negotiating power. I wasn't a purist to the point of being politically unrealistic, so I went along with that tack, but in the next Congress, 1987–88, I and other moderate members of Congress across the aisle renewed our lobby for five significant arms control measures: the Antiballistic Missile Treaty, Salt II, the antisatellite weapons ban, a nuclear test ban, and cuts in funding for Reagan's Star Wars initiative. Every one of our arms control bills were watered down in conference negotiations with the Senate, but the success of our efforts significantly increased pressure on President Reagan to conclude some sort of arms control agreement with the Soviet Union. At the December 1987 Washington summit, Reagan and Gorbachev signed the International Nuclear Freeze Treaty, which was ratified by the Senate in 1988. Small steps forward are better than no steps at all.

The effort to raise awareness about the correlation between domestic conditions and unrest in Central America, particularly in Nicaragua, Honduras, and El Salvador, was an arduous one but eventually paid off. I had traveled extensively through this region in various capacities and had become convinced of the need to counter the threat of instability and Communist involvement through a balanced policy that would take into account the economic, health, educational, and environmental needs of the people as well as the political and military realities of this troubled region.

In March 1982 I traveled to El Salvador to observe the constituent assembly elections. I was quite concerned by the irregularities I observed and the clear potential for retribution by the Salvadoran government against those voting against it. A year later I returned on a human rights trip with Congressmen James Oberstar (D., Minn.) and Bill Richardson

(D., N.Mex.) and was quite discouraged by the deterioration we saw in respect to human rights and the rising social strife of the people. I was shocked to learn firsthand of the extreme violence that had been perpetrated a few weeks before against the people of Las Hojas, a small town in the departamento de Sonsonate. On February 22 the army massacred between eighteen and seventy-four peasants.

We discussed this massacre with the regional army commander, with friends and relatives of the victims, and the U.S. embassy. We also expressed our concern that napalm was being used by the Salvadoran military against its own people. Our trip report triggered alarm in many quarters, but a majority in Congress continued to disagree with our call to cut military aid to the Salvadoran government and instead increased assistance.

Once, when leaving El Salvador, the embassy made plans to have me driven to the airport. The road to the airport was a dangerous one and the taxi driver drove as if banshees were on our heels. He took off almost before I was fully out of the car. When I got into the terminal, I found that my flight had been canceled and there were no more flights out that night.

There I was, alone in the airport, with no one else around and the next plane not scheduled to leave until five-thirty in the morning, hours later. It was a rough night. Miracle of miracles, the plane showed up. The pilot and I took off and eventually I found myself home, safe and sound. It is instances like this that fully bring home how relatively safe we are in this country. People everywhere have faced terrorism and threats to their lives, not on the level of September 11, but more constantly than anything we can begin to imagine.

About the same time tensions were escalating between Nicaragua and Honduras. I became involved in meetings organized by the Contadora group that was attempting to generate support for a regional peace initiative among Latin American nations. I hosted a meeting between members of Congress and ambassadors from Nicaragua and Honduras, attended by both the Mexican ambassador and the Venezuelan chargé d'affaires. Everyone present agreed it was very important for the United States to actively and overtly support the peace effort.

Meanwhile, the central issue of the 98th Congress (1983–84) was the proper role for the United States in terms of whether to give military or economic aid to the area and whether to give covert assistance to the contra rebels in Nicaragua. I was convinced that the economic and social problems of the region required a positive approach in which we would encourage democratic reform and social development—help build roads, improve water and health conditions, support education and the like— rather than support a heavy-handed military presence. I believed that the best way to counter the pull toward a Communist-oriented government was by capitalizing on the strengths of democracy rather than arming countrymen against one another. These sentiments, however, fell on deaf ears.

President Reagan's request for renewed aid to the Nicaraguan rebels dominated the next two years of Congress. In the final days of 1986, Reagan's request for funding for the contras was finally approved—over my and too few other congressmen's strenuous objections.

In February of 1986 I sent my foreign policy aide Laurie Schultz Heim to Nicaragua to investigate reported human rights abuses by both the contras and the Nicaraguan government. She and others on the mission found that both sides were abusing human rights but that the contra troops were much more blatantly and seriously doing so. I called on Secretary of State George Shultz to withdraw the administration's request for $100 million in military aid to the contras while the administration studied the allegations.

Debate on the issue reached a peak that spring while three of us—Lee Hamilton (D., Ind.), William Richardson (D., N.Mex.), and I—fashioned an alternative policy that relied on rewards and penalties, the proverbial carrot-and-stick approach, to pressure and encourage the Nicaraguan government to adopt more acceptable approaches in return for some aid. Rather than further militarization of the region, our alternative called for the use of diplomatic tools and adherence to a clear set of foreign policy principles and humanitarian policies. We battled long and hard through three divisive legislative debates but in the end our amendment was defeated in late June by a slim twelve-vote margin.

The next March we got a moratorium placed on the release of $40 million in military aid passed in the House, but the action was blocked in the Senate and the money went south. Meanwhile, I kept working on the

Contadora proposal. Costa Rican president Oscar Arias became an active ally in the effort to bring peace to the region while I worked on the White House to support the Arias peace plan. Momentum for a Central American agreement was building throughout the summer, culminating in the Guatemala Peace Accord signed by the five Central American presidents in August 1987. Our government undermined that agreement almost immediately, I believe, when Congress approved roughly $90,000 a day to maintain the contras through February of the next year. Then, on February 3, 1988, the House was allowed an up-or-down vote on the administration's contra policy. We got a refreshing victory when the House rejected the president's request for yet another $56 million in aid. We continued to work on the peace effort.

Seven weeks later, in Sapoa, Nicaragua, the Nicaraguan government and the contra leadership agreed to a cease-fire and began the process of national reconciliation. The House reacted quickly and, on March 30, overwhelmingly passed a resolution that contained the primary components of the nonmilitary alternatives that Hamilton, Richardson, and I had originally offered. The very next day, the Senate approved the bill, contingent on adherence to the cease-fire. It provided $17.7 million in food, medicine, and clothing for the contras and $17.7 million in medical aid to help children who had been injured by the war. One could be bitter that so many more millions were spent on military aid than on improving food, medicine, and clothing, but, given the climate of the time, we saw this as a tremendous victory that just as easily could have gone the other way. In these efforts, I knew that I had the support of many Vermonters; a score of towns had gone so far as to voice opposition to U.S. military intervention in Central America at their traditional town meetings.

Honduras, a country sandwiched between Nicaragua, El Salvador, and Guatemala, has had special interest to me for many years. Vermont adopted Honduras as a sister state in the Alliance for Progress program, created in the 1960s as part of President Kennedy's one-on-one diplomacy movement that also spurred the creation of the Peace Corps. I was a member of an international delegation of official observers for the November 1981 presidential elections in Honduras, during which I spent a week discussing the political, economic, and social situation with a broad cross section of Hondurans. What a wonderful people. Despite adversity the Hondurans have an innate sense of optimism that I found refreshing. While there, I helped local music enthusiasts start a children's orchestra. When I arrived home, I hunted down Laura's old clarinet and promptly sent it off to the band. I believe President Kennedy was right— small efforts like these do as much for world peace as military engagements. Perhaps they do more.

In late November I was one of the six official witnesses to Honduras's first election in more than a dozen years. In instances like this, I often took hope from the people themselves. Their enthusiasm for the election made me jealous. I wished Americans at home would recognize how important each vote is and how much we take for granted our own election system.

The 1981 election was an essential start toward building a democratic political system in Honduras, but I was also very aware that the country faced serious challenges if it was going to avoid the violence of its neighbors. In some cases, I felt that U.S. foreign policy was doing just the opposite—drawing Honduras into a regional conflict involving Nicaragua, El Salvador, and possibly Guatemala. Honduras, a country of about two million people, followed Haiti as the second most impoverished nation in the Western Hemisphere.

After I joined the Senate in 1989, during Bush's administration, I became involved in the discussion of U.S. policy toward El Salvador. Because of my trips there and my concerns about human rights, I became one of four sponsors of legislation to withhold 50 percent of El Salvador's military aid pending negotiations for a peace settlement. In these and other relative efforts, Senator Patrick Leahy (D., Vt.) and I worked closely together. It was a dark time. Leahy had succeeded in amending the appropriations bill for military aid but opponents of the cut restored full funding on the Senate floor.

Six weeks later the Salvadoran guerrillas, known as the FMLN, launched a major military offensive that was harshly beaten back by the Salvadoran military. On November 16, 1989, six Jesuit priests were dragged from their beds and brutally murdered by a battalion of American-trained members of the elite Salvadoran army. Four days later, during consideration of the conference report on the Foreign Operations bill, we again attempted to cut military aid to the country by 30 percent. Again, we failed.

I was outraged by the murder of the priests and wanted to do whatever I could to support a negotiated solution to the civil war. I went to El Salvador on a human rights trip the following January. The death of the Jesuits had awakened many Americans to the suffering of the Salvadoran people. That spring I cosponsored legislation to withhold half of El Salvador's military aid—one would perhaps want to withhold all of it but that would never fly. I was also pressing the U.S. trade representative to review Salvadoran workers' rights practices and consider revocation of the country's trade benefits. Slowly, haltingly, the Salvadoran government and the FMLN began to make progress on peace talks through 1991 and 1992. On January 16, 1992, after twenty months of negotiation, the Salvadoran government and the FMLN signed a peace accord. In 1994 we again were pressing the government to withhold military aid as a way of encouraging a free and fair electoral process in the 1994 balloting.

Similar events brought me to Guatemala on several occasions and led to deep concerns over human rights abuses, particularly under the government of President Jorge Serrano who took office in 1991. Here again, there were murders—most notably of Myrna Mack, a Guatemalan anthropologist, the previous year. In 1992 I urged Secretary of Defense Dick Cheney to press the Guatemalan military to cease its support for and investigate the killings and disappearances of human rights activists. We were successful in getting the U.S. Trade representative Carla Hills to formally review violations of U.S. trade laws in Guatemala. The following May, Serrano was forced to resign. Those of us who were involved in the issue tried to raise consciousness and support for an end to the civil war. Today, conditions have improved—or so we believe. Our eyes and vigilance are surely on another part of the world, but we must not forget the history of our involvement in this region.

I believe we must change our focus from searching for military solutions to these and other problems. Political foment, terrorism, and anarchy thrive when there are leaders who do not have legitimacy with the people, when there is poverty, and, particularly, when there is great disparity between the haves and the have-nots. To win the hearts and the minds of people for democracy, we would do much better by helping countries improve their health, transportation, and educational systems than in arming them.

Vermonters supported my efforts throughout these troubled times by repeatedly sending me back to Congress. In April of 1981, I announced I would run for the U.S. Senate if Bob Stafford decided to retire. There was no way I would have campaigned against the man who has done so much for our state and our country and, especially, for education, which is why the federal student loan program was named after him. I did briefly consider another race for governor in 1982 but declined. I felt my energies were best spent in the House of Representatives where I stayed until 1988, when Stafford resigned. I ran for the open seat and won my current position in the U.S. Senate.

CHAPTER 15

The Second Time Around

LIZ LIKES TO TELL stories about her family and especially her parents, who were openly affectionate, brutally honest, and about as real as you could get. They were gregarious and fun-loving but, like most couples, they had their conflicts. Liz's father, John Daley, loved people and people loved him. He hated conflict and loved his church. When there were problems at home, he didn't take himself to the corner pub to drown his problems but rather went to church and prayed.

Now, Liz's mother was devout enough, but one can well imagine how aggravated she might become with a husband who went running off to church whenever there was disagreement rather than staying put to see the battle to its end. He often left it to her to deal with problems or to discipline the children; he was a man who wanted to be loved by his children.

One night there was a particularly testy exchange between Liz's parents, and her mother was angry as a wildcat at her husband, who had taken his problem to God. The next day Liz joined her mother for lunch in downtown Burlington. As they walked along Church Street, Liz's mother suddenly grabbed Liz's arm and exclaimed, "Look, there's John, Elizabeth. There's your dad." She had a huge smile on her face and was as excited as a teenager in love. For his part, as soon as he spied his wife, Liz's dad hurriedly crossed the street and embraced her. Liz watched dumbfounded as her parents kissed and chatted like two lovebirds. When they finally parted, Liz asked what had happened to the argument. Liz's mother dismissed the squabble with a wave of her hand, making a subtle comment that left Liz with little doubt that the couple had more than kissed and made up the night before.

Liz likes to tell that story with the added message that all obstacles between two people can be conquered if they have physical chemistry between them. That physical attraction, Liz believes, is more powerful than common sense and more essential to happiness than chocolate or a healthy bank account. She also believes it's essential to a successful marriage.

Liz and I have that chemistry. It's probably the only way I can explain how, despite all our trials and tribulations, we have survived as a couple. Let's face it: There is much about me that drives her nuts and much about her that I simply do not understand and cannot tolerate. But through the years from 1978 when we separated until 1983 when we began to make our way back to life together—despite our economic and political disagreements—we never stopped loving each other.

In some ways our separation was fairly easy, as we had agreed on several things: the children came first, we would spend holidays and birthdays together, and we would try our best not to disagree in front of the children. They had seen enough of that.

During our separation Liz had rediscovered herself and found a whole host of hobbies and activities that gave her pleasure. After those earliest culinary disasters, Liz had become an accomplished cook. During the years of separation she learned how to cook for pleasure not necessity. She became completely free of alcohol and prescribed tranquilizers. She rediscovered reading and knitting and gardening and public service of her own. She took time to think about what she wanted from life. Liz had always had a close relationship with her family. After our divorce her sisters and brothers literally wrapped her in love. Each of them played a part in her healing. She took college courses and worked at a local travel company. Most of all, she felt good about herself.

Meanwhile, I, too, had done some growing. I'd been very busy with my congressional work but I missed talking to her, sharing my successes and disappointments. I admired her growing self-confidence and could see how much she cared about the children, her community . . . and me. We tried another round of couple's counseling and we began to discover that there was a way for Liz and I to be a couple.

For Liz it meant simply doing her own thing as much as possible. For me it meant being more aware of my responsibilities to my wife, of not being so driven about work. Of course, by now, the children were older and in college and needed less of our time. But during our second courtship we made a commitment to talk our problems out rather than let them fester. Liz has often reminded me of this promise, but I think she'd agree that I have improved.

We were married on August 26, 1986, with Leonard and Laura as our best man and maid of honor, on what would have been our twenty-fifth wedding anniversary. Indeed, sometimes we just say we've been married for forty-two years or however many years it would be if we had never divorced. Liz has told me that she told one suitor that she couldn't be serious about their relationship because she always knew that she and I would get back together. I'm glad she had that belief because I think it also helped us heal. I'm also thankful that we got married on our original date. Like the proverbial screw-up husband, I often forgot that important date, but had finally gotten it planted in my memory before our divorce. Replacing it with another anniversary date might have been difficult.

Our wedding ceremony made news far and wide and our picture and stories about our second-time-around romance appeared in most of the big newspapers. There was Liz, outspoken as usual, telling the *Boston Globe* that there had been times when she got so angry at me she could barely speak but that she loved me anyhow. The story was accompanied by a photograph of us walking together, arm in arm. And smiling.

As part of the divorce Liz had gotten some of the land in Shrewsbury and we immediately set to building a house in our favorite town. Our friend Jim Kachadorian designed efficient and attractive passive solar houses and we found one that fit us to a T. It's a rugged cabin by D.C. standards and certainly not the gracious abode in which many would imagine a U.S. senator living. Our solar-heated mudroom, however, is perfect for starting the spring seedlings. The woodstove keeps the house toasty warm and I don't mind that the cat has nearly shredded my favorite chair.

For Liz and me, our return to Shrewsbury was like starting all over again. I have a blue, forty-horsepower Ford tractor that I like to drive around. It has a Woods Dixie Cutter attached to mow the brush and keep my small meadow open. Our property is located between Gould Brook and Shrewsbury Peak. There's not much I like better than to sit atop that tractor and bring some order to my small piece of paradise. As I did with the first house, I've made a little pond that's fed from the brook. It has a dam that I'd hoped might produce a little hydroelectric power—very little—but I've not had time yet to work it all out. I've a very small windmill as well, a token to my plans to garner a little wind power from the chilly blasts that often blow down from the mountains. Both the pond and the windmill await my retirement—if I ever retire. In the meantime, I spend whatever spare moments I have out in the woods, where I cut our firewood, or otherwise tinker around the property. Liz has planted flowers and usually has a vegetable garden. When we're in Shrewsbury, life slows down and we become aware again of the important things that so often get missed in the hustle and bustle of Beltway politics. We both became very close to the Pierce family and, as they aged, continued our habit of stopping by their little general store more for a chat than to buy groceries.

Marjorie was the last to die, two years ago. She had closed the store by then but was still quite active, keeping abreast of local and national news, always opinionated, always savvy, with nearly a century of information and experience tucked away in that wise brain of hers.

Liz is quite active in the Shrewsbury Community Church and I pretend to be a member of the volunteer fire department. In reality, I can only offer my help for them and other similar volunteer organizations through whatever federal support I can garner for volunteer fire departments. The most important thing about living in Shrewsbury is that it remains my link to a real community, one where everyone knows your name and perhaps a bit too much of your business, but one in which people care for and about one another. Ours is a quirky place, which makes it even more interesting. The key to town hall is kept on a peg on a building across the road. Residents can use the hall for a function with little fuss or bother. This is a true community—with contra dances, where local musicians play, and evening performances on the lawn outside the elementary school in summer. Shrewsbury residents are serious-minded but also extremely fun-loving. They know about and are often involved in environmental battles near and far. They're committed to recycling. The manager of the town dump is called the dump master and each year the town celebrates its successful recycling program with a Dumpling Day in which residents show up dressed in all sorts of recycled items. I'm lucky to call this town my home.

After our second marriage, Liz began coming to D.C. on occasion, but she kept those visits to a minimum until shortly after I seriously injured my back in yet another car accident in the late 1990s. These days, she spends much of the winter with me in Washington but the remainder of the year in Vermont. It's where she is happiest.

When I ran for the U.S. Senate for the first time in 1988, I was very glad to have Liz by my side. She and her sister, Jane Mendicino, campaigned door to door and attended many of the GOP functions together. She was meeting more and more Republicans and finding many that she felt she could support.

My opponent was William Gray, a Burlington attorney who had been a U.S. attorney during the Carter administration, a nice fellow who ran a bit of a negative campaign. It wasn't much of a race, as I was so well known in Vermont, having been a U.S. congressman for seven terms. By 1988, I had campaigned in every election since 1968 with only one loss, that of the 1972 GOP gubernatorial primary. So Vermonters knew me well. And regardless of the fact that I ran under the Republican Party banner, Vermonters knew that I would vote my conscience not the party, and they seemed content enough with that.

The most daunting thing really was the office itself, and the man whose seat I was vying for, my political mentor Robert Stafford. Bob's public service had spanned four decades. He served the Republican Party and residents of Vermont well and I was less than confident that I could live up to his record. Looking back on the articles written about me during that campaign, one can see that the seeds to my switch from the Republican Party had already been well planted. One article pointed out that during my fifteen years in the House I had voted for more legislation favored by Democrats than that favored by Republicans; that I'd consistently supported the ERA and a woman's right to choose despite the official party line; that I'd voted against Reagan's tax cuts and six years later, in 1987, supported a $12 billion tax increase introduced by the Democrats, which passed by only one vote.

CHAPTER 16

Protecting Tradition, "The October Surprise," Clarence Thomas, and Working for an International Nuclear Test Ban

ONE OF MY GREATEST challenges started almost my first day in the Senate in 1989, when I became involved in a huge battle with the new Bush administration over the selection of federal judges. Bush had decided to end the long-standing custom of allowing the Senate to have the final say on replacing federal judges in their state. Vermont federal judge Albert Coffrin was the first in the Bush administration to announce his desire to retire.

Under the Constitution, the president appoints all federal judges, from district courts to the Supreme Court. The Senate, however, has the duty to approve the president's nominee under the Advise and Consent Clause in the Constitution. Under long-standing tradition, the senior senator of the same party as the president from the state of the vacancy makes the recommendation to the president. Unless there was a serious problem, the president would honor this recommendation and appoint the person to the judgeship.

Since I was a Republican, I had the honor of making the selection. In the early 1980s, Senators Leahy and Stafford had agreed to a procedure to follow in determining who would be recommended to the president in the case of a Vermont vacancy. I agreed to follow this procedure, which called for nominees to be made by both state senators and a screening committee that worked in conjunction with the Vermont Bar Association to assess possible candidates. The name we put forth to replace Coffrin was Fred I. Parker of Middlebury. Fred, as you may remember, had been my deputy attorney general and was a highly respected attorney with a wonderful record of public service. He had been the most highly recommended applicant for the job.

But the president insisted that we send down three names, not just Parker's. Although I made it clear he was my first and in fact only recommendation, I complied and sent the names of two other highly qualified Vermont attorneys, Robert Rachlin and Dean Pineless.

Over the course of weeks, Susan Russ, my chief of staff, and I made several calls to the White House and provided additional information as requested. We received less than satisfactory responses to our inquiries as to the progress of Fred's nomination. I began to think that the White House had someone else in mind and, through the District's ever-present grapevine, learned that the president's family was interested in the lifetime position going to a Vermont lawyer who was the son of a close friend.

If the candidate the president was interested in had been one of the search committee's recommendees we might have considered him. But he was not. And I was quite determined to protect Senate tradition; my Senate peers urged me not to give in. The White House agreed that their choice was not the best nominee, but they wanted yet another recommendation from me. I made it clear that I had already recommended the very best candidate, as well as two additional names who were well qualified. I did not intend to send any other names.

The White House contact was C. Boyden Grey. He was adamant that the Senate tradition was going to end. Being brand new to the Senate, I was concerned about what to do and sought advice from colleagues. I've never had an easier cause to get unanimous Senate support. I let it be known I would block all judicial appointments until Fred Parker was appointed.

As the session was coming to the year-end break almost a year after the debate had begun, I was still blocking all judicial appointments. Of course for the members who had nominees ready for appointment, there was less enthusiasm for my method, even if they agreed with my motive. On the last legislative day, I released all but two judicial nominees and made it clear that when we returned in January, I intended to fight with every weapon at my disposal to ensure that Fred was appointed and that the tradition was upheld. During the debate I made more than forty-one phone calls, wrote eight letters, held seven meetings with the White House and Justice Department personnel, and initiated at least two lengthy Senate floor discussions on the Parker nomination. It was not until the following spring of 1990 that the White House finally capitulated. It didn't help my relationship with Boyden Grey or those judges I held up. Every once in a while I meet a judge who will groan about the money he lost because of my actions.

I think my colleagues had an inkling then that I was more than a little determined when I felt I was right. I had been a pest, but I was a successful pest, and the federal judiciary has been well served because of it. Judge Parker was later appointed to the 2nd Circuit Court of Appeals and continues to impress everyone who has occasion to deal with him. But more important, I had upheld the Senate's tradition and protected states' rights in the selection of federal judges.

My success in this effort might have ill-prepared me for my next great challenge—investigating the ten-year-old allegations that the Republicans had interfered with the release of the hostages from Iran during the 1980 elections in order to help defeat President Carter. Because President Bush's actions during that election would be scrutinized, it was a particularly awkward situation, one that resurrected a difficult chapter in recent U.S. history.

Almost immediately after Iran lost interest in seeking an agreement with the Carter administration, people began to allege that it was because Iran had received some sort of assurance from the Republicans that the military pipeline between the United States and Iran would be reopened if Reagan were elected. This implied that the Republicans had sought Iranian help in defeating Carter by getting Iran to simply delay the release of the hostages until after the election. Allegations also circulated that the Reagan administration later circumvented a congressional ban on arms shipments to Iran by sending military equipment and supplies to Iran through Israel. For ten years arms dealers and journalists explored these allegations in numerous articles, TV shows, and books.

The allegations of a partisan political conspiracy at the expense of jeopardizing American lives led to many requests for a full congressional investigation.* The situation came to be known as the October Surprise in recognition of the fact that the Reagan people feared Carter would pull a surprise in October by gaining the release of the hostages a month before the election. One of the more disturbing questions that kept being asked was whether George Bush had participated in efforts to keep this from happening. He flatly denied any involvement in any such effort.

In June 1991, eight of the fifty-two Americans held hostage in Iran asked for a formal investigation. Reagan muddied the waters by telling reporters, "I did some things, actually, the other way to try and be of help in getting those hostages—I felt very sorry for them—of getting them out of there." Asked whether that entailed direct contact with Iran, Reagan said obliquely, "Not by me."

On August 5, 1991, Senate majority leader George J. Mitchell (D., Maine) asked the Senate Foreign Relations Committee to investigate the October Surprise allegations through its subcommittee on Near Eastern and South Asian Affairs. That was my committee and I was ranking member, meaning it fell on me and Senator Terry Sanford (D., N.C.), the chair of the committee, to decide whether to conduct the inquiry. Sanford was a terrific partner in the inquiry. A Democrat from North Carolina, he had served in the army and had been an attorney in private practice, an educator, a state senator, governor of North Carolina, president of Duke University, and, for a brief time in the early 1940s, a special agent with the Federal Bureau of Investigation. On October 16, Mitchell, Sanford, and I introduced a resolution requesting investigatory powers to pursue the issue, including $596,000 in funding as well as subpoena power. That resolution was approved on a close vote,nine to eight, by the full committee but nearly a month later, by a vote of fifty-one to forty-three, a motion to close debate on the issue failed in the Senate.

---

*First came Debategate, in which a subcommittee of the House Committee on Post Office and Civil Service investigated whether there had been unauthorized transfers of information from the Carter administration to the Reagan campaign, and whether Reagan's campaign director William Casey intended to monitor Carter's activities in relation to an October Surprise. The Albosta Report, issued on May 1, 1984, detailed preparations undertaken by the Reagan campaign to respond to an October Surprise, including assigning retired military officers who were given the job of monitoring possible U.S. shipments of arms to Iran in exchange for hostages.

Sanford and I wondered how to proceed. The tally clearly indicated that we would not get enough votes to conduct a full investigation. Sixty votes would be required, but fifty-one members *did* want us to proceed, a sizable number. We decided that we would conduct a more limited sub-committee investigation—limited not only in funding but also in scope and authority.

Few decisions I have made before leaving the GOP in May 2001 have angered my fellow Republicans more than the decision to pursue the October Surprise investigation. After all, George Bush, one of the people we would be investigating, was now the president of the United States.

I suppose I could have walked away from the investigation. After all, we had not received clear Senate approval and it had been made clear to us that if we had asked for it, it would have been denied. Yet I felt that if we didn't conduct the investigation, the allegations against Reagan and our party would forever haunt us. And didn't the hostages and the American people have a right to know?

As it turned out, the Republicans had little to fear. Or did they? To this day it's hard to say what is true. The material in this chapter is based on the report written by special counsel Reid H. Weingarten and delivered to Sanford and me on October 15, 1992, twelve years after the events we were looking into actually took place.

Our task, we thought, was to focus on four important allegations:

- Did William Casey, Reagan's 1980 campaign director, develop an elaborate intelligence operation to monitor and perhaps influence the Carter administration's handling of the hostage crisis to ensure that the Reagan campaign wouldn't be caught off guard by a so-called October Surprise? An Iranian expatriate arms dealer and businessman named Jamshid Hashemi alleged that he and his late brother Cyrus Hashemi met Casey several times in Madrid in the summer of 1980 to discuss the hostage situation and offered to help in arranging an arms for hostages deal.
- Did prominent Republican campaign operatives—including Bush, Casey, Richard Allen, Robert "Bud" McFarlane, Donald Gregg, and Robert Gates—meet with Iranians and Israelis in Paris in October 1980 to finalize an agreement to delay the hostage release in return for an agreement to supply Iran with American-made military equipment

via Israeli channels, as alleged by several individuals who claimed to have either attended the meetings or to have received details about them?

- Did Allen, McFarlane, and Laurence Silberman meet with an unidentified Iranian emissary at L'Enfant Plaza Hotel in Washington, D.C., in fall 1980 to conduct unauthorized negotiations with the Khomeini regime relative to the hostages, as some sources alleged?
- Did the Reagan administration tacitly authorize overt shipments of large quantities of American-made spare parts and military equipment from Israel to Iran in return for the Iranian regime's cooperation in delaying the release of the hostages until after the 1980 election?

Our investigation was hampered by the fact that we had to operate within the resources of our committee and by the constraints placed upon us due to not receiving Senate approval for the inquiry. We were not allowed to spend money for foreign travel to interview the dozens of prospective witnesses we wanted to talk to nor could we subpoena them to come to us. Ultimately, eighteen subpoenas were granted, allowing us to talk to forty-seven witnesses and make inquiries of fifteen entities—mostly government agencies believed to have relevant information.

The FBI was helpful in providing some information. It had conducted extensive surveillance of Cyrus Hashemi for most of the time in question. However, the most important tapes of Hashemi's activities—ones we considered crucial to our investigation—had been missing for many years, indeed from 1984. In 1992, as we were finishing our investigation, 450 of the missing Hashemi tapes were found in an FBI storage facility, essentially too late for us to use them. As we were writing the report, the FBI informed us that they had found no conversation between Cyrus Hashemi and Reagan, as Hashemi's brother had alleged, on the tapes they had reviewed thus far. We were never able to review the tapes ourselves.

Another problem we encountered in our investigation was the fact that the most important person in these allegations, Cyrus Hashemi, the arms dealer who claimed to have been the go-between between Casey and the Iranians, was dead, as were many other people we wanted to talk to. Casey, who went on to become director of the CIA, died in 1987. John Shaheen, a Lebanese-born international businessman defined in Weingarten's report as having "a taste for high-risk, high-yield oil ventures," had served for a time in the Office of Strategic Services along with Casey during World War II and would have been the likely person to have introduced Hashemi to Casey, but he, too, was dead. Houshang Lavi, a wealthy international arms dealer who, along with Ari Ben-Menashe, came forward to claim that the two had met with Allen, McFarlane, and Silberman at L'Enfant Plaza, was dead. And so, too, were several other minor but important sources of information who claimed to have either been at these meetings or to have learned details about them from those who were.

We were also hampered by a lack of cooperation from many governmental entities and officials. Secret Service records for the dates in question when these meetings were supposed to have taken place were eventually provided, after many requests, but in a redacted form on a read-only (no copies to be made) basis. The Secret Service also eventually agreed to supply information regarding agents who had been assigned to Bush on the dates in question, but our request to question the agents directly was denied. Much of the information we needed regarding travel arrangements for the people named in the allegations was no longer available because of the passage of time. In the case of Bush, however, there was substantial indication that he had not traveled overseas during the times in question, but we were never able to confirm where Casey was on the days the meetings were alleged to have occurred.

We requested documents from the National Security Agency and the Department of Defense that might have answered some of these questions, but they didn't supply us with the requested information until too late in our inquiry to give them proper review. We had no luck finding Casey's passport, which would have told us where he was when. Despite considerable effort trying to track it down through the CIA, through Casey's former secretary, his daughter and widow, it never showed up. We also tried to get copies of his personal diary and calendar pages. The documents were finally provided but, in both cases, pages for important dates during which the alleged meetings would have occurred were missing. The same was true for Shaheen's Pocket Diary and passport, as well as his financial ledger pages from 1980.

Reagan was less than cooperative. Despite repeated attempts to get his campaign records, diaries, schedules, expense reports, and other documents relative to the 1980 Republican presidential campaign, the Reagan Library delayed access to his papers until late August 1992, when our investigative staff had already been reassigned to other duties.

Perhaps most disturbing was President Reagan's declination to grant us an interview. His written reply, issued by his attorney John A. Mintz on August 26, 1992, was wholly inadequate. Mintz wrote that Reagan "has advised that he has no recollection or other information relevant to the issues raised in any of your questions." Reagan's memory may have been affected by Alzheimer's at this point.

During our investigation some sources told us that Carter had used the hostage situation to his own advantage in his primary fight with Ted Kennedy. These witnesses speculated that Carter's optimistic announcement on April 1, 1980, that he expected good news about the hostages was timed to influence the outcome of the Wisconsin primary. But there was equal information that he did have good reason to expect the news. We were unable to learn why the negotiations later fell apart.

There was also adequate evidence that many of the people who made allegations against Reagan and his team had shady pasts and had in one way or another tried to profit not only from the hostage situation but from the complex political situation in the Middle East. And there was also evidence that people in both the Carter and Reagan administrations knew many of the people we interviewed. On January 5, 1980, for example, at the urging of Carter's State Department, the CIA provided $500,000 in cash to the Hashemi brothers for a sensitive covert operation in Iran.

In the end, we were left with nearly as many questions as we had had in the beginning. The special counsel concluded that there was insufficient evidence to support allegations that the Republicans orchestrated a delay in the release of the hostages until after the election. The timing of the release could simply have been a deliberate and final insult to President Carter on the part of the Khomeini regime.

At the same time, however, there was ample and disturbing evidence that Reagan campaign officials had extensively monitored the Carter administration's every move with regard to the hostages in the hopes of anticipating an October Surprise.

On the issue of whether the Reagan administration allowed arms to be shipped to Iran against the congressional prohibition, the special counsel found that the administration had acquiesced to limited Israeli transshipments of American-made weapons to Iran. Weingarten, however, found no evidence to link these arms shipments with the late release of the hostages. (Independent counsel Lawrence E. Walsh subsequently ruled in 1997 that a 1994 sale of arms to Iran under the Reagan administration contravened U.S. government policy and may have violated the Arms Export Control Act.)*

I was very disturbed by the lack of cooperation from U.S. government officials and agreed with Weingarten's recommendation that a more thorough investigation be done, but that was never undertaken.

In the end, the animosity I encountered for going through with the investigation was not warranted. While we did not find conclusive evidence to clear the Republicans, we did put the issue at rest for most people. Perhaps, if everyone had cooperated and we had been allowed a more thorough investigation, we may have been able to issue an even more positive—or at least complete—report.

I was already concerned with the conservative and overly technical trend in Supreme Court decisions when Bush nominated Clarence Thomas to fill the seat of Justice Thurgood Marshall, long a champion of people's rights. The Thomas nomination really made me reexamine the role of the Senate in the formation and composition of the court. I concluded that, when it appears the philosophical makeup of the court has swung so far to one way or the other that it is at odds with a clear majority of the Congress, then the nominee must be someone who can restore balance to the court. That is what the Founding Fathers had in mind when they created the three branches of our government.

---

*Walsh's summary said, "The Iran operations were carried out with the knowledge of, among others, President Ronald Reagan, Vice President George Bush, Secretary of State George P. Shultz, Secretary of Defense Caspar W. Weinberger, Director of Central Intelligence William J. Casey, and national security advisers Robert C. McFarlane and John M. Poindexter; of these officials, only Weinberger and Shultz dissented from the policy decision, and Weinberger eventually acquiesced by ordering the Department of Defense to provide the necessary arms . . . large volumes of highly relevant, contemporaneously created documents were systematically and willfully withheld from investigators by several Reagan Administration officials."

But I felt that Thomas's nomination would swing the court further to the right and, thus, must be rejected. To say and do otherwise, I believed, would allow the executive branch to wrest control of the judiciary and make the highest court an agent of a particular president's political views rather than an arbiter of fairness. I simply could not support this kind of domination of the one branch of government that is intended to be the arbiter between the remaining two branches as well as the balancing wheel in social exchanges.

Quite frankly, I also found little in Thomas's record to suggest legal excellence. The bar association's recommendation had been tempered and there was little evidence of legal or intellectual distinction. Measuring legal qualifications is a relatively objective process compared to the more subjective analysis of character or judicial temperament. In the latter two, however, I was certainly not reassured of Thomas's qualifications.

I believe a president should look first to the finest jurists in the land without regard to philosophical or political bent or an attempt at homogeneity with the president's own persuasions. That was the standard I applied to Thomas. It was not so much the Anita Hill allegations or Thomas's conservative stand on issues that made him an undesirable candidate in my mind, but rather that I believed the Supreme Court was already too conservative and, for the good of the country, needed a more moderate and gifted candidate who could bring balance to the court.

The closeness of the Senate vote on his confirmation, fifty-two for and forty-eight against, and the seven to seven tie in the Senate Judiciary Committee showed me not only that there was not overwhelming support for Thomas but that public opinion was split on the matter as well.

My vote on this, in retrospect, is reminiscent of the process I went through in my decision to leave the Republican Party and wrest support of the Senate from the Republicans. Then as now, I believe government should reflect more evenly the opinions of the people of our great nation, who are more centrist and even-handed in their beliefs and opinions and certainly less polarized than our government has become.

President Bush and I maintained a fairly productive relationship despite my decision to take on the October Surprise investigation and despite my opposition to his nomination of Clarence Thomas to the Supreme Court. Near the end of his term of office, I warned Bush that he was moving too far to the right to be reelected. He later apologized to me and said he should have followed my advice and been more moderate.

People have asked me in recent years why, if I opposed the nomination of Thomas for Supreme Court judge, I didn't also oppose the nomination of John Ashcroft for U.S. Attorney General. Indeed, I also believe that Ashcroft is more conservative than most Americans, and I remain wary of his propensity for bringing church into state matters. However, my philosophy is that a president has the right to choose his staff—his attorney general, his secretary of state, and the like. These are nominations that remain in place as long as a president chooses or as long as he is in office. A Supreme Court justice, however, is named for life. Their influence on the nation can extend over decades. That is why we need individuals who are not partisan, who can step beyond the political fray and see issues objectively, ruling for what is best for America, not the president and party who put them in office.

Defense issues always seem to be a priority, and that was true during the Bush administration. During the 101st Congress, moderate colleagues and I worked hard on passing a comprehensive nuclear test ban. In 1990 I joined forces with seven other parliamentarians from the United States, Great Britain, and the Soviet Union on a five-day trip to the capital of each country. We met with Gorbachev, Deputy British Foreign Minister Douglas Hogg, and National Security Adviser Brent Scowcroft. We presented each official with a petition signed by more than 2,050 elected officials from the three countries in support of the Comprehensive Test Ban.

In Moscow, Gorbachev greeted us warmly and invited us to join him when he made his economic forecast speech. We watched him from an adjoining room as an interpreter translated his lengthy speech into English and then he joined us to talk long and earnestly about the importance of our mission. I had brought a pint of maple syrup—one of the elixirs of the gods—with me and gave it to him with the comment that maple syrup makes a person feel serene and peaceful. He asked, "Do you have a liter?"

While our group didn't get everything we wanted, the Senate in 1992 voted to enact a nine-month moratorium on the testing of nuclear weapons and indicated that all testing would be terminated by the end of fiscal year 1996. President Bush signed the bill into law in October 1992.

•   •   •

All this happened with the Persian Gulf War as a backdrop—one of the most disturbing times in recent American history. It began in early August 1990 when Iraq invaded its tiny neighbor, Kuwait, after talks broke down between the two countries over oil production and debt repayment. Iraqi president Saddam Hussein annexed Kuwait, declaring it a nineteenth province of Iraq. President Bush believed that Iraq planned to invade Saudi Arabia and take control of the region's oil supplies. Not only were we allies with Saudi Arabia but Bush was concerned about oil supplies and began organizing a multinational coalition to seek Kuwait's freedom and restore the government.

The U.N. Security Council authorized economic sanctions against Iraq, a move I strongly supported. Bush quickly responded to a Saudi request for help and ordered U.S. troops to protect Saudi Arabia. Operation Desert Shield began August 6 with 230,000 American troops sent to Saudi Arabia to take defensive positions. I didn't have a problem with that. I felt we had to do something. But I and many Americans became quite concerned as Iraq continued its huge military buildup in Kuwait and the president ordered an additional 200,000 troops deployed for a possible offensive action by a U.S.-led coalition force. I felt not enough time had been allowed to let the sanctions work and that we might force Saddam Hussein's hand if we acted too soon. Yet the president had already acted, and the last thing I wanted to do was to undermine him at this crucial time.

As fall turned into winter, constituents at home and across the nation began to show the same division as during the Vietnam War. On New Year's Eve 1990, the Brattleboro Sane Freeze representatives came to see me in Rutland, bringing reporters with them. I explained my strong belief that we had much to lose if we went to war and vowed to continue to work on developing alternative energy options and to lobby for a nuclear-testing freeze. Most of all, I said I would strongly oppose the use of ground troops and would push for United Nations–composed forces. Meanwhile France and several Arab nations were negotiating with Saddam Hussein, whom I thought might be crazy but not stupid. I believed that he liked the center stage too much to risk a loss and that he would back down.

On January 8, 1991, Bush obtained a U.N. Security Council resolution setting a January 15, 1991, deadline for Iraq to withdraw unconditionally from Kuwait—or else. Meanwhile, Congress made the decision to insist on a Declaration of War for our armed forces to be utilized. I was really in a tough position. I was opposed to the president's approach but I felt that I had to support him. Quite frankly, he had placed us in a bad position. If Congress voted against him, that would send a message to Saddam Hussein that the American people were not behind the president and that might further embolden him. Phone calls were pouring in to my office with about two thousand to fifty against approval of the declaration of war.

Because I was still undecided, everyone wanted to lobby or interview me. I was torn but I was leaning toward voting with the president as I thought to do otherwise would really pull the rug out from under him and would actually be counterproductive to the interests of peace. I had high hopes that France's independent diplomatic initiative, which favored an international conference to discuss both the Gulf crisis and the Arab-Israeli dispute, would be successful.

One morning, a staff worker looked out the window of the Montpelier office to see about forty protesters marching down the street. They marched right into the office and began a peaceful occupation. They wanted to talk to me and I told them I would do so. Police protection for the office building was supplied for the night but there were no problems inside. Outside, however, was the real shock. Body bags with protesters pretending to be dead blocked the steps. Goats' blood had been poured on the body bags. Inside my office, mothers openly nursed their babies—contrasting new life with the death they believed the war would bring. I promised to come to Vermont and told a *New York Times* reporter I would once again examine my reasoning.

I no sooner hung up the phone than I learned there were more than five hundred people outside the Vermont Capitol building holding a rally against the president.

That night, former New Hampshire governor John Sununu, Bush's chief of staff, called to talk. I told him I wanted an assurance that President Bush was not intending to go immediately to war after the fifteenth. I told him I believed we had not exhausted our options. Sununu promised me that, if any hope of meaningful negotiations remained on the fifteenth, we would hold off on the attack and would not use ground troops. But, he said, Bush was adamant that any agreement with Iraq would have to include the removal of any threat of chemical, biological, or nuclear weapons. This seemed appropriate to me.

The *New York Times* article ran in the Vermont newspapers the next day, with its suggestion that, while I was rethinking my position, it seemed apparent I would back the president. By now, more than 4,000 people had called the office. I was concerned with Bush's national security adviser Brent Scowcroft's statement that the negotiations had broken off.

By six P.M. my concern was so great that I called the president, who called me right back. He started right off assuring me that he would not start hostilities if there was any chance of meaningful negotiations, but he added that at the present there were none. He would give me no guarantees.

Here was my conundrum: I felt Saddam Hussein would accept the French peace initiative because it would allow him to save face and keep him center stage. I also thought this would provide the opportunity to enforce protections against nuclear proliferation as well as chemical and biological weapons. I thought that would be the outcome but that I'd have to support President Bush's show of strength to get it.

My own thoughts went back to the Vietnam War. One of my navy reserve duties had been to represent the district navy commandant and inform Vermont families of the wounding or death of their sons and daughters.

One particular incident kept coming to mind. As I pondered my decision, I could see the faces of the Dexter family of Rutland when I brought news of their son Richard's death. As I walked to their front door in uniform, my heart was very heavy. They knew why I was there. After I made the formal statement, they gave me the last letter they had received from their son, a beautiful letter. He had been a conscientious objector and had volunteered to serve as a navy medical corpsman. He expressed his devotion to helping the wounded Vietnamese citizens and his hope for peace. I was deeply moved and left their house in tears myself.

Later I worked with Vietnam veterans in Rutland who formed the first chapter of the Vietnam Veterans of America, in part in response to their feelings of being shunned by the traditional veterans groups. Since the war, I had supported every effort to gain medical attention for the Vietnam veterans and to investigate the effects of Agent Orange on them and their children. I was often frustrated at the treatment of these veterans—not just by other veterans but by the government as well.

The protesters in my office brought all this back. I understood why they dreaded the thought of another Vietnam. I promised to come to Vermont to meet with them.

Estimates were that as many as 5,000 people would come to protest and listen to me. I flew to Vermont with much trepidation. The staff was really tense—as was Liz. One of our neighbors, a wonderful, now deceased, friend named Red Brigham, had come up to Liz at the Shrewsbury dump and shouted to her that he had not fought in the South Pacific to watch a president go to war over oil.

The White House was so concerned about my safety that they sent Secret Service personnel to help me in and out of the Montpelier City Hall where I was to speak the following evening. Fortunately, a huge snowstorm arrived the day before the meeting and far fewer people attended than were at first expected. I decided to travel to the auditorium from my friend Jim Johnston's house. Jim had been my campaign chairman in the last election; he also was a funeral director. We hadn't thought of the symbolism of my traveling to the auditorium in his black limo, so often used in funerals. On the way out, I got another call from the president, asking again for my support.

At the appointed hour, we set off through the high snowdrifts. The Secret Service limo skidded off the road into a ditch. We loaded the Secret Servicemen into our car and drove to the auditorium. The event was remarkably orderly. Vietnam veterans had formed a phalange between me and the audience in case trouble broke out. They weren't needed but I appreciated the support. I was honest but brief. I told those present I would take their concerns into account but that it might be too late to go backward. They told me it was never too late to stop a war. It was indeed an emotional night.

In the end, I voted for the Declaration of War, not believing that Bush would actually use the authority we had given him. The declaration won by only two votes. Although many of my constituents were disappointed in me, I did not regret my vote, given the circumstances. I think Saddam Hussein had pushed us to the point of having no alternative.

On January 16, we began the most devastating air assault in history against military targets in Iraq and Kuwait. The night we started bombing

Iraq I was in my office with Susan Russ and Mark Powden, one of my top aides. There are few times when I have felt greater despair.

Sadly, the president ordered the ground war to begin February 24. The war was over by March 3 when Allied and Iraqi military leaders met on the battlefield to discuss terms for a formal cease-fire to end the Gulf War. I don't think the American people fully understand the consequences of this war. More than 532,000 U.S. forces served in Operation Desert Storm. There were a total of 148 U.S. battle deaths and 145 non-battle deaths; 467 men and women were wounded in action. The United States estimated that more than 100,000 Iraqi soldiers died, 300,000 were wounded, 150,000 deserted, and 60,000 were taken prisoner.

As the tension in the Middle East between the PLO and Israel is once again at a terrible pitch and the threat of war is present, I still believe that we do ourselves little good by playing the military card while doing so little to end our dependency on foreign oil.

The effects of war are clear enough. I have supported the effort to provide health services to veterans who fought in Desert Storm and came back with health problems much the same as I fought to provide services to Vietnam veterans exposed to Agent Orange and their families and to the veterans who suffered from post-traumatic stress disorder.

There's only one conclusion: The world has got to find some other way to resolve conflicts.

CHAPTER 17

Building the Case for Education in the Shadow of Gingrich's Contract with America

THE 1994 MIDTERM election brought about a sea change in Washington that was dubbed the "Republican Revolution" by its self-styled leader Newt Gingrich. Both houses of Congress had flipped to Republican control; Newt became the Speaker of the House and unveiled the Contract with America. I had just narrowly won a new term in the Senate and was poised to play a strong role in shaping education policy.

Election night 1994 I was at the Burlington Sheraton Hotel with the rest of my staff, family, and key supporters awaiting the final results to come in. The campaign had been a lot tougher and the race a lot closer than any of us had anticipated. I finally made it to the private suite we had reserved for Liz and me and the senior staff.

Susan Russ was there and we turned on the TV, sitting side by side, drained and silent on the edge of the sofa in front of the screen. The final tally was in for Vermont: I had beaten Jan Backus by a slim 51 to 46 percent margin—some would say in spite of my campaign. The broadcast immediately turned to the national report and the congressional races. The Republicans had won the House and Newt Gingrich would be in line to be the next Speaker.

Susan and I completely ignored the news of Vermont and my victory. Both of our jaws dropped simultaneously and we gasped aloud in unison, "Oh my God, Newt Gingrich." I was leaning forward so far I nearly fell off the sofa, and that started us laughing.

"You are the only Republican who would fall off his seat in dismay upon hearing this," Susan said. We were laughing, relieved, and ready to celebrate my return to the Senate, but I had my reasons to be wary of the news that night, and as time went on they were certainly validated.

There was a lot I had to learn in the years after the Republicans took control of the House and Senate. The issues I cared passionately about—education, health care reform, the environment—all cried out for long-term solutions that could only be forged through careful consensus and compromise. I was absolutely certain that the work could only get done if the moderate voices from both parties could be heard. The challenge for me at the start of my second Senate term was to seize the opportunities I would be handed by the Republicans while also making sure my voice was heard and reasonable compromise considered.

As Speaker, Newt Gingrich set the tone not only by defining the issues on which the party would focus but by also embarking on a crusade to define the philosophy of government itself. Who can forget the new Speaker back in those early days? Fired up, an excellent orator and academician, he came out of the box, media-savvy and hungry, using every opportunity to extol a "less is more" approach to government. He was a C-SPAN superstar, passionately filling the screen for long stretches, making appearances at the National Press Club, and orating at podiums at matriculations, commencements, and conferences around the country. The conservative ranks of my colleagues, about to assume powerful positions, were in lockstep.

When the Contract with America was circulated as the "new paradigm" for the Republican message, I publicly and vocally disagreed with it. I think I was one of the only Republicans to do so. The idea was to cut lots of government programs, interventions, and regulations and allow states and municipalities to mind their own business. There was a belief that industry would take up some of the slack of the gutted or cut federal programs and that people would work together to fill the others. I am not one for extremist or moralistic platforms, especially when the crux of the argument was antithetical to what I believed good government should be. Newt's plan to diminish the federal role in governing did not reflect what I saw as the critical need for leadership, especially in education reform. Without leadership, national standards, and increased federal resources, the American education system would never be competitive in the new, globally interconnected economy.

My explanation for countering the House Republicans was that I had a contract with the people of Vermont. I wrote an op-ed piece at the time that was read on NPR that stated, "If we moderates are successful in gaining consensus, change will come. It will be tempered by those of us in Congress who believe our government is neither all-powerful nor evil, that government can work to bring about constructive change to better our lives and our nation's strength."

Vermonters had heard me say all this before. My election had been close but I had won. I felt secure to state my position, which was that the nation's business stood in good stead under the Constitution, the original contract with America, and the normal course of debate, compromise, checks and balances that the system was so brilliantly built upon. If we did our jobs well and listened to our constituents we wouldn't need a gimmick.

Newt had more of a "my way or the highway" approach, and my discomfort with his plan cemented my profile as a loose cannon. As time went on, my fears about Newt were confirmed. He used his perch as Speaker for what I saw as the dangerous practice of moralizing and stretching government's reach into inappropriate places, such as the privacy of the bedroom or wrongly linking church and state, precursors of things to come. He seemed to care more about the issue of prayer in school than our math or reading scores.

During Newt's tenure, the party became more and more conservative and placed increasing pressure on party members to get in step. Those of us with a more moderate philosophy often found ourselves thankful for one another's support, as we found less and less tolerance for our views. In 1996, Nancy Kassebaum, my moderate Republican colleague from Kansas and the sitting chairwoman of the full Labor Committee, announced her retirement. I was personally saddened to hear the news because I had really enjoyed working with her. I respected her immensely, and losing another moderate member of the party would be a real blow.

On the other hand, as I was the next in line in seniority on the committee, her departure would open up the chairmanship to me. Chairmanship of the full committee, then titled Labor, Health, and Human Resources, would give me direct jurisdiction over the country's largest domestic discretionary programs, including education. It was the opportunity to match my passion and commitment for education with direct policy-making power; without a doubt, a pinnacle in my career.

My ascension to the chairmanship, however, was not without difficulty. Indeed, the scenario that follows clearly illustrates what I believe is extremely wrong with our political system today. Instead of respecting the plurality of our country and creating an opportunity for diverse opinions to be aired, what we had come to in Washington was a constant battle over extreme ideology with the party in power doing its darndest to impose its will on the people.

In my case, two other members of the Labor Committee, Dan Coats (R., Ind.) and Judd Gregg (R., N.H.), essentially mounted a coup to usurp my right to the chairmanship and give it to Coats. Both Coats and Gregg were junior to me and part of the new wave of conservatism. For an old-timer like me, this was unheard of.

The sanctity of the committee system in Congress, a system based on experience, seniority, and courtesy, had come under the gun of Newt's "reform." He began to deconstruct the way House committees were assigned, disavowing seniority in the name of iconoclasm. Newt and the camp of conservatives he enjoined had put more stake in ideology than practical experience. It seemed that such thoughts, coupled with skepticism of my ability to tow the conservative line, were at the heart of Senators Coats and Gregg's argument against me. And word came that they had gone to the Majority Leader to make their argument.

I felt bad about this for many reasons, but principally because I had tried to work with Coats despite the fact that he had exhibited a clear disdain for me on many levels. I tried to speak with him to see if we could find some common ground; my staff worked feverishly behind the scenes to open communication and assure him that as chairman I would work hard to incorporate all views on the committee. Coats decided to play hardball and ignore my outreach. The question ended up with Trent Lott.

Many senior staff across the Senate knew what was going on, so it didn't take long for the press to get the story. Trent knew he would alienate the moderate Republicans by anointing Coats, and that would mean the entire block of New Englanders right there. There would be many Democrats, veteran politicians like me, who would be outraged as well. In the end, Trent sided with me. The political scales had been tipped in my favor; I won't flatter myself to think he relished the thought of my tenure as chairman.

Having the chairmanship, however, meant I could rework the structure of the committee to reflect my priorities. I immediately raised education from a subcommittee function to a principal concern of the full committee. This also would put education directly into my portfolio. To reflect the change, we gave the committee a new name, Health, Education, Labor, and Pensions or the HELP Committee. This reflected my contention that four principles are essential to the fulfillment of the American experience—good health, good education, good employment, and a good retirement.

In the new committee structure, Dan Coats became chairman of the Subcommittee on Family and Children and Judd Gregg got the subcommittee chairmanship on aging. The fallout from the failed coup was not all roses for me by any stretch. While Coats's term only lasted until 1998, he and Gregg sought to thwart my efforts and control at nearly every turn. Important pieces of legislation got stalled. The prime example was the reauthorization of the Elementary and Secondary Education Act that we were unable to pass during the Clinton administration.

Education, I believe, really suffered from the tensions between the Republican leadership and President Bill Clinton. Clinton had come into office promising the American people that he would revitalize the sagging economy, not only through fiscal policy but also with a clear mandate for education reform including national standards, job training, and access to technology for all students. I couldn't have agreed with him more, but the political reality of Newt as Speaker pitted Congress against the White House in a more concrete and ideological way than I had seen ever before.

I was anxious to use my legislative clout. The tide was rising against our education system, which was sorely out of sync with the slick rhetoric being employed by the president and vice president about the promise of the Internet and the new millennium. We still had an education system based on the turn-of-the-*old*-century's agrarian model. And if spending was any indication of priority, we had certainly shirked our responsibility. If Clinton was serious about doing something about it, I was willing to help.

The damage had begun back in the Reagan administration. At a time when we needed to be investing more into our educational system and improving the education of our teachers, we instead cut programs and funding. By 1994 federal leadership and spending for education had grown so thin, and our overall level of educational excellence had fallen so greatly, that an international assessment of educational progress by the Education Department showed that America's standing among twenty-six other industrialized nations in math, science, and reading was far from the top. The statistic that jumped out at me—and one that I still refer to—was America's sixteenth place ranking in math performance of thirteen-year-olds. We ranked behind almost all of our European counterparts including Slovenia. But the real question was, who was number one? Not just slightly ahead of the competition, but head and shoulders above was China, the world's most populous nation.

In 1995, Hedrick Smith's *Rethinking America* laid out the theory of global labor markets and the criteria for competing in the new century. I had a chart made of our math performance versus China's and toted it around with me from speech to speech as a wake-up call. But I always noted that our ranking was just the inevitable outcome of having failed to heed the original wake-up call issued ten years earlier, in 1983, by Terrell "Ted" Bell, the secretary of education under President Ronald Reagan. Bell was a formidable man and a thorough one. He issued the now famous report entitled "A Nation at Risk," which said in no uncertain terms that America's public education system needed a serious overhaul. Sad to say, twenty years later the report's ominous title is still accurate and should be required reading for anyone wanting to be an activist for education. The quote that springs out at you is this: "If an outside power were to impose upon this country our current education system, we would consider it an act of war."

Not much has changed in the intervening years, and the future of America is still at risk. We simply can't wait any longer to act. The Third International Mathematics and Science Study (TIMSS), conducted in 1995, involved forty-two countries at three grade levels and was the largest, most comprehensive and rigorous assessment of its kind ever undertaken. In 1999, TIMSS collected data in thirty-eight countries at the eighth-grade level to provide information about change in the mathematics and science achievement of our students compared to those in other nations over the last four years. It showed that in 2000 America came in nineteenth among tested nations in eighth-grade math performance. In that survey, the top nations were Singapore, Korea, Chinese Taipei, Hong Kong, and Japan.

Another fact we saw from TIMSS was that our math scores get progressively lower than other nations as our students go through school. We score above international averages for math and science in fourth grade, fall somewhere in the middle for eighth grade, and well below average by twelfth grade. Just when our students need to be prepared for the workplace, or a challenging postsecondary education, we are at our worst.

My esteemed colleague, former Senator John Glenn (D., Ohio) headed a commission to analyze our great deficiencies in math and science. He issued a report entitled "Before It's Too Late." I think the title says it all. The recommendations in the report included a basic overhaul of how we prepare highly qualified math and science teachers. To reach Glenn's goals on a systematic basis will not be easy or inexpensive. But the cost of not meeting the challenge is far greater. Because of our nation's inadequate education in math and science, our government had to create the H1B visa program to bring qualified high-tech workers, many from Asia, to take well-paying jobs that our own citizens simply did not qualify for. I am currently working on a wide-sweeping proposal to find funds for Glenn's recommendation. But beyond money the answer to our problems is not a mystery.

Esteemed national reports, including "A Nation at Risk," come to the same conclusions: We must extend the school year; we must extend, and make more productive, the school day; teachers must be better prepared and paid better, at least double their salary on average; and we must extend education to younger children and give all three- and four-year-olds excellent pre-K preparation.

Does America have the money to make these reforms? Of course. It's simply a question of priorities. In 1944, Congress enacted the G.I. Bill to provide education and training for more than 10 million returning servicemen. The G.I. Bill cost $3.6 billion by 1949, pushing federal spending on education to nearly 10 percent of the entire federal budget. We found the funds then. During the Cold War, when the Russians launched the Sputnik rocket and America found itself behind in the space race, we found the resources again. Congress authorized the National Defense Education Act to provide more than $1 billion for the improvement of elementary, secondary, and postsecondary math and science education. This large education effort enabled our nation to thrive in the fifties and sixties. Our universities, with federal help, responded to the challenge by educating thousands of our brightest, and thousands from all over the world to help our industries compete and excel. Many foreign students at that time received a higher education from America, and then went home to fuel our competition.

Fast forward almost fifty years to the past decade and federal spending on education has fallen to slightly more than 2 percent of the entire federal budget. Curiously, the drop came after the civil rights movement, when education spending had been rightly directed to the young, poor, and disabled. The current picture is deplorable. Indeed, it is at the center of my dissatisfaction with the Republican Party.

I believe in civil rights for all, and early in my political career I became a supporter of education for a group that had received little advocacy over the decades: individuals with disabilities. The Individuals with Disabilities Education Act, passed in 1975, remains the largest unfunded education mandate, highlighting the shameful dearth of funds and further blighting Congress's ability to make a promise and keep it.

Prior to chairing the Education Subcommittee, I was indignant that funding for IDEA was being ignored. The IDEA mandate, as intended by Congress, called for a partnership between states and the federal government whereby the feds would pay 40 percent of costs with the remainder provided by the states. Because Congress had never lived up to that promise, states and localities were having to chop away at their education budgets for all children. It was a heavy burden in Vermont, and it sickened me to think that the wealthiest nation in the world couldn't make good on its financial commitment to the progressive notion that all children in our society need a chance at a decent education. I still can't fathom how a country built on the promise of human potential would deny any child a shot at reaching his or hers.

Once I obtained a position on the Senate committee responsible for education, I used every opportunity to make this point, including initiating a one-man campaign for One Percent for Education. In 1993 I had been able to pass a "sense of the Senate" ruling by unanimous consent that supported increasing federal spending for education by 1 percent *each year* until a full 10 percent outlay for education had been reached. But as some will know, a sense of the Senate is a nicety and not much more. On April 5, 1995, now as chairman of the Sentae subcommittee on education, I stood at the podium, ready to make my case on the issue once again at a summit we had organized called Key to the Future. Ted Bell had come from his home in Utah to attend. Secretary of Education Richard Riley, Colorado governor Roy Romer, and Michigan governor John Engler, along with key leaders from the corporate community, were also on the panel. I was giving the opening speech to an audience of more than three hundred in a downtown Washington hotel while my words were being sent by the Department of Education's satellite live to twelve cities across the country where similar gatherings of local political, education, and business leaders had been assembled. I had even endured media training prior to this event and the coaching of well-meaning members of my staff to hone my oratory skills.

My speech was well received and became my mantra during Newt's leadership of the Republican Party. The facts still come easily to me now as I list the costs to society of not educating people—billions of dollars in remedial skill training borne by businesses each year; taxpayer dollars supporting prison inmates of whom 80 percent are high school dropouts; societal costs of drugs, crime, and welfare that accrue when half of our public high school graduates are considered functionally illiterate.

The moderator we had engaged for the education summit was Hedrick Smith, the author of the book *Rethinking America* that I think should be required reading for political leaders and educators. He was fantastic. My goal was to have the event help me delineate the direct link between the state of our national education system and the health of our economy. I figured this would be the best way to reach the conservative Republicans. I needed my colleagues to see that there had to be a strong federal role in education if we were going to be competitive. How could we not have national education standards if we were to compete against China and other nations?

The Key to the Future summit took place on the heels of the first new education law passed under the Clinton administration, the Goals 2000

Educate America Act. The law codified six national education goals set out by the governors and provided incentives for the states to set up academic standards to reach the goals. The problem was that there were many in the conservative wing of the Republican Party who wanted no federal standards for education on the grounds that that was meddling in state business. What seemed logical to me was fraught with political land mines, but I was determined to keep building a broad and bipartisan coalition for education reform and funding. And I never stopped plugging full funding for IDEA, because I knew you couldn't achieve real reform without it.

As dawn cracked one morning across a North Dakota plain in October 1995, I felt a strong sense that my work was a privilege—despite the jarring of the van in which we were riding. We were on our way to see a tiny school, Wakpala Elementary, on the Standing Rock Lakota Sioux Reservation. The school served 112 Native American students and was one of 120 that I would visit during a 10-state national education tour over the course of a year and half as part of my work on educational reform. I wanted a geographically and demographically diverse picture of U.S. education—inner-city schools as well as rural ones, including schools on Native American lands. There is no hearing I could have designed that could have had such an impact.

Prior to North Dakota, we had been to schools in Detroit, New York City, Los Angeles, and San Diego. We had taken day trips to tour Washington, D.C., and Baltimore, and had rounded out the schedule with trips to Atlanta and Jackson, Mississippi (including the Mississippi Delta). After the North Dakota trip, we also planned to visit schools in Santa Fe and Albuquerque attended by children of the Pueblo and Navajo tribes.

The inner-city schools we had seen faced plenty of challenges. In some, thirty different languages or dialects were spoken. Some students spoke no English at all, and although they may have been in tenth grade, they were reading at second-grade level *in their native language*. These students, although not mentally handicapped, were often placed inappropriately in special education classes. There were drugs, crime, and gang warfare to contend with. If families had two parents, they often were both working, and some more than one job, so if no after-school program was provided, the children were unsupervised for the dangerous stretch from three to six in the evening, when violent crime skyrockets. The transient nature of many inner-city populations caused many children to move around so much that the schools had no individual history or profile for them, making it even harder to get funding for the kind of specialized programs they needed.

We certainly have the technology and managerial ability to help the schools face such challenges. And we have examples from around the country where, through the energy of a superb superintendent and/or principal and the support of the community, a school was working miracles. The Paul Robeson Academy in Detroit, Michigan, was just one such example. The program is based on an African-American–centered curriculum combined with rigorous academic standards. Originally designed as an all-male school to address the crisis of black male identity, educators had developed numerous community-based programs for male-to-male mentoring and parental and community involvement that could serve as models for the nation if the funding were made available to replicate them. As we walked through the school, the children, all dressed in uniforms, were greeted by the principal with words like "Good morning, doctor!" or "Good morning, lawyer!" or "Good morning, CEO!" as he pumped their hands and smiled into their shining eyes.

As we drove to the reservation school, I was contemplating the enormous peach and gray sky when my eyes were drawn down to a herd of bison thundering along not far from the dirt road we were traveling, the main road to the school. My education staff assistant, Rayne Guilford, who accompanied me on the trips, was mesmerized as well. We were ill prepared for what we saw next.

We had not been anywhere as remote as the Wakpala Elementary School, located an hour and a half from Bismark using mainly dirt roads. Even in mid-October the weather was already freezing. The building was more than a hundred years old and the boiler room was still stoked with coal. A janitor was charged with checking it every hour to be sure it didn't become dangerous. Still, it was cold enough inside the school that the children had to wear coats in the classroom.

There were less then two hundred books in the library and the paint was peeling from the walls. Like many other schools we'd seen around the country, temporary buildings were being employed to house classes.

These students had to walk between buildings to class or to the cafeteria. In the winter, in the middle of Standing Rock Reservation, temperatures can average twenty below zero. The food served to us in the cafeteria for lunch was appalling—no fresh fruit or vegetables, only Department of Agriculture commodity surplus food. That would be the only food many of the children would have all day. The recreation room had undergone a massive flood, and because of inadequate resources for cleanup, it smelled so strongly of mold that it couldn't be used.

The principal and the teachers we met were hopeful for the future and committed to the children, but the poverty of the situation was over-whelming. It was as though we were in a Third World nation rather than the most abundant country on the planet.

Again, the American Congress had made a promise regarding educa-tion and had not adequately met the responsibility. In the 1800s the American government had signed treaties with Native Americans to officially claim their land. The Indians regard these treaties as sacred, since they have been agreed to in return for their sacred land. There were 119 treaties signed that "guarantee education in perpetuity" from the American government; our Public Law 100-297 affirms that education is a right and a part of the trust responsibility for the federally recognized American Indians. Although some monies were being allocated, the standard for education that we would want to have for our own children was not what I was witnessing at Standing Rock, or later on the Pueblo and Navajo reservations in New Mexico.

I could have returned to Washington entirely overwhelmed, but the tour of schools also confirmed something I had seen working beautifully in my home state. When a school becomes a center of learning and social services for an entire community, children truly benefit. I had seen that model at the H. O. Wheeler School in Burlington, Vermont, where a variety of social and education services were offered after school, on the weekends, and in the summers. These programs included literacy educa-tion, health services, expanded library hours, parenting skills, technology education, and recreational and cultural activities—all in a safe, super-vised environment. The H. O. Wheeler School became the model for a nationwide initiative that I created jointly with former congressman Steve Gunderson (R., Wis.) called the 21st Century Community Learn-ing Center's program.

The program had been included in the 1994 reauthorization of the Elementary and Secondary Education Act. The program subsequently gained the attention of the Clinton administration. By the end of the Clinton administration, 21st Century Community Learning Centers were being funded at a level close to $1 billion.

While touring the country, it was apparent to me that a holistic approach to children, families, and communities was excellent for both rural and urban areas in need. Wherever the school was a true hub for the community, strong partnerships were taking place to ensure that children were being supported on all levels. I knew I had to use my leadership to foster such partnerships.

The ugly truth was, I didn't have to go so far afield to witness the sad injustices of our education system. They were glaring at me from my backyard in the nation's capital. I first became involved in the District of Columbia schools in 1996 when I was named to a new position overseeing appropriations for D.C. One day, as I was holding an important hearing, I gaveled abruptly to wrap up the meeting. Witnesses and the media looked at me with surprise. We had at least another twenty minutes to go, but I had a very important appointment. Mark Plotkin, the excellent reporter who covers District politics locally, asked me on the record why I was cutting things short. "Because I have to go read with Diego," I answered, referring to my weekly date as reading partner with a third-grade student at a Capitol Hill elementary school around the corner from the Senate. I wasn't calculating my remark for publicity's sake. But I was glad for the press that came of it because the program for which I was a volunteer—then just seven months old—had already been a winner. Its title reflects the benefits to tutor and student alike. The literacy program is called Everybody Wins!

I usually joke about falling into the job of D.C. Appropriations chairman in the first place. I really had no idea how important the work would become to me. I had wanted to be on the committee to help leverage resources for education overall. But being that I was last on the list for committee members, number thirteen, I was lowest in seniority. The person lowest in seniority traditionally gets D.C.—and that is emblematic of the entire unfortunate circumstance in our nation's capital.

The District of Columbia is not a state or a territory but rather a "federal district" with neither the power of a state nor the full protection and patronage of the federal government. Alice M. Rivlin, former director of the Office of Management and Budget, wrote a book about the plight of D.C. entitled *The Orphaned City*, and that is an apt summation. In terms of pure democratic process and the ability to raise and control its own revenues, the District has certainly been relegated to a kind of national halfway house.

The Founding Fathers, in Article 1, Section 8 of the U.S. Constitution, gave Congress exclusive legislative authority over the District. But as the country and government grew, the District changed from a sleepy southern backwater to a small but thriving metropolis requiring local governance. President Theodore Roosevelt signed the law in 1906 that authorized the creation of an appointed board of education for D.C. public schools. That board was appointed by district court judges, not by the community at large.

It took sixty-two years for the board to become locally elected. The change came in 1968, due to the work of noted civil rights activist Julius Hobson, who charged the board with failing to provide the D.C. public school population, which was 90 percent poor and black, with the same educational opportunities given to white and affluent students.

In 1973, Congress granted the District of Columbia a limited Home Rule charter, giving citizens the right to elect a mayor and city council. Occurring on each other's heels, these major milestones in D.C. politics shortchanged Julius Hobson's dream and the children of the District. The school board became more of a political springboard to the mayor's office or the city council, and the management continuity and institutional knowledge needed to implement school reform was lost.

Congress has final approval over the entire annual budget for the District, and provides some of that money directly in the form of a federal payment. This payment, which was averaging around $600 million a year when I took the subcommittee chair, is what keeps Congress so closely tied to the District's inner workings. The year 1995 was a watershed in D.C.'s relationship with Congress because "reform" was the buzzword and few places could have seemed more ripe for it than our nation's capital.

Years of financial mismanagement in the city had precipitated a general fiscal crisis that extended to the overall management of the schools—

perceived to be politicized to the point of corruption and paralyzed by an entrenched, nepotistic bureaucracy. Political flames were fanned between the school board and the city council over who was accountable for the shortfalls in the education budget. Parent groups formed in outrage over the poor quality of education and, in particular, the corroded school building infrastructure, which kept schools from opening each year. In addition, there were huge problems with special education in the District, with many kids being identified as in need and not nearly enough teachers or programs available. The District also had horrendous transportation problems, especially in terms of getting special needs students to appropriate programs. All this was exacerbated by the skyrocketing attorneys' fees that resulted from the mess.

The mix of local D.C. politics with the overarching structure of Congress presents a series of hurdles and haggles that has kept the turnover rate for the D.C. superintendent of schools inordinately high. Even with all that took place between 1995 and today, there has been a new school superintendent practically every year, which leaves a sore leadership vacuum and general blow to morale. As I was briefed by staff about the state of District politics and the D.C. public schools, I felt a rising sense of anger and indignation.

The District of Columbia is the nation's capital. Its performance and reputation is a reflection of our country and America as a people. Think for a minute how other nations look to their capitals as centers of excellence, history, and cultural achievement. If the local Parisian government was in chaos, the mayor arrested on drug charges, the budget so badly mismanaged that the city's credit was reduced to junk bond status, and the city's public schools easily among the worst in the nation— would most of France just sit back and let it happen? When tourists come to Washington to behold the great buildings, the majestic monuments, the fireworks on the Mall, they pass by the ring of poverty on the city's northern and eastern borders. They usually stay in hotels in the neighborhoods west of the park that divides the residents by socioeconomic level and primarily by race. If they visit Capitol Hill they usually stay safely within the Capitol's policed boundaries. My own home on the Hill of twenty years is in an area that also houses persistent pockets of poverty; my daughter and I have both been mugged on our street and the house was burglarized twice.

Yes, the Mall and the many monuments to our leaders and our servicemen, the White House, and the capital's buildings are beautiful. The Botanical Gardens and the National Galleries of Art contain specimens of both natural and human beauty. But this is not enough. The underlying disparity between the haves and the have-nots that one can find on many sides streets surrounding these symbols of our greatness is a microcosm of what ails our country. Although crime and poverty are nothing new in any urban area, Washington, D.C., is a special case. Here it is clear that the root of disparity is in the public school system, and for the schools in the nation's capital to be a crying shame is a blight every American has to bear. If we can't hold the nation's capital up as all that is great and possible in our land, we really have a sham going on, and in the case of our federal district, I believe Congress and the White House are ultimately responsible.

As a longtime resident of the city and someone who is committed to education, I wanted to take responsibility and make a difference. The time was right. Mayor Marion Barry's tenure had certainly garnered plenty of negative press for the District, and the lamentable condition of its school system had also been fairly well publicized.

As a result of these situations, the federal budget passed in 1995 contained the District of Columbia Financial Responsibility and Management Assistance Act, which effectively stripped the District's elected officials of any power or authority until concrete improvements were made. Strict measures were put in place in the form of a Financial Control Board appointed by Congress. The board was charged with restoring the District's financial solvency and improving all city services, including public education. I had helped craft a specific part of the law that ensured reform measures for the public schools. That part of the law had been contentious, as some of my conservative colleagues pushed for private school vouchers to be included in the package. I was, and am still, deeply opposed to siphoning resources from the public school system, especially before a thorough audit of the system had been undertaken. The compromise I was able to get expanded the number of charter schools in the city. Again, my Republican colleagues were grousing at me as the education community was applauding.

I knew we would get some action from these changes, and I was also prepared for negative local reaction. While some local political officials protested the usurping of home rule, I think the majority of residents were relieved that there would finally be some accountability. This was especially true of the parents who were beholden to the public school system; those who couldn't take part in the rampant "middle-class flight" to the surrounding suburbs of Maryland and Virginia. I would venture to say these parents were at their wit's end, and with good reason.

Test scores in the District of Columbia were appalling. Ninety percent of fourth graders were not reading proficiently, math scores were lower than anywhere else in the country except the U.S. Virgin Islands and Guam. Dropout rates by eighth grade were the highest of any city in the nation. The level of violence in the schools was extraordinary. During my tenure over D.C., a student was murdered in one high school during school hours and the bodies of two other students were found buried on another high school's grounds—not to mention a disturbing number of stabbings and beatings. Gang and drug warfare among school-aged children was constantly in the news. And year after year, the schools could not open on time because of fire code violations and leaking roofs. The students even took to the streets in protest for not being able to start school. Their placards begged for someone to take accountability for their right to a free and appropriate education.

I made huge posters showing the students protesting and brought the posters to the Senate floor. I railed on in long tirades about the plight of the D.C. schools, especially about the infrastructure problems. I needed my colleagues to work with me to find the funds to address the capital improvements, because as more and more information came out of the Control Board's analysis, the worse the picture got. Basically the school buildings were, on average, fifty years old and had not been maintained. They all needed new roofs, among other major improvements, and the estimated cost for the entire job was $2 billion. There was no way Congress was ready to appropriate that much money without someone seriously beating the bushes.

The problem is that no one in Congress has any direct motivation to get the job done. The District has only one delegate elected to the House of Representatives and that position is nonvoting. I saw some of my colleagues rolling their eyes at me as I opened yet another floor statement about school roofs that had absolutely no votes attached to them—not in Vermont or anywhere else we all hailed from. That was fine with me. I had a plan up my sleeve to get some eyes trained on me for this effort, and it worked.

I sat down with Jeff Fox, my staffer on tax and finance issues. I wanted an analysis of the tax mechanisms used in the major tristate areas in the country. In most every instance, nonresidents who work in major cities but commute from an adjoining area pay some tax revenue to the city to support the increased volume of transportation and other city services. Although the idea of a commuter tax for D.C. had been floated at different times, it was always successfully quashed by the powerful senior lawmakers from Virginia and Maryland. And then there was always the argument that any money going into D.C. would spiral uselessly into a maw of corruption. But things were changing; the Control Board was in place, congressional oversight had never been more stringent, and an urgent, concrete need had been identified for fixing the educational system, beginning with the school buildings.

On June 17, 1997, I introduced a bill to "provide a regional education and workforce training system in the metropolitan Washington area, to improve the school facilities for the District of Columbia, and to fund such activities in part by an income tax on non-resident workers to be offset by tax credits."

The next day my phone rang. It was Senator John Warner, a Republican from Virginia. He wanted to meet to talk about my bill, and would it be all right for him to bring two representatives from Virginia—Tom Davis, also a Republican, and Frank Wolf, a Democrat? I also heard from my friends Barbara Mikulski and Connie Morella, both Maryland Democrats, within the week. An article came out in the *Washington Post* with "commuter tax" in the headline. Now things were cooking.

Before long, many more eyes were focused on the financial needs of the District schools. The Clinton administration took a leadership role in involving the entire executive branch in a D.C. revitalization plan. Trent Lott appointed a congressional task force on D.C. revitalization that met through that summer and fall as various city services and systems were to be subsumed by the federal government to free up other funds. The Army Corps of Engineers took a lead role in fixing the schools and reporting progress back to the task force.

You could say my bill went nowhere, for no commuter tax was levied. John Warner, a longtime friend, thanked me for helping him to get reelected. He and his staff had been intrinsic in the task force work, as had the other regional representatives on the revitalization team. But as the saying goes, "all politics is local," and Warner was thankful for the anticommuter tax platform I had provided. I was just pleased that schools were going to be able to start on time the following fall. And although my chairmanship of the D.C. subcommittee had expired, I had become involved in several projects that cemented me to the cause of the D.C. public schools.

While the city's political and fiscal leadership seemed on track, the schools still struggled for resources and reform.

One of the things I wanted to achieve from my national education tour was to bring innovative ideas and programs from around the country to D.C. It would take all kinds of best practices to make the nation's capital a model for education, and I wanted to show some exciting examples of how an entire community could work together to help children.

Literacy is concern number one, in the District and the nation at large. I discovered the Everybody Wins! program while touring schools in New York City. Speaking to city and school officials, I had heard over and over about the pressing need for literacy improvement, class size reduction, and academic mentoring. Manhattan was a microcosm for the country. Kids who weren't learning to read were being pushed through the system anyway, a practice known as "social promotion." If a child hasn't learned to read by the third grade, and receives no remedial attention, the damage is done. From first to third grades you learn to read, from third grade on you read to learn.

At that time the Department of Education had just released national reading statistics that showed that 51 percent of the students who graduated from high school and who were not going on to attend college were considered "functionally illiterate." And the statistics for D.C. were well below average. Functionally illiterate means unable to read and comprehend a newspaper article, unable to read and process a basic math question, and unable to read and follow a bus schedule. That meant that an appalling number of students would be unemployable above the most basic, manual labor positions. Even jobs in the dwindling manufacturing sector were coming to rely upon technology that required a basic level of literacy.

A man named Arthur Tannenbaum founded Everybody Wins! in New York to provide a critical need: adults reading aloud with children in the early grades. Tannenbaum, a retired businessman, and his wife, Phyllis, a former schoolteacher, organized reading mentors from the business community to go into local elementary schools on their lunchtime to read books with kids. On Wall Street and in midtown, one lunch hour a week, employees from huge firms such as Bear-Sterns, Goldman Sachs, Colgate Palmolive, and the *New York Times* were making their way to schools to share books, friendship, and the love of reading and learning.

I asked Arthur to come to D.C. to see how we could start the program. I knew the fundamental benefits of reading aloud. Academic research shows how critical out-loud reading is to language development. But I was also embroiled that winter of 1995 in trying to build support for the District public schools. It is one thing to talk about a problem, another to see for yourself. To get leaders of a community to go into the elementary schools on a regular basis would be a way to build a very important bridge across sectors of the capital community that had little connection. I was convinced I had to launch this program. I called my colleague Paul Simon (D., Ill.), a good friend and supporter of education. I wanted to form a bipartisan group of senators who could lend a little staff time and maybe even some of their own time to read. I wasn't disappointed.

Everybody Wins! D.C. was launched in March 1995 at a small elementary school on Capitol Hill. Forty Senate staffers and a handful of senators were the first reading partners. The program has grown to be the largest literacy and mentoring program in the Washington metropolitan area, serving twenty-seven Title I elementary schools with seventeen hundred reading partners across the region.

I have been reading every week since the start in 1995. Ted Kennedy has been my Democratic partner in leading the program since Paul Simon's retirement, and I usually see Ted at the school reading to his partner every week that we are in session. The kids don't really know the difference between a senator and anybody else, which is terrific for us. It's nice to leave budget wrangling or the stress of an impeachment trial to focus on Blues Clues or dinosaurs for a while. As any parent or teacher knows, the perspective of a second grader can be preciously refreshing. It also reminds me why I am doing my job.

The success of Everybody Wins!, now operating in more than twenty cities throughout the country, including Vermont, is built on leadership and support from the corporate community. One of my main goals in launching the program was to give the business sector another direct vehicle to get involved in education and help schools meet needed reforms.

If it weren't for the great game of golf, I wouldn't have been able to get the attention of so many corporate leaders. There are so many charitable causes, and quite honestly, I was a lesser-known public servant (to put it mildly) before the events of May 2001. Even in places where you would think I might get some respect as a U.S. senator, I am often identified in humbling terms, such as in 1993, at a reunion of the officers from the USS *McNair*. The newsletter prior to the event lamented that the president wasn't going to speak to the group. "The best we will probably be able to do is have an obscure senator from a small state," it said.

I needed a way to draw attention to my cause and to support expanding Everybody Wins! to more children in D.C. I thought of the PGA Tour as a way to pique the curiosity of the corporate decision-makers in town.

Tim Finchem, the commissioner of the PGA Tour, is a generous and astute executive who responded to my request for help beyond my hopes. Tim and his senior staff member Richard Bowers put the word out to the players that an event was taking shape in Washington to support children's literacy and personal appearances were needed. We called the event Links to Literacy and the first year Chi Chi Rodriguez was the keynote speaker, describing his road to success from a poor childhood where education and determination shaped his well-known future. During the following years, Raymond Floyd, Davis Love III, Jim Colbert, Fred Funk, and the late Payne Stewart who was so fantastically enthusiastic, all came to Washington to plug away for Everybody Wins! D.C.

I enjoyed these events immensely also because the spirit of bipartisanship and camaraderie was so great. The Singing Senators, the quartet that Senators John Ashcroft, Larry Craig, Trent Lott, and I formed in 1995, was always a feature during the cocktail reception. There would be a live auction of golf memorabilia conducted by Conrad Burns (R., Mont.), who had been a professional cattle auctioneer at one time. One of the funnier moments I can recall was having Ted Kennedy introduce the Singing Senators to a packed room at the last Links to Literacy in 1999. Politics aside, charisma and good humor carried the day to the delight of the crowd and I was proud to be at the center of it.

The national education tour also catalyzed an after-school fitness and life skills program called Operation FitKids that I started in a partnership with American University, and a regional education and workforce development program called PREP, the Potomac Regional Education Partnership.

I first saw the model for PREP when I was out visiting schools in Long Beach, California, where a dynamic woman named Judy Seal is charged by the Long Beach Unified School District with maintaining an active partnership between the K-12 schools, the business community, and the institutions of higher education to create what is known as "seamless education." This is the notion that all phases of a child's education are linked together so that at each step the student is well prepared for the next. It seems incredible to contemplate that such an articulation between educators wouldn't exist, but it often doesn't. What is especially impressive about the Long Beach model is the way the entire community and the business community are communicating and responding together to support K-12 education reform. I have been able to lead the creation of PREP because of the Long Beach example.

These ongoing public-private partnerships have been a way to bring additional resources to the region and raise the public's awareness of what is needed in the District of Columbia. We can't have a world-class education system in America without having a world-class education system in our nation's capital.

CHAPTER 18

Again the Maverick: Health Care
and Impeachment

JUST AS THE REPUBLICAN Party has become more conservative nationally, so, too, has Vermont's GOP. Fortunately, there were still enough moderates from both sides of the party that I felt comfortable attending an August 1992 fact-finding trip to the former Yugoslavia instead of attending the Republican National Convention.

I had been very distressed about the growing unrest in the region and wanted to arm myself with information to determine if there was a way to condemn the violence there, especially the reprehensible acts of the Serbian and Bosnian Serb armies against Bosnian civilians, without committing U.S. ground troops into the fray. I not only feared a loss of American lives but also believed that we had not used humanitarian aid and international monitoring efforts to their fullest effect. I was one of four members of the Foreign Relations Committee to oppose a resolution to send ground troops into the region. When the motion got to the Senate floor, the more moderate senators like myself were able to modify the motion so that U.S. troops would only be engaged in conjunction with a U.S.-approved cease-fire agreement. Subsequently, Senator George Mitchell (D., Maine) asked me to accompany him and four other senators to assess conditions. I came back convinced that sanctions on Serbia should be tightened but that the situation would not benefit from a unilateral introduction of U.S. troops. For the next several years I strongly supported lifting the arms embargo against Bosnia, but at the same time, over and over, in letters to the president, to Secretary of State Madeleine Albright, and in speeches on the Senate floor, I stressed the importance of humanitarian aid deliveries, war crime tribunals, the need for strong NATO air support, and awareness of the terrible repressive acts in Kosovo.

I had thought there would be a change in attitude on defense issues under a Clinton administration, but that was not a given. In the summer of 1993 I learned that the Clinton administration did not plan to send an envoy to the United Nations Test Ban Amendment Conference. After a number of us senators exerted considerable pressure on the White House, Clinton changed his mind and sent an envoy.

Later, when we learned that China planned to detonate a nuclear weapon, breaking the de facto international moratorium, several of my colleagues and I wrote to Clinton urging him not to resume testing even if China did. We also wrote the French parliament with a similar plea. Throughout 1995 I remained one of the few Republicans to urge the president to maintain the zero-threshold posture and insist on a comprehensive, zero-yield test ban in the Geneva negotiations. The moderates again made a similar plea to the French and believed these negotiations helped achieve a comprehensive test ban treaty.

President Clinton sent the Comprehensive Test Ban Treaty to the Senate in the fall of 1997. Alas, I was one of only four Republicans to vote to ratify the treaty, which failed significantly short of the needed sixty-seven votes.

I write this on the day that the *Bulletin of the Atomic Scientists* moved the hands of the doomsday clock, a symbolic gauge of the threat of nuclear annihilation, two minutes closer to midnight. It is now set at 11:53. As I hear that news, I think about how, in the years following the Cold War until the heinous acts of September 11, my fellow moderates and I argued over and over that global stability is essential not only to our economic health at home but all over the planet. I believe the key to that stability is support for U.N. peacekeeping operations and ratification of treaties to lessen the stockpiling and development of nuclear weapons and other weapons of mass destruction, and that an awareness that proactive steps to improve the lives of people and to forestall crises before they begin are the best ways to maintain world peace.

I had begun my work on a national health care package in 1990 when I traveled to Canada with staff members to gather firsthand information on the workings of the Canadian Medicare system. This was part of my overall inquiry into how it was that other nations had been able to offer universal health care without bankrupting their citizens. Many other senators were also working to understand the problem and we freely exchanged ideas. My plan, which I called MediCORE, began to emerge slowly. The term reflected my belief that all U.S. residents were entitled to a core of basic health care benefits, with concentration on preventive and primary care, as a matter of right. I envisioned an independent Federal MediCORE Board, patterned on the Federal Reserve Board, which would oversee the program. Health delivery plans would be developed and administered by the states under the federal guidelines. My plan called for freedom of choice for consumers and providers with strong encouragement for allowing competitive market forces to set fees. In the early 1990s I sought input—from schools of public health, doctors, the American Medical Association, and health officials from foreign countries—and established a Health Care Reform Advisory Committee in Vermont comprised of twenty-five people with expertise in health care issues. We held a health care conference in Vermont on August 6, 1991, inviting national experts on the issues as well as average Vermonters. What we wanted was to hear what people thought their government ought to do for them in terms of providing access to health care and to gather as many ideas as possible on how it might be done. More comment was sought—from labor groups, industry, educators, and Vermont governor Howard Dean, who also happens to be a medical doctor married to a doctor. It became clear to me that there was overwhelming support both in Vermont and the nation for a major overhaul of our health care system and strong support for a federal program that would ensure basic health care to everyone, regardless of ability to pay. I brought Peter Caldwell, a classmate at Yale, on board to assist me in drafting my plan.

It took until the following October to revise our bill for introduction into the Senate. Essentially, I set five goals: straightforward and equitable financing, cost control at current levels, equal entitlement to all U.S. residents, primary state responsibility for design and administration balanced with federal financial support and policy guidance, and development of state delivery plans that could provide greater choice and market competition. The Tuck School of Business at Dartmouth rated our bill as the best they had reviewed from the dozen or so promulgated in the early 1990s.

In October 1993, President Clinton delivered the administration's thirteen-hundred-page health care legislation. Because the Clinton package shared many of the goals of MediCORE, I had publicly promised first lady Hillary Rodham Clinton that I would cosponsor the bill. As it turned out, I was the first and only Republican to do so.

As a senior member of the Senate Labor and Human Resources Committee, I sat in on the more than sixty hearings held on health care reform in the 103rd Congress. Senator Edward M. Kennedy (D., Mass.), who chaired the committee, held one of the national hearings in Brattleboro, Vermont. Meanwhile, I took part in a bipartisan Senate Working Group on Mental Health and Substance Abuse, where I continued pressing for parity for those suffering from these issues in whatever national health care plan might emerge. On June 9, 1994, the Senate Labor Committee chaired by Kennedy was the first committee in Congress to pass a comprehensive health care reform package. It included many of the essential ideas that my MediCORE proposal favored, including protections of rural health clinics from bureaucratic red tape and rewards for states that begin work on controlling health care costs.

The bill saw many amendments through the summer, but in late September of that year the majority leader, Senator George Mitchell, ultimately abandoned the possibility of the Senate voting on health care reform. Those of us who believed in the importance of basic universal health care didn't give up the battle easily. Working with other moderate Democrats and Republicans, we came up with a bipartisan bill that we called the "mainstream proposal," which relied heavily on incentives in the marketplace to drive down health care costs. In general, our proposals differed from the Clinton proposal in that ours had more balance between state and federal rights. We believed that the federal government should provide uniform guidelines to the states but that the states could best judge how to fit the central elements of the health care delivery system into a program that would meet its citizens needs.

When I ran for reelection in 1994, my two Democrat opponents were Douglas Costle, the former head of the federal Environmental Protection Agency and a president of Vermont Law School, and state senator Jan Backus, a Democrat from Windsor County. Backus and Costle were attacking me as an outsider and saying I hadn't been effective. What a bind to be in? Yes, I'd been independent and voted against Republican efforts as often as not, but I didn't think I'd been ineffective. Who came to my rescue but none other than the standard-bearer of liberal Democrats, Senator Kennedy. He publicly praised my work in forcing bipartisan discussion of health care reform and getting our bill out of committee. I don't know whether Kennedy helped or hurt my candidacy in Vermont—it's just as likely that Vermonters resented his intrusion into our affairs as they appreciated his praise for me. I won reelection but, alas, the health care debate got mired in partisan bickering that I often found disheartening.

Assuming chairmanship of the Senate's Committee on Labor and Human Resources had placed me in a good position to try to do more to improve health care for Americans. I was fortunate to have a strong staff that included individuals with backgrounds in federal and state health administration, as well as a number of clinicians. In fact, since I've been able to attract a Robert Wood Johnson Health Policy Fellow to work on the committee for each of the past six years, the program has described assignment to my office as a tenured position.

My first major health-related success as chairman of the committee came on November 21, 1997, when President Clinton signed the first comprehensive revision of the Food and Drug Administration's (FDA) law in decades. The bill, which I had authored, aimed to reform laws governing drugs, foods, medical devices, cosmetics, and over-the-counter medicine in response to concerns on the part of patients and their physicians, in Vermont and around the country, that the FDA was too slow to allow access to safe and effective medicines and technologies that had been available for years in Europe. Delays in the FDA product review process was also often cited as a reason for drug and device companies deciding to relocate research and manufacturing efforts overseas.

The process leading to enacting of the legislation was difficult since I had strong disagreements with my good friend Ted Kennedy over many of the key components of the legislation. Fortunately, I was able to work closely with many of the other Democrats on the committee, including Chris Dodd of Connecticut, Tom Harkin of Iowa, and Barbara Mikulski of Maryland, to build strong bipartisan support for the legislation.

During my chairmanship, I was also very active in another area that fell under the HELP Committee's jurisdiction: managed care reform. I strongly supported enacting patients' rights protections, like those enjoyed by Vermonters, for all Americans. I believed we could provide the key protections that consumers want without adding significant new costs and increasing litigation.

In 1998 I introduced, with Senator Joseph Lieberman (D., Conn.), the Health Care Quality, Education, Security, and Trust Act, which came to be known as the Health Care QUEST Act. This was the first managed-care bill sponsored by a Republican and was designed to make two important improvements to our health care system. First, it called for comparative information about health plans so that enrollees and employers could make more informed decisions and better understand their coverage. And second, the bill provided all enrollees with an independent external appeals process to resolve disputes and guarantee that providers would inform patients of treatment options.

I believed that this package of reforms would have enhanced health care quality and would have provided necessary consumer protections without increasing costs. I thought it was the best we could do given the negative atmosphere in Washington. Unfortunately, the HMOs and the Republican leadership fought even the modest proposals contained in the QUEST Act. Today, however, I'm sure they would be happy to embrace my proposal given the far more costly and intrusive alternatives currently being considered.

On this issue, I increasingly found myself in the position of being a significant influence in shaping the Republican position and strategy. The first floor action on health issues took place in 1999, when the Senate passed the Patients' Bill of Rights Plus Act, which I had introduced in January.

On October 6, the House passed its companion bill and a Senate/House conference committee was appointed. As chair of the committee with primary jurisdiction over these issues, I was appointed as one of the twelve Senate conferees to iron out the differences between the House and Senate bills. I was committed to working with the other conferees and with President Clinton to bring this legislation to a point where we could reach bipartisan agreement on responsible, low-cost legislation to regulate managed-care plans. If so, we would have, for the first time, a new federal cause of action against a health plan provider or HMO if they failed to comply with the decision of an independent external medical reviewer, or if their decision to delay care caused harm to an individual. The most important part of the Senate version was the creation of a new, independent external appeals process that would allow a patient's health care professional to recommend the best treatment and serve as the patient's advocate. I was committed to keeping that in the bill.

I enjoyed working with my Republican conferees on this issue—especially Bill First (Tennessee), the only physician in the Senate, and Don Nickles (Oklahoma), the chairman of the conference committee. We held daily meetings beginning at 8:45 A.M.—immediately after my rehearsals with Trent Lott and the other Singing Senators. An amazing amount of work went into the conference discussions and we found ourselves immersed in a level of detail that is unusual for senators.

As we prepared this legislation, I had three goals in mind: first, to give families the protections they want and need; second, to ensure that medical decisions are made by physicians in consultation with their patients and are based on the best scientific evidence; and finally, to keep the cost of this legislation low, so it did not result in someone being unable to get health care coverage.

Unfortunately, the conference committee collapsed under partisan fighting and the 106th Congress adjourned without an agreement.

Clinton suffered a tremendous defeat when his and his wife's universal health care proposal failed to gain momentum in Congress. That failure, of course, had followed on the debacle of the "don't ask, don't tell" approach to whether openly gay people could serve in the military and signaled the bitter years to come. Of course, the Clintons brought much of this on themselves, but the Republican party, I fear, should take some of the blame for the nasty, partisan politics that are the legacy of the Clinton years.

But despite these disappointments, early in 107th Congress under George W. Bush, I joined with Senators Bill First and John Breaux (D., La.) in introducing my third managed-care legislation, the Bipartisan Patients' Bill of Rights Act of 2001. Since it met the patient protection principles outlined by President Bush in his campaign speeches, I felt confident that he would sign our bill into law.

Later in 2000, both the Senate and the House again acted and, with the major exception of more expansive liability provisions in the Senate-passed measure, the House and Senate have passed virtually identical legislation. After more than five years of debate, I anticipated that Congress would pass a Patients' Bill of Rights that would be signed by the president.

However, that initiative still has not been enacted as of this writing in spring of 2002.

My other major committee assignment during the Clinton years was on the Senate Finance Committee. It was a unique opportunity to coordinate discussion between two committees that have historically competed with each other over the jurisdiction of health care. One of the areas we tackled was Medicare, whose structure has remained essentially unchanged since the program's establishment in 1965. In 1997, Medicare was spending more money than it received. There were repeated warnings that the Hospital Insurance Trust Fund would go insolvent as the baby-boom generation entered the program. This would obviously have devastating consequences for our nation's elderly, and I was committed to preventing this prediction from becoming a reality.

With my support, Medicare reform legislation was overwhelmingly passed in the summer of 1997 as part of the Balanced Budget Act. The measure ensured the solvency of the Hospital Insurance Trust Fund until the year 2025.

At the same time, I also recognized that the children of America needed better access to health care. Nearly ten million children had no health insurance. Many of these children live in families with parents who work for very small companies or who simply do not make enough money to afford health insurance.

In order to help address this national problem, I cosponsored both the Hatch-Kennedy CHILD Act and supported Senator Olympia Snowe's efforts to promote the Children's Health Insurance Provides Security Act, or CHIPS. The CHILD Act would have established a state health insurance grant program and the CHIPS Act encouraged states to provide uniform Medicaid coverage up to 150 percent of poverty for children of all ages. These two bills were ultimately combined to create

SCHIP, the State Children's Health Insurance Program that has been so successful in ensuring that our nation's uninsured children have health care coverage.

The initiative provided $24 billion to states over the next five years—with $8 billion to come from an increase in the tobacco excise tax. Under SCHIP, states are able to use their allotment of funds to expand or enhance their current Medicaid program or provide for state health insurance programs to cover children. I believe using an increased cigarette tax as the revenue source for this program is especially appropriate since it will have the added health benefit of helping to deter children from starting to smoke in the first place.

The Balanced Budget Act of 1997 also mandated the use of a new Medicare prospective payment system for home health care, beginning in fiscal year 2000. The change was needed because many home health agencies were ripping off the system through overcharges. In the interim, Congress passed an across-the-board cut of 15 percent in Medicare payments for 1997 and 1998.

I was truly concerned about how this interim cut would impact Vermont and other areas where home health care charges were based on actual costs. I feared the interim payment system could bankrupt the thirteen Medicare-certified nonprofit home health agencies in Vermont. The weighted interim payment system favored providers whose costs were extravagant in 1997 but it penalized providers in states like Vermont where the costs were low. I was concerned that Vermont's seniors could lose access to needed home health services.

In October 1998, I cosponsored the Medicare Home Health Fair Payment Act of 1998, introduced by former senator William Roth (R., Del.). The bill sought to revise the beneficiary and visit-payment limits for health services under the Medicare program. The new formula was budget neutral since it cut payments for some of the highest-cost agencies while increasing payments for low-cost agencies. I had considerable leverage in the debate because I was a member of both committees with jurisdiction in the issue—Appropriations and Health, Education, Labor, and Pensions.

I was doing my best to promote the bill—speaking to as many senators as I could and bringing the cause directly to Trent Lott. I finally told him that I would do everything within my powers to ensure the passage of this home health legislation before Congress adjourned, even if it meant the time-consuming reading of the entire Omnibus Appropriations Bill.

When the Constitution was written, great care was given to make sure each state reserved powers to protect its rights. This was done by vesting in the Senate, and in individual senators, the power to protect their state and/or citizens from abuse. The most renowned and obvious way to try to get one's way is to filibuster. A filibuster occurs when a senator takes the floor of the Senate and simply keeps on talking, refusing to give up the floor to any senator or to let the normal business of the floor resume, until he or she gets the desired result. This of course creates havoc for the leadership and also takes huge personal effort, even if you have like-minded senators to help. If you do not have the cooperation of the leadership, it is basically impossible to succeed, except under rare circumstances. However, if you do have the cooperation of the leadership, or even a committee chairman, it can be most effective.

Another approach is to wait until the end of the year or the legislative session, when members have travel plans, vacations, and speaking commitments lined up. If a senator pulls a delay tactic late in the session, in particular on the final day, he can shift the pressure to the leadership to help attain the desired goal.

I was getting nowhere with the Fair Payment Act, so I threatened a filibuster. The last important bill of a session is usually the Omnibus Appropriations Bill, which included the disastrous cut I was trying to remedy. The Omnibus Appropriations Bill is a multibillion-dollar bill covering a multitude of solutions to various problems that were worked out at the last minute in a House-Senate conference. These have to be approved by both houses before Congress can go home. In this case the bill was about three feet high, literally thousands of pages. Every senator has the right to have the bill read aloud. This would not only take hours but days to read. Here was my filibuster material: I insisted on having the huge bill read in its entirety. I had plenty of volunteers to keep the bill being read while I went into the back room to work on a compromise. Senator Lott and Speaker Gingrich had appointed a conference committee consisting of myself and four other Republicans—Senators Roth and Phil Gramm (Texas) and Congressmen William Thomas (California) and Michael

Bilirakis (Florida)—to try to work out a compromise. Senator Gramm and I were both on the Finance Committee—with him being the most conservative member and me the most liberal—and the debate came down to the two of us.

In this kind of standoff we're often asked to find the agreeable middle, which wasn't easy. This required finding savings in other areas to meet the budget demands and provide the additional funds for the Medicare program. We finally agreed on a system that the leadership could accept. Our solution was to allow people who win the lottery to get all their winnings immediately, rather than over time. This quick source of tax revenues would quickly balance the budget. It was a great compromise: The budget was balanced, the home health care agencies were saved, Congress could adjourn. Clinton signed the Omnibus Appropriations Bill, which included the home health care changes I'd demanded. Later, the IRS made changes in this solution but the changes did not affect the home health care agencies.

I was quite fond of Bill Clinton and also very disappointed. I saw him as a brilliant man who had overcome a hardscrabble childhood and represented the first of the baby boomers to assume the highest office. He brought with him the freshness of youth and a promise of great social change. His failure to fully acquaint himself with the workings of Washington and to plunge too quickly into highly contentious battles without first forging ideological and practical coalitions can be blamed on the exuberance of victory and the conviction of his ideals. But it was the opposite, a lack of personal conviction and ethics, coupled with an inability to simply admit the truth and be done with it, that resulted in his impeachment.

Clinton's second term was a difficult time for me. We accomplished so much in those years—a raft of educational reforms that included more money for grants for needy college students, a lowering of interest rates for college loans, reauthorization and funding for Head Start, vocational education and literacy programs. We won $500,000 to help Vermont's volunteer fire departments, approval of the Northeast dairy compact, $7 million to the Veterans Administration hospital in Vermont, secure funding for home health care and nursing home care, and approval of a bill to help speed new drugs and medical devices into the marketplace.

Of course, I am happy about all these developments, but they are overshadowed by the long and divisive impeachment hearings. It was a difficult time for Liz and me as well.

In 1997, Liz was diagnosed with ovarian cancer and she told me she didn't think she was going to go through chemotherapy. I went into research mode and, armed with all the studies that showed how treatment increased the chances of survival, I was able to convince her to take her medicine, despite its toll. She is a very strong woman and recuperated very well.

Then, in early September 1997, I was involved in a rather serious car accident while driving back from the golf course at the Old Soldiers Home with my daughter Laura. We had stopped at a light when a car behind us lost its brakes and plowed into us at a good clip. Fortunately, Laura received only minor injuries but I got a serious whiplash. I was in pain but I didn't want to miss the opening debate of the Senate. The car ahead of us was full of Department of Education staff and they offered to give us a ride to the capital. My staff arranged to have a doctor examine Laura and me as soon as we arrived at the office.

I didn't get X-rayed until the first break in the session and learned that there had been some misalignment of the backbone and I would eventually need surgery.

In 1998, Liz had a heart attack, perhaps a result from the stress that the chemotherapy had placed on her body. She had joined me in D.C. taking a spring break from Vermont's long winter and had brought our dog, Kariba, with her. She was walking the dog near the Mall when she suddenly felt very strange. She hailed a cab and she and the dog headed for home. But after only a few moments she decided it might be best to stop at the Capitol and check in with the police to see if she was okay. I'm glad she did. They called the Capitol medical team, who then called an ambulance. I was notified and immediately went to George Washington University Hospital. I will never forget waiting with Liz while the medical personnel checked this and that. All of a sudden she said that everything was getting quite dim. I was holding her hand when she said, "Jim, I love you, I have had a wonderful life and if I don't make it, please don't be sad." Then she went into cardiac arrest. Again, we were lucky and she has made a full recovery. Liz is a trouper. She jokes that she's too mean to kill, but I do believe that her wonderful temperament has been an asset through these struggles.

Liz's health problems and the pain in my back and neck seemed to emphasize the tawdriness of the accusations and news reports about Paula Jones and Monica Lewinsky, the whole Linda Tripp scenario, and then the impeachment process. People all over the world were hungry. Kids weren't getting the education they needed. My wife was ill. And the U.S. Congress and all of Washington seemed to be caught up in a never-ending soap opera.

But beyond these personal hardships, I really felt torn apart by the impeachment trial and the damage it did to America, both at home and abroad. In many ways I had remained an idealist who believed that each person can make a difference and that there was value in public service. I saw both the Gingrich years and the Clinton debacle as disasters in terms of creating a positive image of political life and responsibility for young people. These times just deepened the distrust Americans had toward their politicians and further exacerbated the national apathy.

As for me, my entire political career had been spent in the middle, but now the middle felt like a big squeeze—squeezed between the GOP leadership in the Senate and the defense of the Democratic president in the White House who, quite frankly, had let me down.

The president had often referred to me as his favorite Republican senator. Just two months before the impeachment vote, at a breast cancer awareness event at the White House, he told the crowd he "used to refer to Senator Jeffords as my favorite Republican and then I was informed that I had endangered his committee chairmanship . . . and his physical well-being."

He was right in that. The Senate Republican leadership, especially Majority Leader Trent Lott, put tremendous pressure on me and other GOP senators to toe the line in order to give the appearance that the pro-impeachment forces were stronger than they actually were. One thing that was apparent to me, something that later contributed to my decision to make the switch, was the realization that one has more freedom to defy the leadership in the House of Representatives than in the Senate simply because of the numbers. It's not as if I was actually marching to their drum. In 1998, I voted with a majority of Senate

Democrats against the majority of my Republican colleagues 41 percent of the time—the highest defection rate among the GOP. I went along with the leadership and voted against a motion to dismiss impeachment charges against President Clinton. I voted in favor of a motion to depose three witnesses before the Senate. Pundits speculated at the time that I did so against the backdrop of the 2000 elections, when I would be seeking a third term as senator. As one article said, "If Jeffords had been the sole Republican to break ranks this past week, he surely would have faced a primary election challenge next year." But that was not my primary concern. As with the October Surprise decision, I felt it was better to air the evidence than to cover it up and forever leave questions unanswered.

But the testimony did little to solve my dilemma. Here I was, believing that the prosecution's case was very strong and that the president had lied. There was little doubt about that. But he had lied about something that wasn't a crime—consensual sex. Should someone be impeached for lying about something personal that wasn't a crime? Is that grounds for throwing a president out of office? More important, what kind of a standard would this establish for future presidents to be removed from office?

It was awful. I awoke every night drenched from nightmares. Liz once woke me because in my sleep I'd been shouting "Watch out for the machine guns. They're firing." I'm sure the pain medication prescribed for my ongoing back problems contributed to my condition. I often felt very disoriented and tired. I was also very worried about my wife.

It didn't help that just about my every move was being recorded for a special edition of "Dateline." The crew had set up a camera in my office, where once a day I made a kind of oral diary notation to record my emotions and responses to the ongoing impeachment drama. Because I was considered one of the Republicans most likely to vote against removal, photographers and the press were in and out of my office or camped outside at all hours of the day. Once I got stuck in a tiny elevator with a couple of staff members, two or three cameramen from "Dateline" and their equipment, and a reporter. Before we got the emergency button to work, the elevator went up several floors at what seemed like breakneck speed then fell several floors equally quickly and then back up again. When it finally stopped, we were stuck between floors for quite a long time. By then, it was about eleven-thirty at night and, quite frankly, I was exhausted. But the "Dateline" crew kept interviewing and filming.

Throughout the impeachment process, the office phones rang off the hook with constituents back home calling, each fiercely arguing one side or the other. They all had an opinion. And the question, day after day, was how was I going to vote?

As the impeachment proceedings began to wind down I became deeply concerned that Clinton would mishandle the final days. The House had impeached him; however, it was becoming clear that the Senate would not remove him from office. I was worried that the president would misunderstand that vote as clearing him of guilt. My Everybody Wins! reading partner at the time was a very intelligent young girl named Sherryl. We had been talking about the impeachment. I asked her how her friends felt about the president. I was surprised by her vehement response: "They're mad, real mad. He lied. He should be punished. He should apologize." I was sad for the president, and felt I should do what I could to make sure he understood how the children felt. I hoped he would be humble and contrite when he responded to the Senate vote.

I met with Joe Lieberman and expressed my concerns. I suggested we try and meet with the president. He agreed. Because of my work with Hillary Clinton on health care I felt at ease in talking to her. I expressed my concerns to her and my desire to meet with the president along with Joe. She said she would help. A meeting was arranged for the following evening. I was concerned about the press seeing me going into the White House and making the meeting out to be something it was not. Plans were made to prevent that. I arrived at the agreed upon time after parking near the Executive Office Building. I was ushered into a small room off the main hall leading to the upstairs. I was all alone. No one seemed to be around as I spent time examining all the items on the walls' shelves. It seemed like a long time before Joe arrived, but very soon after he did we were ushered upstairs to a sitting room. After about fifteen minutes President Clinton joined us. I explained why Joe and I wanted to talk with him, how important we felt it was that he handle the "no removal" vote with sincere apologies for what he had done. I relayed the comments of Sherryl without using her name. I asked him to keep in mind the young people who admired him but were deeply disappointed.

They were upset, as all of us were. But the accomplishments of his administration could more than overcome the disappointments if he would sincerely apologize.

We then had a lengthy discussion on the postimpeachment situation and how to handle it. The president started talking at length about Joseph Conrad's *Heart of Darkness*. It had been many years since I had read it so I had a hard time following what he was trying to say. Later, when I refreshed myself, I still had difficulty. He seemed to be saying he had been overwhelmed by the opportunities his position provided and was sorry he had let us down. We talked for well over an hour. We again urged a sincere apology. Joe and I left and went home separately. We hoped we had helped.

The president's apology speech was not all I hoped for, but I felt it was adequate. It was a relief to get back to work with the president, especially on education. There was much to do.

In the end, I concluded Bill Clinton had lied under oath and may have obstructed justice but that the offenses weren't enough to undo the two elections and that impeachment could set a devastating precedent. On February 9, 1999, I announced I would vote to acquit on both counts. I felt censure would be more appropriate and signed on to the motion to do that, which ultimately failed. During one interview, I committed one of my famous abuses of the English language by saying Clinton had committed "a noncrime crime." I was trying to explain that he'd lied under oath—a crime—about having a sexual relationship with Monica Lewinsky, a severe lapse of judgment but not a crime.

"Our Founding Fathers intended impeachment only for the greatest offenses," I told a reporter. "The facts and circumstances of this case are low and tawdry, but these same circumstances do not, in my opinion, cause his offense to rise to the level of impeachable acts. Constitutionally they do not nearly fit into the definition of either high crimes or misdemeanors."

In my official statement I acknowledged that my decision would not be a popular one; I added that "I [was] willing to go the extra mile for those of my colleagues who are still truly wrestling with these issues." For the Republicans who were losing steam for impeachment, my vote was perhaps the last straw—not just in their effort to impeach Clinton but also in their tolerance for me.

You can see the strain on my face in the "Dateline" piece. I'm surprised I sounded as coherent as I did. I was glad the piece was dramatically cut at the last minute due to new revelations in the ongoing debacle. What these were, I can no longer recall. I was more than willing to step back out of the limelight and let someone else—Ken Starr, Linda Tripp, Monica herself—be the focus of America's attentions.

CHAPTER 19

The Singing Senators

DESPITE ALL THAT has come to pass, one of the most exciting and enjoy-able experiences in the Senate was being part of the Singing Senators. It all began quite by accident. Among those who attended a birthday party/fund-raiser for Bob Smith, a Republican senator from New Hampshire, in the spring of 1995 were fellow Republicans John Ashcroft from Missouri, Trent Lott of Mississippi, and myself. With lit-tle prompting and no planning, we started singing "Happy Birthday." Connie Mack (R., Fla.) joined in the harmonizing, which gave us the idea for a quartet. We didn't sound that bad. After the event, both Trent and I enthusiastically talked up how great we sounded to our respective staffs.

Later in the summer we learned that Senator Mark Hatfield (R., Ore.) was having a seventy-third birthday party with a gathering of well-wishers. I called Trent and suggested that he, John Ashcroft, Connie Mack, and I get together to sing at his birthday. He thought it was a great idea. Connie declined to join us but fortunately Larry Craig (R., Idaho) could. Larry has a superb voice.

Unbeknownst to me, my press secretary Erik Smulson had called the congressional newspaper *Roll Call* and they sent a reporter and photogra-pher. We sang pretty well, I think, and found ourselves on the front page with the funny caption, "Sen. Hatfield's Lonely Hearts Club Band." We were called "a power quartet." The next day we got a call from a group having a fund-raiser at the Kennedy Center. Would we appear?

Appear? What a question. What were we, a performing group? Well, I guess we were because later that year, on October 22, we sang at that fund-raiser. Again, unknown to us, word got out—this time to CNN—and the next thing we knew we were on national TV. The next day the producer of the "Today Show" called to invite us on. We appeared on December 12, right before Christmas 1995, and had so much fun that we began practicing regularly and really worked on our harmony.

"Elvira" was our fame maker. We borrowed this song along with a few others from the well-known country performers the Oak Ridge Boys. Fortunately, Trent's Mississippi state director, Guy Hovis, was a most talented musician. Some of you may remember him as "the little boy" on Lawrence Welk's show. He whipped us into shape.

He had his challenges, especially with me. I was singing first tenor, a range I had never sung before. We all needed a bit of Guy's attention, although Larry and John both had experience and musical talent. I had not trained for public performance or public singing. My last performance had been in high school. The music had to be rearranged to match our talents—or at least not overdramatize our shortcomings, especially mine, in terms of range.

Guy donated many, many hours helping us reach reasonable success—time I'll always be grateful for. But our main job was to help people have fun—and you don't need much training for that.

We had a bit of a scare when we got a call from the Oak Ridge Boys. We had been using their music without permission. Were they angry? To the contrary, they loved it and wanted to sing *with* us. Thus, on Monday evening, April 22, 1995, the Oak Ridge Boys joined us at the Capitol in an event that was so wonderfully American it's almost impossible to describe. There were the four senators—sounds like a fifties rock group—singing next to considerably hairier professional musicians—Duane Allen, an avid basketball player and antique car and motorcycle buff; "Mountain Man" William Lee with his long gray hair and beard and appreciation of Native American people; Joe Bonsall, a Phillies die-hard who loves the boating life almost as much as music; and Richard Sterban, an owner of the Nashville Sounds, the White Sox AAA team. What a country we live in—four senators and this group of interesting country musicians, playing together in the U.S. Capitol. The caption above the photograph of us that appeared the next day in the *Hill*, a Capitol Hill newspaper, said "Congressional Harmony."

But the high point of the evening occurred after we had sung to our fellow senators. After the performance, we took the Oak Ridge Boys on a little tour of the Capitol. We moved slowly toward the rotunda. The building had been closed and it was dark. Someone, I'm not sure who, started vocalizing. Then, spontaneously, we started singing God Bless America. When we finished, our words were reverberating up to the Capitol dome and back again. We were all dumbstruck. It was a spiritual moment.

The following morning I was to escort the Oak Ridge Boys and their spouses to the top of the dome. This is an often-requested but rarely granted request. Usually a member of Congress must accompany the tour to keep down the number of tours, which are long and a bit dangerous. I have made the trek only a couple of times. However, since I have a hidden desire to fly off of high places, it is not without some trepidation that I went. One of the Oak Ridge Boys' wives had the opposite problem, equally nerve-racking. She was afraid of heights. She was also exceptionally attractive. I thought I must not let her miss this opportunity so I went up with her holding tightly on to my arm.

Obviously, we managed to make it up and down. I bid the group adieu, happy to have performed my various duties so well. The next morning, as I showered, I noticed the deep blue bruises in the shape of her fingertips on my arm. Liz got quite the kick out of that. We went on to have many other appearances with the Oak Ridge Boys, at fund-raisers for Republicans and other groups.

But our next big ego builder was singing at the Republican Convention for Bob Dole in 1996. When we appeared, the audience roared. We were well aware that it was not who we were but what we were—a Senate novelty act—that made people love us. Yet we certainly didn't want to blow it with twenty million possible viewers watching and listening. We did our best and it went off without a hitch. Trent was especially upbeat with his banter. The applause was loud enough that we figured we'd been a hit; we later learned that the major TV networks had used almost all of our time to run ads.

During the five years that the Singing Senators were together, we usually practiced in Trent Lott's hideaway office almost every Tuesday and Thursday we were in Washington. Few people know that the members of Congress have an official office and also another lesser-known office, usually called hideaways, where we go to get away from the press, have more private meetings, or simply to be alone.

We had quite a thrill when we appeared with the Oak Ridge Boys at the Charley Pride Theater in Branson, Missouri, on a stage famous for musical performances, the following September 21, 1997. Unfortunately, I wasn't in the best of shape because of my car accident. I had decided to put the surgery off because my HELP committee was conducting the first serious review of the Food and Drug Administration and I wanted to stay with that until it was completed.

But my back pain was terrible. I wanted to go to Missouri for John Ashcroft's fund-raiser—and, of course, I wanted to perform at Branson. As it turned out, the Oak Ridge Boys took care of everything, organizing places for me to rest between events up to the big night at Branson. Once on that stage, I forgot my condition, but when we finished, I was finished. I returned to Washington and made arrangements for the operation that has helped me get active again.

The Singing Senators really came to end on December 4, 2000. Larry Craig had come to my office to ask for my support for the chairmanship of the GOP Policy Committee. I considered Larry a friend, which is why I answered him honestly and told him no, I'd be voting for Pete Domenici from New Mexico. I explained that I thought Pete would provide a more moderate voice, which I felt we dearly needed in the Senate. The next day, I voted for Pete.

Although John Ashcroft's failure to be reelected to the Senate and his subsequent nomination for attorney general would have meant the end of our little group sooner or later, I was never invited to sing with the Singing Senators after my vote for Domenici.

I was a little dense on the snub. Over the weekend leading up to President Bush's inauguration, for example, we were scheduled to play with the Oak Ridge Boys at several events. My staff and I kept calling to nail down time and place and kept getting vague answers. Finally, during the inauguration, our family was attending an event. When it was announced that the Oak Ridge Boys and the Singing Senators were going to perform, my daughter-in-law Maura literally elbowed our way up to the stage. The Oak Ridge Boys, who did not know I was now persona non grata with my fellow quartet members, were thrilled to see me. They quickly helped me onto the stage and it wasn't until I learned that I had missed two previous performances that I realized I'd been cast out from the inner circle, or that small part of it that I'd been allowed to inhabit as a member of the Singing Senators.

It was petty grammar school stuff. I was stunned. But it was a precursor to the insults, large and small, that brought home to me how far I was from this Republican Party to which I had belonged for my entire political career.

CHAPTER 20

The Days Before the Switch

I HAD BEEN QUIETLY mulling over my growing discontent with the direction of the party throughout the spring, but contrary to my usual habit of talking decisions over with my staff, I was keeping my own counsel. Of course, the signs of my discontent were obvious enough.

The GOP saw the election of President George W. Bush and the thin grasp Republicans maintained on the House and Senate as a wonderful opportunity to fundamentally change the direction of government. I did, too, but only because I was hopeful that we could, as the president had promised, change the tone of Washington and escape the poisonous relationship that had grown up between the Clinton administration and the Republicans in Congress.

Instead, the Bush administration headed down the very same path that the Clinton administration had trod eight years earlier, taking a plurality of the vote as a mandate and attempting to reward its political base with a largely partisan budget. President Bush publicly drew a line in the sand, signaling that whatever else happened, the budget must contain $1.6 trillion in tax cuts over the next ten years. Privately, the White House made clear that any Republican who thought otherwise was morally or mentally deficient—a foreshadowing of the lock-step mentality of the war on terrorism.

Just a few years previously, President Clinton's proposed budgets, which perennially called for familiar and unachievable budgetary savings while also supporting pet projects, were greeted with Republican howls and equal measures of incredulity. The election of President Bush had changed the dynamic considerably. Instead of greeting the president's budget submission with derision, Republicans acted as if it bordered on the divine. For the first time since the Eisenhower administration, Republicans found themselves in control of both houses of Congress and responsible for enacting the president's agenda. For Republicans serving in Congress, this was the first time in their careers they would have the opportunity to do so, and they were not about to let it slip from their grasp.

Not only had the Republicans' fortunes changed but so, too, had the economy, which had been growing steadily over the last few years. Deficits were no longer the hammer that would keep spending in check as they had through the Reagan, Bush, and Clinton administrations. While the surpluses of 1998, 1999, and 2000 were novel, by the time the second George Bush came into office, most of Congress believed the surpluses were here to stay for the foreseeable future if we didn't screw things up too badly.

As often happens in politics, changed circumstances caused the parties to change places. Democrats, who normally would like nothing better than to spend whatever money was available, suddenly began sounding like small-town bankers in their fealty to paying down the national debt. Republicans, who had taken exactly that approach in the face of the previous administration, just as suddenly decided that we really shouldn't pay down the debt too much or too fast.

Both sides were shaping their economic arguments to suit their larger political ends. Republicans wanted to shrink the size of government by cutting off revenues. Democrats knew that any dollar not raised could never be spent. Once taxes were cut, it could be political suicide to try to increase them in any significant way later on.

And so the stage was set for the budget and tax debates of spring 2001. There was precious little contemplation of where our national needs lay, and little or no examination of any long-term consequences of our actions. Our decisions often seemed driven by a simple and almost instinctive approach to government, as something to be revered or reviled, nurtured or neutered.

I found myself out of step with both approaches. It seemed to me that you could have it both ways, a substantial tax cut directed at helping working Americans and substantially increased spending on the sorts of things that both presidential candidates had talked about in the fall.

This was not some new revelation. It was exactly what I had campaigned on in the fall of 2000. As I had put it in the text of a speech to the Burlington Rotary Club in October:

The surplus has created a whole new set of headaches, as some of my colleagues want to devote it to either a new spending spree or to unsustainable tax cuts. I disagree, and here is what I would do with the surplus.

First, we should set aside any surpluses in Social Security and Medicare into a lockbox for each. What this means is that more than half the surplus—over $2.7 trillion—will be used to pay down the debt, reduce interest costs, and give us some room for borrowing when the baby boomers retire.

The remainder—about $1.8 trillion—should be broken into thirds.

The first third should be set aside for both the expected and the unexpected. . . .

The second third should be spent on important national priorities like fully funding special education and providing a drug benefit under Medicare.

The final third should be given back to the taxpayers in the form of both targeted and broad-based tax cuts, like repealing the marriage penalty and providing limited estate tax relief for farms and small businesses.

At the time, I thought this speech was a pretty good statement of my views and those of moderate Republicans generally. But as the surplus grew, Republicans seemed to move away from that position, while the Democrats moved toward it.

Without much discussion or debate, Republicans as a whole decided that virtually all the new funds should be dedicated to tax cuts, and almost none would go to reversing the decline of domestic discretionary spending. But the fact that our children lag behind their international peers strikes me as a bigger long-term threat to our national security and economic stability than the rate of taxation paid on multimillion-dollar estates. In my mind, the education we give to *all* our children is far more important than the size of the fortunes left to a fortunate few.

In April, since the evenly divided Budget Committee could not agree on a budget resolution by the usual majority vote, the budget came to the floor of the Senate. The problem for the Republican leadership and the White House was that the budget lacked a majority on the Senate floor as well.

In the first few days of February, I tried to signal my concern about the size of the proposed tax cut, which was double what I had campaigned for and a direct threat to increased spending for education and health care. I bluntly told a reporter for CNN that as far as the $1.6 trillion tax cut was concerned, "Right now, the size of it, I think, is too high, so I would vote to cut it." My staff privately conveyed to the White House that it should not base its budget strategy on the assumption that it would hold all fifty Senate Republican votes.

Through March and into early April, the pressure increased on me and my fellow wayward Republican, Senator Lincoln Chafee of Rhode Island, to support the president's call for $1.6 trillion in tax cuts. One day I was invited to a meeting with Majority Leader Trent Lott, Assistant Majority Leader Don Nickles, Budget Committee chairman Pete Domenici, and Senator Chuck Grassley of Iowa—my old friend from the post-Watergate days. They wanted to discuss what it would take to get my support for the budget. I listed one area after another where I saw the need for greater investment, from early education, to math and science instruction, to coming to grips with the nursing shortage in our country.

I could see my Republican colleagues drift farther and farther away. When I mentioned the need for nearly $200 billion in increased spending on education for disabled students over the next ten years, Trent asked if I meant for the funding to be guaranteed. I replied, "Yes, of course I do." What else could he think I meant? As the meeting concluded, Don Nickles left the room cursing me in a very loud stage whisper.

My colleagues had trouble believing I was serious, and I had trouble making yet more empty promises on special education. While I would not have had the audacity to expect close to $200 billion for special education a year or two before, it seemed to me that, in the context of a $1.6 trillion tax cut, this was not an unreasonable request. In the days that followed this meeting, I decided to winnow down my list of spending priorities to this one. It seemed to me the most fruitful avenue, in part because it was the most Republican.

In March and early April I made my case to the Republican leadership and to the White House, saying we should triple the amount of money we spend on IDEA, the Individuals with Disabilities Education Act, over the course of the next few years so that we could finally meet the 40 percent commitment we had made to the American people in 1975. At the same time, I thought it was critical that we convert the program to a so-called mandatory spending program, on a par with social security or student loans. This would almost guarantee that the funding wouldn't be cut later on.

As it stands today, IDEA is a "discretionary" program, forced to compete every year for funding with hundreds of other worthy education, health, and social services programs. The result of this twenty-six-year experiment is obvious. Disabled children are not a potent enough lobby to receive their due. Given the size of the tax cut, the increases in defense spending that the Bush administration wanted, and the aging of the baby-boom generation, I felt there would be tremendous pressure on domestic spending over the next decade. I didn't want kids with disabilities to have to repeatedly compete with these other, powerful lobbies. Actually, the real losers are all children. A child with a disability has a constitutional right enforceable in court to an "appropriate" education.

I was never sure that the Republican leadership believed I was serious, even though I had always done my best to be straight with them about how I would vote on a given issue. And I think the White House may have been relying on its ability, or Trent Lott's, to turn me around. But I was quite serious, and my staff and I tried to make that point repeatedly so they would not mistake my intentions.

They worked assiduously to win the votes of moderate Democrats for the president's $1.6 trillion tax cut. Indeed, at times their interest in working with me seemed inversely proportional to the success they felt they were having with Democratic senators Ben Nelson of Nebraska, Bob Torricelli of New Jersey, or John Breaux of Louisiana. They weren't having much luck there, however. Early on they had won the support of Senator Zell Miller (D., Ga.), but having lost my vote and that of Lincoln Chafee, they were down one vote.

The White House had painted itself into a political corner. It had defined the $1.6 trillion figure as the difference between success and failure. And since the president's advisers felt this would set the tone for the entire Bush administration, they were unwilling to deviate from it. My argument that we should scale back the tax cut and devote the funds to special education fell on largely deaf ears in the weeks leading up to consideration of the budget in the first week of April. The $1.6 trillion figure had become the Holy Grail for the White House, and in this environment I was something of an infidel.

As the day of reckoning arrived, the Republican leadership and the White House had not found the Democratic vote they needed, and so they came back to me with newfound interest in reaching an agreement on special education funding. Debate began on the afternoon of Monday, April 2. Behind the scenes I worked the phones and walked the halls to try to secure the IDEA funding.

That morning I had met with Senator Lott, and by the end of our meeting I thought I had secured an agreement to reduce the tax cut to $1.4 trillion, fully fund IDEA at a cost of $180 billion, and hold to that arrangement when the Senate ironed out its differences with the House in a conference committee. My optimism was short lived.

About an hour later I met with Pete Domenici in the so-called Marble Room, the senators' private lobby just off the Senate floor. Because I had supported Pete over Larry Craig, I thought he would at least listen. I did my best to persuade him of the importance of the issue, spending about ten minutes laying out in detail the history of IDEA, our commitment, its importance, and the possibilities within the budget. When I finished, Pete clasped his hands together, rocked forward, leaned toward me in his chair and exclaimed, "God, Jeffords, you are so damn passionate about this thing, aren't you!" His staff then jumped in with a new offer, no better than the last. But I said I would look at it. The proposal was a hybrid plan that, in my estimation, could not work given the realities of budget negotiations.

Still later that day my legislative director, Ken Connolly, was trying to find me in the Capitol and mistakenly walked in on a budget meeting under way in Senator Lott's office. While there, he asked Senator Domenici's staff about the status of our negotiations. The meeting was breaking up and, as Domenici rose from the table, his staff relayed the question. Not recognizing Ken, Pete replied, "What Jeffords wants is crazy. He'll never get it. I'm done dealing with him." Lott's chief of staff tried to signal to Domenici that he was speaking to a Jeffords staffer, but Pete waved him off by saying "I don't care who heard that."

A little after five that afternoon I met in the Vice President's Room off the Senate floor with Vice President Cheney. I had served with Dick in the House when he was the minority whip and I was the senior Republican on the Education and Labor Committee. Our relations were cordial, though we were not particularly close. The vice president wanted to try again on the hybrid proposal that I had rejected earlier in the day in my conversation with Senator Domenici.

I started to get the sense that the Bush administration was simply trying to find a way to survive the next few days, promising me something, almost anything, that they would then throw overboard once the budget reached the conference committee that would resolve differences between the House- and Senate-passed bills. About an hour after I left the meeting with Cheney, I put an outline of my bottom line on a piece of paper and gave it to Pete Domenici on the Senate floor. I needed full mandatory funding for IDEA, and the White House and Senate leadership must support both it and the necessary authorizing language to effect the change throughout the entire legislative process.

It continually amazes me how people's perceptions can be so starkly different. What seemed to me to be a simple restatement of what I had been talking about for weeks was greeted by at least some in the White House as an eleventh-hour apostasy. The idea that the president would *actually sign* the legislation needed to make the funding real was seen as a new, unreasonable demand on my part.

Given the White House reaction, I wondered whether the White House thought I was after nothing more than a symbolic victory. I certainly didn't want nor need anymore feel-good press releases on IDEA. I wanted exactly what I had said I wanted—full, guaranteed spending for IDEA. The next morning I met with Senator Domenici in the Republican cloakroom off the Senate floor again. I left the meeting guardedly optimistic. I told him I could live with a small reduction in funding if the rest of the agreement was as I understood it.

Sure enough, in the middle of the afternoon I met with Pete again in the Vice President's Room where he delivered the news that we had no deal. Some of the more conservative Republicans in our caucus had balked at the idea of a "new" mandatory spending program, overlooking the fact that IDEA was already very much in place in every school district in the country, mandated by the federal government and paid for by state and local property taxes and other funds. My agreement to a small compromise had only brought more opposition.

Finally, I spoke with Senator John Breaux, the moderate Democrat from Louisiana who had been trying to marshal a small band of centrist senators around a compromise budget. I told him I would likely join him at a press conference he had planned for the following afternoon with a few other Democratic senators and Senator Chafee. That group later came to be known as the Centrist Coalition.

Although Senator Lott's chief of staff indicated that night that they still wanted to talk, the next morning passed without a word. Just after midday I spoke with Chuck Hagel, who thought I should give it more time, but I wasn't sure time would change much of anything. Still, it's not in my nature to refuse people, so when I was asked to meet with Senator Domenici in his Capitol hideaway at two that afternoon, I agreed to do so, asking that the White House be involved as well.

Pete and everyone else involved with the budget knew I was planning to attend the Breaux press conference at two forty-five that afternoon, so he didn't waste time getting to the point. Neither did I. I knew my problem was with the White House, not him, so I was surprised that no one from the White House was present.

Pete and I spoke for a few minutes before he left to get the president's representatives and bring them into the room. Strangely enough, though the halls were full of key White House staff in these critical days of the budget debate, finding them proved to be a difficult task. About ten minutes later, Pete returned and told me that the White House staff was on their way but that he had to return to the floor.

Ten more minutes passed. It was now two-thirty, just fifteen minutes before the Breaux press conference was to begin. Finally, a representative of the vice president and a White House legislative liaison staffer appeared. They informed me that the vice president had "just two minutes ago" authorized senior White House staff to sit down and see if they could work things out. I was informed that they were on their way. Asked if they had anything new to offer, they said no, but repeated that more senior policy staff was on the way. Susan Russ, Mark Powden, and I waited, with growing frustration and rising anger.

As the clock ticked, it became clearer and clearer to me that the White House was playing a game of stall ball by having lower level staff keep talking with me until the Breaux press conference had passed, thus stealing some of his thunder and buying a few critical hours to figure out the next maneuver.

Senator Breaux's staff was understandably exercised. His press secretary called my press aide Erik Smulson on his cell phone at about two forty-five, wondering how long Senator Breaux would have to keep telling bad jokes before beginning the press conference. Erik, who was standing outside in the hallway between the Domenici and Lott offices, couldn't tell her whether I would even attend.

Inside Pete's office, with the Breaux press conference already under way, my staff and I were finally forced to ask the White House staff to leave the room. We had come to the same conclusion—the White House was stalling for time to scuttle my appearance with Breaux, and had no intention of changing its position on IDEA spending.

With my usual aversion to accepting the worst of others, I wasn't sure what I should do. Susan cut through the clutter and asked who best represented what I thought was the right approach to the budget. Without hesitation, I answered the centrists headed by John Breaux.

With that we were on the move. Susan went across the hallway to inform Senator Lott's staff of my decision. Erik went to summon the elevator, signaling with a thumbs-up to the press gathered at the public end of the off-limits corridor that I was heading up to the centrists' press conference.

Minutes later, I went up the tiny elevator, twentieth-century technology squeezed in a former ventilation shaft from the nineteenth. In the third-floor press gallery, the news conference was under way. I had had no intention of making a dramatic entrance but the result was unavoidable. If the Democrats held their ranks, Linc Chafee and I represented the votes to defeat the president's budget. The usually jaded press corps reacted with an audible gasp, Senator Breaux's press secretary with tears.

A huge smile broke out on Breaux's face when he saw me. The White House would have to moderate its demands and abandon its strategy of ramming a budget through the Senate on a near party-line vote. And I had reached what I thought was the point of no return on the budget.

I concluded my remarks at the press conference with the observation, "I feel very comfortable here, first time in awhile." Amid the crowd's laughter, Senator Chafee responded, "I feel comfortable that you're here, too." I regretted that I had not been successful in my goal of securing White House agreement for full funding of IDEA, but I had no regrets for supporting a budget that might leave room to make that goal still possible.

In the midst of the press conference, the Senate began to vote on a key amendment of the entire budget debate. It was offered by Senator Tom Harkin (D., Iowa), another of my colleagues who entered Congress with me in the Watergate class of 1974. But even though he represented the same state as Chuck Grassley, the two were very different. Tom is the prototypical Watergate baby, a populist Democrat, as liberal as Chuck is conservative.

The Harkin amendment proposed to knock the tax cut back by $450 billion, spending $250 billion on IDEA and other education and training programs, and applying $200 billion to debt service. It was just the sort of approach I had been advocating in my discussions with the White House and the Republican leadership.

Since I had struck out trying to win the support of the administration for greater education spending, I cast my vote for the Harkin amendment without hesitation. Combined with the votes of Republicans Lincoln Chafee and Arlen Specter of Pennsylvania, the Harkin amendment was on its way to adoption when I left the Senate chamber and headed to a meeting already under way on the education bill that we had voted out of the education committee a month before.

The meeting was one of several that took place among a group of senators that Trent Lott and Senate Democratic Leader Tom Daschle had informally designated to try to work out as many areas of agreement as possible. The education bill was slated to be the next order of business following completion of the budget.

We went back and forth, seeming at times to talk past one another. The president's head of congressional relations, Nick Calio, made appeals to past support and spoke darkly of the future if I opposed the president. At one point, another of Bush's senior advisers asked me what their incentive would be to deal with me if I proposed to reduce the tax cut below $1.6 trillion. "How about educating children?" I responded, not intending to be sarcastic but probably coming off that way. The argument finally ended, as did our fruitless meeting.

Trent had cast his vote on the side of the Democrats to preserve the parliamentary option of voting again on the Harkin amendment. Under the rules of the Senate, any senator on the winning side of a question can move to reconsider it. By voting with the Democrats, Trent could beat the Harkin amendment if he could turn two votes around. The White House promised to put a new proposal on paper, and I agreed to meet with them later that evening.

Ever the optimist, I thought the White House might finally make some proposal for full mandatory spending of IDEA. I was mistaken. The next meeting produced a rehash of the proposal Vice President Cheney had made two days before. Not only did it involve the flawed hybrid funding of Monday's proposal, but it would displace, not add to, discretionary funds. Moreover, the president would not agree to any mandatory funding unless an unspecified set of reforms recommended by a yet-to-be-named commission were adopted a few years hence. I broke off talks with the White House that night and thought we were done. But the next morning, Thursday, I got a call from Trent asking me to meet with him and Vice President Cheney during the vote scheduled to occur at nine forty-five. While nothing had changed overnight, I felt I should hear them out one more time. Once more I went to the Vice President's Room, which my staff had dubbed "the Torture Chamber" during the budget deliberations.

The Thursday morning meeting in the Vice President's Room produced nothing new. If anything, we moved farther apart as the White House, no doubt echoing my demand for clarity, laid out all the procedural and other votes they expected me to cast in return for their rather flimsy offer on special education funding.

The next day brought an end to the week and the budget debate. On Friday the Senate adopted a truly bipartisan budget with sixty-five votes, which included a tax cut of $1.25 trillion. By almost any reckoning, the president had achieved a tremendous victory. He had won the vast majority of the tax cuts he had sought, and he had done so with the support of fifteen Democratic senators, exactly the kind of governing coalition he would need with his narrow mandate and the even narrower margin in the Senate. Instead, given the inflexibility of the White House, it was treated almost as a loss.

Before we had even completed action on the budget, hints had emerged from the White House and elsewhere that I would be forced to pay a political price for bucking the president. After the budget was voted on, the head of Vermont's Associated Press bureau, Chris Graff, interviewed me by phone for a weekend public television news program. At the end of his questions, he asked me about possible reprisals. My response contained what I thought was a statement of the obvious, that it was a short walk across the aisle.

While we waited about a month for the conferees to complete action on the budget bill, the Senate took up the reauthorization of our nation's elementary and secondary education programs. This bill, which I had drafted with my colleagues on the education committee and which had been adopted by the committee by a unanimous vote, could represent a remarkable achievement or an unmitigated disaster.

While the federal government's role in elementary and secondary education is financially small, supplying about 7 percent of all funds, it can have a tremendous impact, particularly in the poorer schools where most federal funds are focused. The bill debated and adopted by the Senate, like its companion in the House, will substantially alter the federal role, by insisting on far greater accountability from states, school districts, and individual schools, while also providing them with greater flexibility in many respects.

The bill also embraces President Bush's early reading initiative, which is designed to help children acquire the basic building blocks needed to become proficient readers. As I had seen in D.C., this is tremendously important, both in its own right and in reducing the need to steer children who have reading difficulties into special education.

That's the good news. But there are two pieces of bad news. First, we run the very real risk of setting the bar of achievement so high that *all* schools will be labeled failures. This, of course, helps no one. But so many of our deliberations to date had been so divorced from real world experience as to astonish me, even after all my time in Congress. President Bush, to his great credit, understands this, and so far has ignored the ill-founded criticism directed his way. Second, wherever we set the bar, it is unlikely that the funds will flow from the federal government in anywhere near the amounts that would be necessary to actually ensure success. Every dollar in tax cuts is a dollar unavailable for education. On this point I cannot be so complimentary. I sincerely wish it hadn't turned out that way.

The White House and I had started out a little rocky on this legislation, as the administration was wedded throughout February to a strategy of ignoring the deliberations in the committee and concentrating its attention on the House and the Senate floor. This seemed unwise in my view, as the committee could, would, and did give the president most of what he sought. Ignoring the Democrats and most of the Republicans on the education committee struck me as an odd way to go about the bipartisan education reform President Bush had told Americans he sought.

The last week of April was filled with events designed to promote the education bill. The first was the announcement of the National Teacher of the Year on Monday, April 23. The award requires a rigorous screening process and really does recognize exceptional individuals and all their high-achieving colleagues across the country.

The 2001 honoree was no exception. Michele Forman, a high school history teacher from Salisbury, Vermont, is a remarkable person. She puts in long hours and, more important, she inspires her students with her own infectious love of learning. I was so pleased that she had won and I was eager to attend the White House ceremony in her honor. I was fully expecting an invitation. This was the first time in the fifty-one years of the competition that a Vermonter was to be honored, and for a small state like ours it was very big news. When no invitation was forthcoming my scheduler, Trecia McEvoy, called the White House and was informed that no member of Congress would be joining President Bush at the White House ceremony.

I left it at that. Clearly it was Ms. Foreman's day, and whether I attended or not mattered little. I got a chance to visit with her and her family and Vermont's then education commissioner David Wolk for an hour in my office after the ceremony, and chalked it up to the inexperience of a new White House. But it was hard not to wonder if the decision not to invite me was designed to send a message. Members of Congress are routinely welcomed to these events, I was chairman of the education committee, and I was managing the president's education bill on the Senate floor. It seemed only right to invite the entire Vermont delegation—Patrick Leahy, Congressman Sanders, and me.

As the press began to focus on the decision of the White House, the rationale for why I had not been invited began to sound a little thin. White House spokesman Ari Fleischer responded to press questions by saying I could not be invited because of space limitations. It was a bit hard to stifle a laugh. As Pat Leahy had remarked of the tiny, three-man Vermont delegation, "We could all ride down on a Razor scooter if we had to."

Far from upsetting, the event made me something of a martyr in Vermont. I tried to brush it off but the press carried the story for days, showing yet again how dumb little mistakes can have outsized consequences. Ironically, instead of attending the White House event, I fulfilled my previous commitment to make fund-raising calls from the Republican Senatorial Committee on behalf of the President's Dinner, a big fund-raising event designed to help Republicans.

For much of May, I managed the education bill on the floor of the Senate. The White House, meanwhile, tried to promote the bill and the importance of education generally, which had been such a successful issue for the president on the campaign trail the previous fall. This success was due in large part because the president is genuine in his commitment to education and education reform.

On May 9, the debate on the education bill was interrupted to consider the final conference agreement on the budget. In the end, the conferees had agreed to a tax cut of $1.35 trillion. Before the agreement came to a vote in the Senate, I sat down with Pete Domenici on the Senate floor. With a yellow sheet of paper in his hand, he outlined the broad concepts. I asked what happened to the $450 million for education. I was shocked. He tried to reassure me that hundreds of billions of dollars in contingency funds from surpluses over the next ten years could be available for education. I felt betrayed and let down. Too many competing interests would lay claim to those funds, if there were any, before they ever reached our schools.

Not surprisingly, the tax cuts put substantial pressure on any new spending for education. The agreement between the House and Senate conferees provided for a little more money for education in 2002 but no increase whatsoever in the years beyond. Meanwhile, the wealthiest Americans would receive substantial reductions in their tax burden. It was a repeat of the Reagan tax cut with education getting short shrift.

I don't practice class warfare. I think the genius of the American system has been to encourage risk with reward. It's not surprising that a tax code that generates most of its revenues from the affluent will yield like benefits for them when scaled back. But it seemed to me that if close to

$1.4 trillion could be found for tax cuts, some substantial amount could have been found for education.

For most Republicans, I was speaking a foreign language. A self-styled budget watchdog group with ties to the Republican leadership labeled me "Porker of the Month" for my refusal to support the president's tax cut without increased spending on special education. Only in Washington, D.C., I suspect, is spending for educating disabled students across the nation considered a pork barrel project.

I voted against the budget agreement, but my disappointment was more profound than that one vote indicated. Here I was, the chairman of the Senate's education committee, at the outset of a new millennium, when knowledge was becoming more important to individual and national success, when our society was becoming more stratified in many ways, when a major reform of education was about to take place, and yet my party couldn't find any additional money to invest in education.

It was a bitter disappointment and I knew then I needed to do something.

On the last Friday of March 2001, I traded calls all day with Senator Chris Dodd (D., Conn.) in an attempt to discuss an amendment on child care we were planning to offer to the budget the following week. Since we were both staying in town that weekend, we finally decided to meet in person.

Late that afternoon, when most senators were on planes heading to their home states and their staffs were breathing a collective sigh of relief, Dodd's office was dark, quiet, and relaxed. For close to an hour we discussed poverty, schools, child care, the solutions, the prospects. I allowed as how I simply could not support the Bush budget without mandatory funding for IDEA. Dodd was convinced it would never happen and suggested that I should announce my opposition to the budget. I wasn't ready for that, but I wondered aloud whether there was room for me in the Republican Party anymore. Chris moved to the edge of his seat, almost rising. He quickly assured me that there was always room for me in the Democratic Party, and that they'd love to have me. I told him I could never be a Democrat, but that I could be an Independent. Neither of us knew whether to take the discussion seriously, and we left it by joking about the commotion such a decision would cause.

As long as I had been in the Senate my Democratic colleagues had kidded me about switching parties. And when Alabama senator Richard Shelby switched from the Democratic to Republican Party in 1994, one of my conservative detractors suggested that he be swapped for me so the Republicans could be rid of me.

Indeed, my family was so used to the constant rumors and speculation that as one of our annual April Fool's Day jokes in 1993, during the Clinton administration's better days, my wife, daughter-in-law, and I cooked up a scheme to convince my son, Leonard, that I was going to make the switch. For days, they uttered innuendoes and even got staff members to go vague when Leonard repeatedly called looking for me. When he couldn't reach me, he called Liz who said, "I can't talk to you right now; there's too much going on with your dad."

But these had been good-natured, or at least whimsical, suggestions. Not until it came out of my mouth in Chris Dodd's office that Friday had I spoken aloud what had been on my mind.

Probably not by coincidence, a month after my meeting with Senator Dodd, Senator Bill Nelson (D., Fla.), with whom I had also served in the House, called to ask me to meet with him. On the morning of April 30, we met and he talked at some length about the party switch of Senator Shelby years before. I mostly listened.

Then, the night of Monday, May 14, Tom Daschle asked me to meet with him and Harry Reid of Nevada, the Democratic whip, the following morning. Tom and I had followed similar paths to the Senate, by first winning our small states' at-large seats in the U.S. House of Representatives, where we had worked closely together on Vietnam veterans' issues. I talked about my increasing discomfort in the Republican Party. They talked about how eager they were to have me join their ranks, at least for organizational purposes.

As soon as I arrived at my office in the Hart Building, I went to see Susan Russ. I was not really sure how she would respond but I had no doubt she would be surprised. In the past, whenever this subject came up, no matter how casually, Susan would always cover her ears and say she didn't want to talk about it. I am not sure what was different this time but when I entered her office and told her I had just met with Daschle and Reid, she put her head in her hands and said, "Let's talk."

It was clear to her, without even asking, that I had already determined leaving was something I should do, and she did not feel any need to give me encouragement in that direction. Instead, Susan went through the impact a switch would have on my staff, career, and relationships in the Senate, and the fallout from and for Vermont. Mark Powden's reaction was typically somewhat more subdued than Susan's, but he, too, was clearly concerned. I left for lunch around one and can only imagine the conversation that ensued among the staff I left behind. When I returned almost two hours later, they were still meeting. Susan's list of concerns had grown as Bill Kurtz, my state director, had arrived and was focused on the logistics of where, when, and how such a decision would become public.

I remember clearly two things that came up at that brief meeting. Bill reminded me that I would be giving up the longest continually held Republican seat in history, and Susan had a list of my closest colleagues and what my move would cost them. Many had finally become chairs of committees they'd long served on, due to the Republican control of both the House and the Senate. These positions would be lost if I took control from them. My anxiety was beginning to return.

Liz arrived later that afternoon to work on a project for the Senate spouses, at this point unaware of the discussion. Although I had talked to her at some length over the past months about my frustrations, and had vented my feeling that I should leave the party, we had not discussed this as a real possibility. I had wanted to talk to Liz privately about this the night before my meeting with Daschle and Reid, but because of our busy schedules, I hadn't had the chance. Or perhaps I was afraid to hear what she would have to say.

It did not take a nanosecond for Liz to see that something big was happening. She asked what was going on, and as I searched for just the right words, Susan rather bluntly informed her that "Jim just told us he is seriously considering switching parties." I quickly corrected her and said I would leave the Republican Party and become an Independent.

Liz expressed her concerns while acknowledging that she knew how frustrated and miserable I had been. Her concerns were more of a personal nature than those expressed by staff. She had become very close to many of the Senate wives, particularly Republican spouses like Tricia Lott, and was keenly aware of the hurt this would cause them and their families. She also was very concerned about how all the attention would affect Laura, Leonard, and Maura.

As I listened to the arguments that afternoon, I looked around at Liz and the staff and felt a profound sadness but a growing sense that what I planned to do was right. I was not sure it was right personally, but I was very confident it was the right thing to do for the country.

Over the next ten days I would revisit that decision several times as the news began to leak out. CNN called to ask about a possible party change. A columnist for an alternative weekly in Vermont, Peter Freyne, asked the same question. Erik was ready to make the same flat denial he had made for years when Susan reeled him in so he wouldn't be put in the position of lying to the press. Instead, he put out a statement that should have served as a neon sign. On Wednesday, Freyne's column came out quoting Erik as saying that "Senator Jeffords is comfortable as the most conservative member of the Vermont delegation, and regardless of party label, will do what he thinks is right for Vermont and the nation." As Freyne aptly concluded, "That didn't sound like an absolute 'no,' did it?"

So, realizing that I could not contain either a decision or press specu-lation much longer, I called former Vermont senator Bob Stafford, the one person outside of my immediate circle with whom I would discuss my possible switch. During the years Bob had preceded me in the Senate, he had chaired the Senate Education Subcommittee that I chaired a few years later. We share a belief that an educated populace is essential to a free country and a stable economy. Bob was instrumental in strengthen-ing federal education efforts, and had sat across from me in many confer-ences between the House and Senate on education, beginning with IDEA in 1975.

Beyond all that, as someone I had known virtually all my life and as a Vermont Republican, I knew I could be perfectly honest with him and that he would understand my struggle. Bob told me he would support whatever decision I made. By the next day, even though I had told both Liz and Susan that I would wait until after the recess, I knew it could not wait. Liz informed Susan early Monday morning that it was clear to her that my decision was made and we should all just get about doing what we needed to do.

Seeing the growing news coverage, my son, Leonard, called me at the office on Monday to ask my plans. I told him I had not fully made up my mind, but that I was leaning toward becoming an Independent. He gave me some arguments against such a switch, and we left it at that. The next day, his wife, Maura, came by the office to deliver a trivet emblazoned with an elephant and a letter in which they made the tongue-in-cheek vow to name their firstborn child "Reagan Nixon Jeffords" as my replacement if I left the Republican Party.

By Tuesday, May 22, the Republican leadership and seemingly the entire Senate was fully aware of my thinking. As we cast vote after vote throughout the day, various senators stopped by my desk to chat. Don Nickles admonished me to stop drinking whatever funny water I had found. Trent Lott and Larry Craig talked about reviving the Singing Senators. Democrat Jay Rockefeller of West Virginia went away beaming when I told him of my intentions. Republican Phil Gramm of Texas, who had switched from the Democratic to Republican Party while a House member in the 1980s, allowed that he might do the same thing if he had my political views. "Just don't screw up the tax bill," he volunteered.

In the midst of the visits and the votes, I met off the Senate floor with Trent Lott at ten, Vice President Cheney at noon, and in the Oval Office with the president at two. I told each of them I was strongly considering leaving the party, and I tried my best to describe my thinking. By the time I met with the president Tuesday afternoon, he had been briefed on my earlier meetings and must have known that he faced a nearly impossible task in dissuading me. He was relaxed and charming, and did his best to impress upon me the consequences of handing control of the Senate to the Democrats. I tried to use my time to convince him of the need to govern more from the center. Coming from me, I doubt it was very convincing. But I argued that, like his father, he would be a one-term president if he didn't go beyond the conservative Republican base on such issues as providing greater resources for education.

I called my daughter at her office in an architectural firm in downtown Washington and said I planned to announce that I was leaving the Republican Party the following day. Like everyone close to me, Laura wanted to be sure I had really thought through my decision. When it was clear to her that I had, she gave me her full support. Laura shares my idealism and optimism, and used to send me off to work every morning with the exhortation "Save the world, Jim." I know it sounds corny but I have tried to live up to her rather lofty expectations.

It had dawned on me that by switching to Independent, I would not only be making a dramatic public statement for the rights of children with disabilities but because of this unique situation—one that may never come again—I had the opportunity to open the dialogue on so many crucial issues that our country faces. The even split in the Senate had only occurred in our nation's history once before, in the 1880s. Only once before, during the Eisenhower years, had the Republicans had control of all three branches of government. With the conservative mood of today's Republicans, which I did not feel represented the majority of either party members or the country, I felt that if I did not make the switch, important lasting policies and appointments would be made that would dramatically change the history of our nation. In this, I am not speaking only of education policy but also the crucial areas of a woman's right to choose, environmental policy, defense policy, and the lifetime appointments of federal and Supreme Court justices.

CHAPTER 21

Making History

ALTHOUGH PEOPLE MAY imagine the life of a senator as somewhat glorious, for much of our lives we are first cousins of the traveling salesman. Marriages fail, as mine did for a short time, children suffer, friends are lost, and ideals are often put to the test by the never-ending barrage of deal-making, influence-peddling, and the conflicting pressures placed on public officials. If my mood as I flew home to announce my defection was on the gloomy side, it was because I had just left a series of meetings where I had very likely lost a few more friends. The days leading up to my decision were easily the toughest I have had during my three decades in politics.

Indeed, by the end of the last meeting I'd had with my Republican colleagues, I was in tears, as were many of the senators sitting around me. It had been gut-wrenching trying to explain what impelled me to think of leaving the party, handing control of the Senate to the Democrats, and wresting it from those with whom I had served so long. Several of the colleagues I talked with in those last days had been in the Watergate class with me in the House of Representatives. Many had waited all their lives to chair a Senate committee and had been working hard since the election to put their stamp on issues they truly believed in. And I was about to rip it all from them.

Yet it wasn't until I was headed for Burlington, Vermont, to make my public statement that I began to truly understand the magnitude of what I found myself in the middle of. The morning papers had given the story front-page coverage. The television was running it almost constantly. Even the business news gave it play, attributing some of the movement in the stock market to speculation about my pending announcement. My press secretary had been so deluged by reporters and producers' phone calls that some other staff members had to come to the rescue.

273

But I was still unprepared for the scene that awaited me as I left the waiting room the airline had made available to me and my staff prior to our flight. A hundred yards away, dozens of reporters had staked out the little gate to our plane, with TV cameras and microphones pointed my way. On both sides of the broad aisle, passengers awaiting their flight stood on their chairs and started cheering and applauding, while others pushed forward to shake my hand. This for someone who a few days before may have ranked about ninety-ninth on the U.S. Senate celebrity scale. Here were scores of people who not only recognized me but also approved of what they thought I would be doing the next day in Vermont, who literally wanted to reach out and touch me. How had what I thought or done to that point so touched these people?

I had tried throughout the past few days to keep a level head, but my family and staff took no chances. Lest I invested too much meaning into the reception I had just received, Susan pointed out that the people cheering me were waiting for a plane to Boston, hardly a political cross section of the country.

The plane to Burlington usually has a Vermont flavor—a few students from the University of Vermont, an engineer from IBM, a state employee or two heading home from a conference in Washington, sometimes even Ben or Jerry. It is pretty common to know a few people on the trip—such is the size of my state. Along with the usual cast of characters, tonight's passengers also included reporters from the network news shows; newspapers from London, Dallas, Los Angeles, and Tokyo; and camera crews from who knows where.

Liz was usually quiet. Yes, she had been an early supporter of Reverend Jesse Jackson's bid for the presidency, and she had placed a yard sign for the Democrat running for governor the same year I was running as a Republican for the U.S. Senate. But tonight, as she had the last few days, she was thinking about the many Republicans who would lose their Senate chairmanships because of my actions and of the staff people who would leave our office, either because they had to or because they chose to. She had told me she supported my decision and I believed her. But she was also thinking about herself and the friendships she had managed to establish with some of the Republican wives, despite the disparity in their views. Liz has a big heart and is capable of loving people with whom she strongly disagrees—after all, she's put up with me all these years. It had taken her a long time to learn to leave politics out of the discussions and to get to know these people outside of their political views. And she was enjoying herself in Washington. I was about to take that away from her, too.

So, on this flight, while I knew she was with me, she was also worried about the people who would be hurt by my decision. It is this characteristic—the ability to see the scope of a problem—that is one of the reasons I love her.

And she was worried about the upcoming reception, too. Neither of us could know how the public, and particularly Vermonters, would receive it. Would I be seen in a harsh light, as petulant or prideful, or would people come to understand my reasoning? What kind of repercussions would flow from it? As Liz knew better than anyone, rocky relations with the Republican Party were nothing new; indeed, they have characterized my entire political career in Vermont and Washington, D.C. For years people had asked me why I called myself a Republican, and I had tried to talk about the Republican Party of Vermont. We had coped with it for thirty years. Why now? My speech had to tell why and it had to speak to Vermonters first because they were the ones who had elected me and they had the right to an explanation.

My critics are right about one thing: I am not God's gift to oratory. I envy those of my colleagues who could talk a dog off a meat wagon. But that's not me. There is a small humor book called *The Vermont Owner's Manual,* written by Frank Bryan and Bill Mares, that tries to explain the state to natives and newcomers alike. In its section on which laws are to be taken seriously and which are not, it describes a twenty-minute high school speech by our governor as a misdemeanor and the same by me as a felony.

The more I went over the speech, the more I thought about the reasoning behind it. Just as my colleagues couldn't understand how I could go ahead and switch, I couldn't understand how I could stay a Republican. The gulf between me and the current national Republican orthodoxy had become too wide. My first allegiance could not be to my colleagues; it had to be to my constituents and my conscience. As I had made clear in my Senate campaign six years before, my contract was not with America, but with Vermont.

I had tried to effect change within the party. I had tried to accommodate my beliefs to the party as a whole. I had tried to be fair to those with whom I had formed friendships over the decades. And I had tried to balance my decision against the impact it would have on my colleagues, my family, and my staff, many of whom would soon be thrown out of work. But in the end, I had to be true to what I thought was right, and leave the consequences to sort themselves out in the days ahead.

I thought back to a statement Senator Aiken had made in an open letter sent to the Republican National Committee on December 4, 1937. I don't for a minute believe that he would have left the Republican Party— his widow, Lola, has made it clear that she believes he would have disapproved of my actions—but still, I think if he knew what I was up against, he might have some empathy. In that letter, the man I consider the epitome of the moderate wing of Vermont's Republican Party wrote: "To purge the Party organization of its reactionary and unfair elements, to focus its forces on the recognition of the youth of our nation, to prepare immediately an affirmative program—that is the demand which the Republican leadership of Vermont makes on the Republican leadership of the nation.

"If that demand is not met, we must look elsewhere for an organization through which thoughtful and devoted Americans of North and South, East and West, can join together to work for the good of all."

I looked for that other organization and I found it in one word, a word that has always symbolized my state and my nation and now defines me: Independent.

When we walked from our plane at the Burlington airport, we could see a mass of people and cameras in the main part of the airport and knew we could not get through the crowd unassisted. Erik went ahead to find the two members of my Vermont staff who were to meet us, Jeff Munger and Bill Kurtz. When they returned, Erik told me that he had never seen such a crowd of press in Vermont and we would just have to keep our heads low and plow through. There were the familiar faces from the Vermont press corps and an awful lot of folks we did not know. We also heard the cheers from beyond the cameras and saw numerous signs, both positive and negative.

At the hotel that night I worked on the speech with Erik and Susan, using the hotel's printer. Finally, at midnight, Erik slipped the finished speech under my door. I read it once and promptly fell asleep, sleeping soundly for the first time in weeks.

As we drove to the hotel where I would be giving my speech, Susan joked that it was not too late to change my mind. Liz reminded me to speak slowly. Erik called to say there was a huge crowd awaiting us, but I could scarcely believe the sight that greeted me as we turned the corner. A dozen satellite trucks were parked on the street that ran between the hotel and Lake Champlain. Hundreds of people had gathered. At the front of their ranks stood a costumed Benedict Arnold, making me believe for an instant that the entire crowd had come to protest my decision. But as we drew closer I could see that the signs of supporters, greatly outnumbered those in opposition.

Once I got out of the car there was no mistaking the positive energy of the crowd. The Burlington police had their hands full keeping the people back so we could make our way into the hotel and through the lobby. I was incredibly touched by all the familiar faces of friends and former staff who had made the effort to be with me, and buoyed by the cheers of the crowd. I was tremendously grateful I had come home, to Vermont, to make my announcement.

Even though we had been forced by the sheer numbers to allow only press into the banquet room of the hotel, it was mobbed—and not just with reporters and photographers with local and regional press passes but reporters from press organizations from around the world. Seven months earlier, when I had delivered my speech to the Burlington Rotary a few blocks away in the final weeks of the campaign, perhaps two reporters had attended.

Just outside the room, the hotel lobby was jammed with hundreds of people who had come for the event. And as I began my speech, I could hear their applause and shouts of support. Not expecting members of the public to be at the press conference, I had not anticipated any vocal response to my words. Awkwardly, I found myself apologizing to the press in the middle of my remarks for the interruption. But it sure felt good.

I found my rhythm. Thanks to Liz's encouragement to study the speech and focus on each word, the words were by now familiar. More important, they came from the heart. I believed then that I was absolutely doing the right thing for the country, my state, and myself. The full text of what I told my fellow Vermonters on May 24, 2001, can be found in the appendix.

CHAPTER 22

The Reaction

ANYONE WHO KNOWS ME knows that I expect no special favors or fanfare for being a senator. My staff and my constituents call me "Jim." I'm more comfortable in jeans and a sweater than a suit. Before the switch, few people outside the insulated confines of the Senate enclave and my home state knew who I was. That was fine with me. I am shy by nature, and I avoid the public spotlight unless it is a necessary part of the job.

Garrison Nelson, a Vermont political scientist, is fond of telling the press this story about me—I don't remember the event he refers to but I've heard the tale repeated so often that it must be true. Apparently, while serving in the House, I was sitting in my office with my leg sprawled over the arm of the chair wearing one of my less than tailored suits when a young congressional aide from another office burst in.

The aide said something like, "I've got to give this important letter to the congressman."

I apparently said, "I'll see that he gets it."

"No," the young fellow insisted. "This is really important. Congressman Jeffords has to get it right away."

Whereupon, I said, "Okay. I'll make sure he gets it quickly." And the aide left without ever knowing he'd been talking to the Vermont congressman.

As a senator, I've had to accept that the media is an integral part of the job and of the democratic process. I choose my media engagements carefully, get my point across about the issues or policy I am working on, and usually leave it at that. I don't do the Sunday talk shows and I don't take too long at the podium at press conferences. The focus should be the issue at hand, not the person speaking.

Thus, despite my long political career, I was totally unprepared for the attention, both good and bad, I was about to receive. I had no idea how much my world had changed.

While I was meeting with the Vermont reporters after my speech, we received several calls letting us know that death threats were beginning to come in from a variety of quarters. Apparently the phone lines in my offices were so jammed that some individuals who wanted to make death threats were unable to get through. Being more eager than clever, a few callers began dialing randomly any Vermont phone number, including those of the Vermont State Police Barracks and the Vermont State House.

Soon after, both an officer from the Vermont State Police and an agent from the Federal Bureau of Investigation were assigned to protect me. This was just the beginning of three weeks of around-the-clock security. Although for the most part I felt I was safe and knew that most of the threats were harmless venting, it was unsettling for me, my family, and my staff to know there were people who might really try to hurt me or those close to me.

After the press conference, I decided to go back to my room in the hotel and rest a few hours until my flight back to Washington. My staff decided to go down to the Sheraton lounge to watch the news, and maybe have a drink. After about an hour, I realized I could not sleep. With my new security entourage accompanying me, I joined Erik, Bill, and Susan.

Earlier that morning, as had been planned months before my decision, I had addressed by videotape the annual Vermont Business Expo under way at the hotel. Immediately following my taped address, almost the entire crowd at the Expo watched my live speech on a television screen that had been brought into the hall.

Many of the Vermont businessmen and -women attending the convention were now gathering in the lounge. When I entered it, their heartfelt expressions of support were overwhelming. I made my way to the table where my staff was sitting and watched the early edition of the local news. My announcement was the lead story. There was the usual buzz of conversation in the room until a reporter on the television interviewed a man who expressed the opinion that someone should shoot me for what I had done.

The room went silent. It is one thing to learn you are receiving anonymous death threats; it is quite another to hear those words from a fellow human being.

The next day, when we landed at Reagan National Airport, two marked Capitol Police cars and one of their large black Suburbans awaited us. We piled into the Suburban and headed home. A security detail leaves almost nothing to chance. But they hadn't counted on a temperamental garage door opener that I should have fixed or replaced a long time ago. As we drove around the back alley of my house, I saw a number of Capitol Police officers at my garage. One of them had the door opener and when he saw us, he pushed the button. Nothing happened. I had gotten out of the Suburban to help but knew immediately, from prior experience, that no amount of pushing the button was going to open the door.

We got back in the Suburban and went around to the front of the house. The small motorcade drew attention and, as I got out of the car, many people walking along the street stopped and began clapping and calling out to me. I was tired but I surely appreciated this spontaneous show of support. I was looking forward to sitting down, having a cold beer, and relaxing. However, after giving me a big hug and asking how I was feeling, Liz said, "Put on your old clothes, we've got a lot of work to do. Your little dance with destiny this past month has put us way behind and company is coming tomorrow!"

And so I ended one of the most momentous days of my life in old clothes, painting and cleaning the house.

Because of security concerns, I wasn't allowed to walk to work the next day. It was probably just as well. When I got to the Hart building, my press team met me at the parking lot to steer me through the throng of media crews that lined the hallway to our office. The crews were staking out the front hall to our office, boom microphones swinging as they shouted questions at me. Three major photo shoots had been scheduled for that day. *Time, Newsweek,* and *U.S. News and World Report* wanted me for photo shoots (only *Newsweek* actually put me on the cover). Time.com named me its Person of the Week.

I felt an enormous sense of lightness as I went through that incredible day, Friday May 25. I wore three different ties for the magazine photo shoots and had to have makeup put on and my hair combed and sprayed. My press team was wrangling with every major media star calling for an interview, but I had decided to do no television at all, just let the Vermont statement speak for itself. I know I disappointed many good reporters, but I really had nothing more to say. I did grant an interview to *Rolling Stone*. For a while there was even talk of me being on the cover. Now that would have really impressed the kids.

It's amazing to be treated as a celebrity by celebrities. I'm sure Sharon Stone would not have stopped by my office before the announcement. When I met her, she said, "The reason I came to Washington was to meet you," As I told Liz, I *had* to console her, she was crying so hard. After she left, people had to tell me who she was. I hadn't seen *Basic Instinct*. I have now.

The office looked like a florist shop. Bouquets ranged from bunches of sprightly carnations to mammoth affairs fit for a palace. Potted orchids and huge exotic plants with shining leaves arrived. We had no place to put them all. The most astounding thing were the notes attached. From all over the country, people thanked me for my courage and wished me well. One family from New York City thanked me on behalf of their two children and the future for all children. Someone in Texas told me I was his hero. It was these personal notes, written by busy Americans, that touched me the most.

In the midst of the forest of green, my two phone assistants tried valiantly to get to all the calls. E-mails poured in. Most were positive, but not all. The staff began circulating the most beautiful ones, like the American English teacher who e-mailed from Indonesia that my actions inspired her to see the beauty of our democracy from so far away, or the pregnant woman from Vermont who changed her choice for the baby's name from Charles to James. It was astounding. It continues. Sometimes the caller wants to express his hatred of me, but for the most part they are positive.

Now, a year later, I am still amazed by how much my switch affected people I have known for decades as well total strangers. One of the funniest accolades is a Web site called I Heart Jim Jeffords (iheartjamesjeffords.com), in which I'm described as something of a heartthrob. I learned a few things about myself on the site, including that my Asian astrological sign is the Wood Dog. According to famous Web astrologer Shelly Wu, Wood Dogs are "champions of the underdog," and "famous for complete loyalty towards their friends and loved ones." Wood Dogs are also "Low on ego, high on soapboxes. The Dogs' curt tongue and fair-minded humanitarianism is legendary."

Relationships with many of my Republican colleagues have remained strained. The weekend before my announcement, Trent Lott described our relationship by saying "We are friends and have been for a long time." On a conservative radio talk shows eight days later, he bitterly denounced my decision as "a coup of one." Aside from the rather regal implications, it showed the instinct to which he inevitably turns, of partisan battle where Democrats are the enemy rather than the loyal opposition. A week later, he drafted a memo calling for a "war on the Democrats," a posture I responded to viscerally after the death threats I had received and one that, after September 11, I hope has been abandoned.

At one point early in my chairmanship of the Health and Education Committee, Trent Lott had handed me a small, cut-out photo of Senator Edward Kennedy on which he had used a felt pen to draw a red circle with a diagonal slash through it, the international sign for prohibition. It was meant as both a joke and a message: Don't cooperate with Democrats, especially Ted Kennedy. Although I do not agree with him on everything, I count Kennedy as an ally in the battle to preserve the American educational system.

President Bush's top political adviser, Karl Rove, along with some of his colleagues, responded to my decision by trying to smear me, suggesting that my motivation was for a better committee assignment or some such nonsense. I'm sure part of his motivation was to deflect blame from the White House, but I think that he may have believed it. For a purely political creature, there didn't have to be more to my story. What's conscience got to do with it?

Vermonters weighed in at my offices about ten to one in support of my decision. A year later, the local newspapers continue to receive letters to the editor praising or pillorying my switch. I thought it fair that Vermonters who had supported me financially in last fall's campaign should be provided refunds if they wished for them, not knowing how much money would be sought by former supporters. So far thousands upon thousands of people from Vermont and across the country have sent me contributions, while only a handful of Vermonters have asked for their money back. Lest this be the final verdict, at least one conservative organization has sent a mailing to my contributors decrying my decision, urging them to request a refund, and giving them a preprinted, prepaid request form to do so. I suspect the real purpose, as it usually is with these mailings, was to generate revenues for the organization doing the soliciting. So far, it has cost them far more than it has cost me.

Unfortunately, my switch has not yet brought the benefits to education that I had envisioned. I was one of ten senators to oppose the compromise education bill that had been fashioned by top-ranking Democratic and Republican lawmakers in the fall of 2001. As a Republican, my HELP committee laid the groundwork for the bill.

But my new Democratic allies were unable to do anything more for the cause than deliver impassioned speeches. The Senate-passed measure to guarantee tens of billions of dollars in additional special education funding over ten years—the very thing that I had campaigned so hard for before and after the switch—was stripped from the final bill.

Have we given up? No. I'm still working for more funding for education and for an entire reform of our educational system. I'm still working for support for a dairy compact. And, once again, this spring, I introduced a national bottle bill. While I have changed my party affiliation, I have not changed my issues.

CHAPTER 23

September 11

THE MORNING OF September 11 was to be a busy one. We were having a "stakeholders" hearing on four pollution-control provisions and CNN was to attend. The meeting was scheduled to begin at 9:00 A.M. I got there around 8:15 A.M. to meet with Ken Connolly, the Environmental and Public Works Committee (EPW) staff director. The TV was on and tuned to CNN.

When the first plane hit the World Trade Center we were just heading down to the hearing. Moments after we arrived at the hearing room, the second plane hit. The Capitol Police were beginning to evacuate the Capitol as I headed to my office in the Hart Senate Office Building. When I walked into my office, my entire staff was waiting for me with their bags packed, ready to leave. Susan Russ told me that the Pentagon had been hit and the entire Capitol complex was being evacuated.

Just before I left the building, Ken reminded me that the Federal Emergency Management Agency, FEMA, was under the jurisdiction of the EPW. I walked home passing the roadblocks that were being set up to keep traffic from blocking police checkpoints all around the Capitol buildings. When I turned on the TV at home and heard that United Airlines flight 93 had crashed in Pennsylvania, I wondered if the Capitol was the next target.

I called Ken and told him that I wanted to go to the Pentagon. We knew the worst thing to do at that point was to get in the way, but I had spent many weeks there on reserve duty and wanted to give moral support to those handling the disaster and I wanted to know if there was anything my committee could do right away.

We went to the Pentagon early the next morning. It was shocking. The plane had struck a newly reconstructed area. There were people buried in the still burning debris and there was hope that some were still alive. I talked to rescue workers from nearby areas and some from as far away as Nebraska. I asked what their worst problem was and the response was simple and clean: "We couldn't talk to each other." It became clear to me that there was nothing I could do then, but in the coming months I would be busy working with others to develop plans to protect not just government buildings and our transportation system but also our sources of water, electricity distribution systems, and nuclear power plants. FEMA has overview over natural and man-made disasters. Our work was cut out for us.

My deepest concern was immediately turned to New York. I had already spoken to Senators Charles Schumer and Hillary Clinton. I had over the years come to know and respect New York's mayor Rudy Giuliani. I contacted him and we set up a trip to New York as soon as possible for me and the ranking Republican on my committee, Senator Bob Smith of New Hampshire. I reassured the mayor that I would do everything I could.

That evening, in a joint session, President George Bush gave a superb speech that built confidence in the public but also raised my concern that his war cries would exacerbate the country's already slumping economy and further erode confidence in air travel. I thought, not for the first time, in the upcoming months that we needed to be more circumspect in what was said publicly so that we would not buy into and further the terrorists' goals of weakening our economy and our trust in modern technology.

The next week, as my train pulled into Penn Station, I tried to steel myself for what was to come in the hours ahead. Like just about everyone in America, I had seen the televised images of the devastation left by the terrorist attacks, but seeing it firsthand, I knew, would be awful. As a New York City Police boat piloted us to the docks near Ground Zero, it wasn't so much the missing towers or the smoke that struck me but the sense of loss.

With Mayor Giuliani we made our way through the rubble. A small group of firefighters escorted two sobbing women, both with firefighters' jackets draped over their shoulders, toward us. A virtual city of first-aid stations, food and clothing supply stations, and communication centers had been set up. Cardboard signs saluted the Ground Zero heroes. Dozens of bulldozers and bucket loaders plowed through the streets.

There were the blown-out windows and blackened facades of surrounding buildings, the flower beds now patches of ash, then the skeletal remains of the South Tower still reaching into the sky and the debris hanging from trees and girders. A war scene on our soil.

In the midst of all the devastation, I was thinking what could be done to help. It was clear that the cleanup and recovery effort here and at the Pentagon might be the largest public works projects this nation has ever seen, which is why I was there.

I felt overwhelmed by the challenges that lay ahead. Visiting the site had put life and politics in perspective. I prayed that we would put aside our differences. We will rebuild our structures and our spirit. We must continue to work in this cooperative manner for a very long time to come. May the rescue workers in New York, the Ground Zero heroes, be our role models.

Shortly after September 11 we found ourselves with another crisis, one of lesser magnitude but with potential for great harm. Senator Tom Daschle and my Vermont counterpart, Senator Patrick Leahy, were the intended recipients of anthrax-contaminated letters. The sender of the letters seemed particularly cynical, using for the return address Fourth Grade, Greendale School, Franklin Park, NJ.

Fortunately, both senators are fine but others who have handled or who came in contact with the letters are not. For me, it was a matter of inconvenience. We were not able to use our offices in the Hart building for several months while it was decontaminated. It was a stressful time, as my staff and I tried to conduct business from my little hideaway deep in the bowels of the Capitol.

In late October, we got an update on the anthrax situation. A new hot spot had been identified, the freight elevator on the south end of the Hart and Dirksen buildings. I realized that I had used that elevator several times the previous week. My son, Leonard, and I went to the Baltimore Ravens game on Sunday, and I couldn't get the anthrax in the elevator out of my mind. I also felt quite tired, but I passed that off to the busy week. I lectured myself about trying to be macho, and realized that not to do the sensible thing and visit the Capitol physician was stupid. I started the sixty-day regimen of Cipro the following Monday.

Since then, my Environment and Public Works Committee has worked on various aspects of national security. A top priority is to improve communications among the various emergency response systems, both regionally and nationally, so that when disaster strikes those in command have as much information as possible, can make well-informed decisions, and can work in conjunction with one another. September 11 showed us many of the inadequacies of our communication system. For security reasons, it's best not to reveal these. But also for security reasons, we must make the necessary improvements.

Within days of the attack, I met with the Nuclear Regulatory Commission and we began what has proven to be a lengthy study of the vulnerability of our nuclear power plants and the necessary steps needed to safeguard them. To this end, I introduced legislation along with Senators Hillary Clinton and Harry Reid (D., Nev.) to make security forces at nuclear power plants federal employees.

The committee has worked hard to develop new protocol to safeguard the country's water supplies. The first step toward that end was a bill I introduced to increase funding for water-supply security. None of this will be accomplished easily. Our infrastructure is complex with many overlapping municipal, state, and national groups involved in regulation, monitoring, and maintaining our highways, water supplies, and power plants. Probably a thorough review of how our utilities do business was long needed. Now we have no choice but to do it and do it right.

A bright spot during these dark days came on October 26 when I received the Ophelia Settle Egypt Award from Planned Parenthood for my work in support of health care, especially breast cancer research and treatment, and a woman's right to choose at the group's convention at the Capitol Hilton. More than six hundred people were there. Security was so tight that the keynote speaker, actress Kathleen Turner, couldn't get in without her official name tag. It had been a frightening time for everyone, but domestic terrorism is nothing new to Planned Parenthood.

My only regret was that Liz was not with me. I opened my response after receiving the award by saying that Liz should be there instead of me as all I did was follow her orders on women's issues. This got resounding applause and laughter.

As usual, I was again asked to explain my reasons for my switch. I talked about the elimination of all money for education from the Bush budget and how disheartened I was to have to start that battle again. But close behind that important reason, I said, were my concerns about Supreme Court and federal court appointments. Many positions will open up over the next few years. Appointees must be people who will continue to protect the rights of women and maintain *Roe vs. Wade.* That decision is the foundation upon which women have been able to make such wonderful strides in the past thirty years in terms of access to education, job security, and job advancement.

My concern is not only for women in the United States but around the world. Actions of the Bush administration in this area had already disturbed me, especially the cutting of our support for overseas health programs that included family planning. Family planning, I believe, is essential to the health of the planet, which cannot sustain uncontrolled population growth and the accompanying strain on the environment and food and water supplies.

One of my worries since September 11, quite naturally, is the amount of money that is being spent on defense and my concern about where the money to pay for it is coming from, and what other programs will suffer as a result. I have been lobbying for fuller disclosure and discussion of our response, both militarily and financially. For the most part, my comments have fallen on deaf ears.

But there are areas where I can do good and that is where I am putting my attention—restoring funding for education, working to develop alternative sources of fuel, upholding and even improving our clean air standards and decreasing acid rain.

Senator Edward Kennedy, who chairs the Education Committee, and I are working on a new plan to review the president's school-testing program and ensure funding. Three new initiatives will aim to improve our preschool education programs, the teaching of math and science, and the overall quality of the nation's schools.

The issue of energy is crucial to our future, not just because of dependence on foreign oil but because of environmental concerns. As I said at a press conference on February 26, 2002, our crisis isn't really about having enough energy but a crisis of relying on outdated fuels that pollute our environment, threaten the health of our children and seniors, and create a dangerous dependence on foreign imports.

U.S. electricity generation is the leading source of carbon emissions, accounting for more than 40 percent of the U.S. total. We have a crisis of power plant emissions of nitrogen oxides, sulfur dioxide, and mercury, which contribute to acid rain, smog, respiratory illness, and water contamination. All this when domestically produced renewable energy such as wind, solar, geothermal, and vegetable matter can supply a substantial quantity of clean, reliable electricity at costs comparable to our current energy prices.

President Bush claims to support renewable energy, but his administration is doing everything possible to block efforts to promote it. His policies would allow the continuation of harmful emissions and continue business as usual. His administration has refused to endorse even a modest federal renewable energy standard.

My press conference was timed to coincide with the beginning of Senate debate on comprehensive energy legislation introduced by Majority Leader Tom Daschle. The proposal that he and Senator Jeff Bingaman (D., N.Mex.) put forth called for making positive steps in the areas of global climate change, standards, efficiency, and low-income energy assistance.

However, because that bill didn't contain enough in terms of renewable energy, I offered an amendment to the energy bill that would require U.S. utilities to gradually increase the portion of electricity produced from renewable resources such as wind, geothermal, and solar energy. My amendment would provide that by the year 2020, 20 percent of our electricity production would come from renewable resources. This proposal would create nearly $80 billion in new capital investment, almost $5 billion in new property tax revenues for local communities, and $1.2 billion in lease payments to farmers, ranchers, and rural landowners. It's remarkably similar to proposals I made twenty-five years ago as a young House member.

I brought with me several CEOs from leading renewable energy producers and distributors who testified that renewable energy production is both technologically and economically feasible and could save American consumers up to $4.5 billion on their energy bills from 2002 to 2020. Two leading consumer advocate groups, Consumers Union and Consumer Federation of America, have endorsed my proposal.

In hopes of moving S. 556, the Clean Power Act along, I wrote President Bush on February 7, 2002, and made the letter public. I felt that the Department of Energy's Environmental Protection Agency could do more to provide data and much-needed technical assistance to my committee.

Those agencies had cooperated during the development of the Clean Air Act amendments of 1990 but, as I wrote President Bush, they "have not provided or have been prevented from providing useful help" to my committee.

I was also upset that, when the industrialized nations of the world had met in Marrakech to discuss self-imposed carbon limits, the United States, the largest polluter, sat idly by without a plan for redressing the problem.

On top of all that, I said in my letter, I thought it very unwise to relieve polluters from compliance with existing Clean Air Act requirements, as the administration was suggesting. Now is not the time to lessen the standards.

Since September 11 I've also been trying to reopen the dialogue on carbon dioxide emissions, an issue of particular importance in Vermont, where acid rain from Midwest power plants has seriously harmed our deciduous trees, especially the maple, whose turning leaves in autumn not only make our state beautiful for residents but are a major draw for tourists. The health of the maple is also crucial to our maple syrup producers.

One year after President Bush formally notified the world and the Senate of his decision to unilaterally abandon the Kyoto Protocol, I spoke out for a sensible, market-based approach to reducing carbon emissions.

This issue doesn't just affect Vermonters. People everywhere should be concerned about the potential impacts of acid rain and climate change on public health, infrastructure, agriculture, wildlife, and sea levels. The rising sea level should be of particular concern to everyone. In December 2001, the National Academy said, "Greenhouse warming and other human alterations of the earth system may increase the possibility of large, abrupt, and unwelcome regional or global climatic events."

I suspect that I'll be working on these issues for the remainder of my political life—and long beyond. But I have other concerns as well.

During the holiday season Liz's cancer came back. During the spring of 2002 she underwent an operation and began her chemotherapy. It's a busy time in Washington, what with the war on terrorism and all the other problems of the world. But my perspective has changed. Now in our sixties, Liz and I have had our share of joy and sadness and we have chosen to focus on the positives.

One of our greatest joys, of course, comes from our children, who have grown to be bright, interesting adults. They both live near us here in Washington, which is quite wonderful. Leonard attended the University of Maryland, where he got all As before transferring to Georgetown University. He earned his master's degree in business administration from Duke. His wife, Maura Blue Jeffords, graduated from Catholic University Law School and went on to Georgetown for her master's in law.

My daughter, Laura, received a tennis scholarship to the College of Boca Raton in Florida. She loved the school and the sport—until her ankles gave out. After an operation to repair the tendons, she transferred to George Washington University. It wasn't until then that we discovered she had severe dyslexia. She'd been smart enough to compensate all those years, but one of her professors figured out from the way Laura took tests that she had the disorder and he suggested that she have herself tested. That discovery changed her life. She learned strategies for improving her reading and her grades immediately improved. After graduating from GW, she went to Catholic University School of Architecture and is now working to be a licensed architect. A couple of years ago Laura decided she wanted her own home and bought a house near the navy yard. The house was in, shall we say, disastrous shape, but the area was beginning to improve and did so fast. She and her boyfriend Jan, a marine, have converted the building into a most livable row house and the whole neighborhood is now dramatically improved.

This summer we'll return to Shrewsbury and put in the garden. I hope to have many uninterrupted afternoons on the tractor and an occasional picnic with my wife in one of our meadows. I'm learning to put things in perspective.

CHAPTER 24

My Challenge to the Country

I SOMETIMES THINK about our young people and wonder how they feel about our political system and their place in it. After fifty years of assassinations, Watergate, and so many other scandals, and the contentious race for president in the last election, it would not be unreasonable to be jaded about democracy and public servants. Indeed, I worry that our best and brightest youngsters are already turned off to the concept of public service.

But I am here to tell you that, despite the obstacles that are inherent in our system, despite the polarization that too often infects the White House and Congress, and despite the shenanigans and gamesmanship of Beltway politics, I have faith. I still believe that one person can make a difference. My life proves that.

Sometimes it's little things that have sustained me—the ability to make the difference in one person's life, such as my recent effort, along with fellow Vermonters Senator Patrick Leahy and Congressman Bernard Sanders, to gain the early release of former Middlebury College Tibetan music scholar Ngawang Choephel, thirty-four, from a Chinese prison where he had been serving an eighteen-year prison term on espionage charges. In the life of a senator, there are big losses and successes, but few are as satisfying as the moment when I saw his joyful face as he exited the plane on January 20, 2002, as a free man.

In another incident, we were able to play a pivotal role in the rescue of three young girls in Egypt who had been abducted by their father. I was able to get the signatures of more than half of all senators on a letter to Egyptian president Hosni Mubarak, urging him to enforce an Egyptian court ruling that the children be returned to their American mother. They were returned.

I believe in the value of dedicating your life to something greater than yourself. And perhaps more than ever, I believe if we are to preserve our open and free society, each of us must do more.

We have to dedicate ourselves to the right of all children to a quality education. Greed, expediency, and immediate gratification have too often dominated the discussion of budget allotments. Quality education is the foundation of a free society. That has to be our top priority.

We must also, each of us in our own way, do what we can to ensure that all citizens are given the tools they need to take part in our wonderful society. We cannot rely on government alone. It doesn't take a lot to be part of the solution—know what's going on in your community's schools. Volunteer. Read to a child. Donate books to the library. Sponsor a field trip. Start an internship program in your business. Join the PTA. Attend school board meetings. Put simply: be involved.

Back in 1979 I came under attack after I gave a talk to the Sons, Daughters, and Children of the American Revolution in which I said that American citizens have to be ready to sacrifice to meet upcoming economic and political challenges. This was at a time when the economy was in a slump and the nation was suffering from an energy shortage. My advice was that we should tighten our belts, spend money on future programs like education while simultaneously doing our best to reduce inflation and our dependency on foreign oil and expensive, unneeded luxury items.

My speech was greeted with hoots. The *Rutland Herald* reported that one woman said, "I'm sick and tired of the sacrificial animal bit" and went on to lament that the middle class was once again getting the shaft.

The *Herald*'s editorial writer, Kendall Wild, agreed with me. His editorial said what I'd been trying to express, only better: "Learning to discard the old myths is the hardest act of rejection for people, but it must be done intelligently and it must be done soon. We will have to prepare for some sacrifices, and it will be on us as individuals. To fret about whether 'the other fellow' will be making the same sort of sacrifice is pandering to the worst instincts of greed and selfishness that afflict humans everywhere.

"When everybody stands around waiting for 'the other fellow' and we ourselves still don't move, and then a break comes—shortage, anarchy, starvation, dictatorship, or war, depending on the seriousness of the circumstance—to take matters out of our hands and settle things for good.

"Face it," Kendall Wild wrote, "there are economic and political problems the like of which this country has not experienced. It will take imagination and a willingness to experiment with something new. . . . [I]ntellectual laziness has many manifestations. . . . It is in those who didn't realize that Vietnam was a bottomless political and economic morass for this country. It is in those who deride development of solar power as useless when their own short-term prosperity depends upon promoting other energy means. It is in those who waste energy and money on gas-guzzling automotive status symbols or recreation frills. It is in those who would keep . . . shahs and juntas in power without . . . national aspirations within those countries. It is in those who ignore the Panamanians because the canal is 'ours.' It is in the municipal union which, having spent great effort obtaining a raise in pay, has replied by giving us the worst winter-maintenance street service in recent city history. It is in all those, in other words, who say 'bunk' when asked to put some personal hard work into creating a United States that is not just more muscular than other countries, but is more intelligent. Rep. Jeffords was right, and we will ignore his advice at our national peril."

Scary, isn't it? Change a few names and places and you've got today. Everywhere I go, people are frustrated with business at home and abroad. They're worried about the world. They're disgusted about Enron. They're sick of all the telemarketers who call during dinner. They're concerned about our young people. They're embarrassed about the homeless. They're afraid of war in the Middle East. They want the government to do something about these problems but they don't want to pay another red cent in taxes.

As I told that group in Rutland in 1979, there are things each and every one of us can do to improve conditions at home and abroad. The five areas that should be our priorities if we are to ensure a safe, prosperous, and healthy world for our children begin with education. We cannot guarantee that all people will have the same successes; all we can do is work to ensure that the tools are there for our citizens to succeed if they choose to use them. That means equal support for women and men, the right of women to choose, passage of an Equal Rights Amendment, and laws to ensure that all people have the opportunity to advance themselves in all the ways that we measure success—in jobs, in athletics, in arts, and in academia.

There is a way for us to achieve a world-class education system for all American students.

Throughout my years in Congress I have had the opportunity to travel to various nations to observe their education systems. In China I learned that the school year was 255 days long and that the school day lasted for eight hours. The long school day, even for elementary school, is modulated with rigorous academic work, physical exercise, resting and social time, and art and music each day. Each subject, even in elementary school, is taught by a teacher specifically trained in teaching that discipline, be it writing, reading, mathematics, science, or art. Is it any wonder they crush us in international exams?

In Germany, I saw training schools located near the headquarters of the Daimler-Benz factory so that young people are trained for existing jobs while still in the public education system through comprehensive internship and training programs that put our country to shame. The same was true in China. I modeled our workforce investment model after their examples.

We have to get rid of our agrarian calendar, in which students have as long as ninety days away from the classroom. Studies show after a twenty-day gap children's retention decreases rapidly. Vacations should be more evenly spaced out over the school year. Our school day must be based on the holistic model of providing a well-rounded curriculum, like the Chinese, and like the Chinese we must be sure to have well-qualified teachers at every level of the system.

The next huge challenge we must accept is to provide quality, educational child care for all infants and toddlers. This is the only way that *all* children will truly come to kindergarten ready to learn, as stated in our long-standing national education goals. Right now the playing field for young children is destroyed by the abysmal mishmash of child care options that parents face after maternity (or paternity) leave ends. In our society today, most families must have both parents working to afford housing and an acceptable quality of life. Some parents can afford the best child care, averaging $1,200 a month, but most cannot.

Why should children be penalized from the beginning of their lives? We need national standards and training for qualified child care providers for all children and the federal government must assure that all children have access to quality care. Every other industrialized nation has an age 0–4 system in place to ensure a parent's return to the workplace and every child's optimal readiness for elementary school. The ultimate irony is that it is American research on brain and learning development in infants and toddlers that is the basis for many other countries' national child care systems. How can we continue to place our children at such a disadvantage?

The next sweeping change we must make is to improve the skills of our teachers; those currently at work in the classroom and our future teaching workforce in our schools of education. While chairman of the Senate Education Subcommittee, I was able to make some major legislative changes to hold institutions of higher education accountable for preparing teachers. We also created avenues to recruit highly qualified individuals, including individuals from other occupations, into the teaching force.

The final piece of the education puzzle is the keystone to it all. An essential mechanism for creating a first-rate educational delivery system requires an increase in the financial contribution of the federal government to education. Our international competitors pay a much higher percentage of the overall education costs than our federal government does. Japan's federal government and most others for example, fund up to 40 percent of their educational costs compared to only 7 percent paid by the federal government in the United States.

If Congress would fully fund IDEA, the extreme burden on states and localities for educating students with disabilities would be lessened, thus allowing reforms such as the extended school day and year. The estimated cost of universal quality child care is $55 billion a year. As part of my vote for the Economic Growth and Tax Relief Reconciliation Act of 2001 (George Bush's tax bill) my provision to increase the child care tax credit for families most in need was included. Child care tax credits need to be substantially expanded. If we postponed the tax rate reduction for the highest income brackets, we could make a great dent in the cost of providing a sound start for all of our nation's children over the next ten years. We have to be willing to recognize that improving the lives of all children ultimately improves our own individual destiny.

Our second priority must be peace. We must do what we can to make the world a safer place. I do not think that means name-calling or further alienating one group of people from another. Yes, we must fight terrorism and do all we can to make sure another September 11 doesn't happen. But we can't focus all our resources and energy on this one problem. To make the world safer, I believe, we must do what we can to help other nations improve the lives of their citizens in terms of health, education, welfare, and their environment. Not to do so will increase our vulnerability.

In this new era, it is even more important for us to learn about and show respect for all the cultures of the world. That is the very basis of a democracy—tolerance, not hegemony.

Rogue nations, military dictatorships, and terrorists thrive in a society in which political leaders do not have legitimacy with the people, in countries where people live in squalor, where children go to bed hungry, and where the comforts we take for granted are denied. If we are to have a safe world for our children, we must do what we can to share the world's resources and to help other nations help themselves to provide adequate food, water, health resources, and education to their citizens. That is the proper role for a democratic leader. The war on terrorism must include these elements if it is to succeed in the long term.

A democratic leader must also care about the planet and be more aware of the limitations on natural resources. Thus our third priority must be protection of the environment, which has suffered drastically as we've placed so much of our resources into growing our economy and supporting our defense systems. It is only common sense to think about the future of the planet if we truly want to leave our children with a world better than the one we came into.

This means that we must preserve the natural wonders and resources of the world. Protecting our national parks is part of this. Protecting important historic sites is also important. To that end, I've led the fight in Congress to protect Civil War sites and other historic places and buildings.

Protecting our air and water is even more essential. A country that destroys its water destroys its lifeblood; we have been too cavalier about our responsibilities for the wonderful natural resources with which we've been blessed. I do not mean to damn the industrial world—our agricultural community and our military have done their share of damage to our waters. The government is the number-one polluter in our nation. We must rectify the damage done and change our future practices.

But, again, each of us must do his or her part. This means not putting poisons into our environment heedlessly. Yes, we want healthy, productive crops, but we must not poison our soil and water simply to get crops that look good but are loaded with chemical residues.

When I made my switch, my primary reason was my concern for the lack of support I received from the Republican Party for funding education. After September 11, my personal responsibility and position as chairman of the Environment and Public Works Committee shifted to problems of pollution. This was a shift from helping to provide children with a good future to protecting the health and lives of all people. The public concern and attention dramatically increased, not only in this country but also all over the world.

The U.S. Environmental Protection Agency's administrator is Christine Todd Whitman, the former governor of New Jersey. I considered her a friend and an environmentalist. However, over the past months, the administration has pushed her to difficult positions. I'm still hopeful she will prevail on crucial issues. That hope gets dimmer each week.

To exacerbate the problem, the president's preoccupation with the war on terrorism has taken resources and attention away from environmental pollution and education to defense.

His actions to reduce environmental protections are even worse, especially his recent "roll back" of New Source Review. This allows extensive new releases of pollution from existing plants, resulting in a considerable increase of deaths.

The September 11 results were horrible with thousands killed or injured. But the annual deaths through power-plant pollution amount to tens of thousands each year. In New York City alone, approximately 2,290 deaths occur from power-plant pollution. Why is there no outrage?

Terrorism is terrible and we must do what we can to defend ourselves. But the most serious threat to Home Land Security is at home from our own power plants.

We need to invest both money and brain power into solving our energy problem. As long as we are dependent on Middle East oil, we cannot be neutral on the politics of the region; we have too much at stake. We must support the development of sustainable and alternative fuels. Here, too, each and every one of us can make a difference: turn off the lights, lower the thermostat, car-pool, recycle, compost. It all adds up.

And we cannot continue to create nuclear waste at nuclear power plants unless we have a way to properly dispose of these wastes. Otherwise we leave our children with a poisoned legacy. Germany recently voted to do away with all nuclear power plants in the next decade, replacing them with clean, sustainable fuels. While this seems like an overly optimistic goal, why isn't this country involved in a dialogue to solve our energy-consumption problems?

Our next priority must be equal access to core health care. A free and civilized society is based on the notion that all people deserve primary care for both their physical and mental health needs. I mean this in a holistic sense that includes education, outreach, and commonsense delivery approaches. A civilized society should seek to educate young mothers about the importance of a healthy diet, good dental care, and exercise. These are not costly notions but the payoffs are great. A civilized society cares for its mentally ill. A civilized society recognizes that addiction is an illness and provides programs to end cycles of substance abuse. The great number of homeless people living on the streets of our great cities shows our great failure in this regard. It is shameful.

Here again, each of us can do our small part. We can give blood. We can volunteer at health clinics. We can read to the elderly in nursing homes. We can teach a nutrition course at the library. We can give excess vegetables from our gardens to needy families. We can volunteer at homeless shelters. It's a matter of accepting our part in making the world a better place.

Lastly, I want to talk about our country's responsibilities to the small farmers of America. I don't want to get into a dispute about farm factories versus the family farm. We need both. We have to meet the demand for produce and dairy products. But the family farm is also an important part of our heritage and it deserves special protections. Family farms help us remember where products come from; they keep alive our connection with the land and the animals that help us in so many ways. And family farms are part of the landscape in so many parts of our country; they contribute to our natural beauty. They not only represent solid American values such as hard work being its own reward but they represent a way of life that is inherently wholesome and worth preserving. That's why environmental laws like Vermont's Act 250, a land-use law that seeks to protect prime agricultural land, and dairy compacts that provide essential funding for small dairy operations are so essential. It's not just an investment in a particular industry, it's an investment in a way of life that is core to the American experience. This, then, must also be our priority, to support those who grow the food that sustains us all.

I hope this book is not just about me. I hope you'll see that one person can make a difference, not just on the political landscape but in the priorities I believe are essential to a democratic nation—education, environment, the safety of the planet, health care, and the support for our agricultural community—and that you can have one heck of a good time doing so. I have.

Afterword

It has been more than a year since my decision to become an Independent. The number of contacts of support has increased, not decreased. I have received thousands of communications from all over the world, and small gifts of appreciation have come from as far away as Australia.

A few days after the switch, Liz and I traveled to Italy with other members of Congress to the "Conference on U.S. National Security and the Global Environment," hosted by the Aspen Institute. As we waited for our baggage, I noticed my picture on the front page of the local Florence newspaper. There were many representatives from various European nations at the conference and I was greeted by applause when I walked into my first meeting. Many Europeans expressed deep and growing concern about U.S. environment policies.

I returned to the United States and immediately attended the "Global Conference" in Maryland, which consisted of a legislative organization for a balanced environment of more than twenty European and American countries. Here again, representatives expressed deep concerns over President Bush's environmental policies. We agreed that we are in One World and the fate of all would be determined by the ability of all to do their part. I came away fully convinced that as chairman of the Environment and Public Works Committee I had the tremendous challenge of defeating the Bush administration's laissez-faire attitude. Without U.S. leadership, such problems as global warming will accelerate, and tens of thousands of needless deaths will occur due to preventable problems.

As of this writing, we have taken the first step with the Environment Committee passing out a bill covering all major pollutants, including carbon related to global warming. Passage in the near future is dim, but this is a major step forward.

Appendix: My Declaration

MAY 24, 2001, BURLINGTON, VERMONT

Anyone who knows me, knows I love the State of Vermont.

It has always been known for its independence and social conscience. It was the first state to outlaw slavery in its constitution. It proudly elected Matthew Lyon to Congress, despite his flouting of the Sedition Act. It sacrificed a higher share of its sons to the Civil War than perhaps any other state in the Union.

I recall Vermont Senator Ralph Flanders's dramatic statement almost fifty years ago, helping to bring to a close the McCarthy hearings, a sorry chapter in our history.

Today's chapter is of much smaller consequence, but I think it appropriate that I share my thoughts with my fellow Vermonters.

For the past several weeks I have been struggling with a very difficult decision. It is difficult on a personal level, but it is even more difficult because of its larger impact on the Senate and the nation.

I've been talking with my family, and a few close advisers, about whether or not I should remain a Republican. I do not approach this question lightly. I have spent a lifetime in the Republican Party, and served for twelve years in what I believe is the longest continuously held Republican seat in the U.S. Senate. I ran for reelection as a Republican just last fall, and had no thoughts whatsoever then about changing parties.

The party I grew up in was the party of George Aiken, Ernest Gibson, Ralph Flanders, and Bob Stafford. These names may not mean much today outside Vermont. But each served Vermont as a Republican senator in the twentieth century.

I became a Republican not because I was born into the party but because of the kind of fundamental principles that these and many other

303

Republicans stood for—moderation, tolerance, and fiscal responsibility. Their party—our party—was the party of Lincoln.

To be sure, we had our differences in the Vermont Republican Party. But even our more conservative leaders were in many ways progressive. Our former governor, Deane Davis, championed Act 250, which preserved our environmental heritage. And Vermont's Calvin Coolidge, our nation's thirtieth president, could point with pride to our state's willingness to sacrifice in the service of others.

Aiken and Gibson and Flanders and Stafford were all Republicans. But they were Vermonters first. They spoke their minds—often to the dismay of their party leaders—and did their best to guide the party in the direction of our fundamental principles.

For twenty-six years in Washington, first in the House of Representatives and now in the Senate, I have tried to do the same. But I can no longer do so.

Increasingly, I find myself in disagreement with my party. I understand that many people are more conservative than I am, and they form the Republican Party. Given the changing nature of the national party, it has become a struggle for our leaders to deal with me, and for me to deal with them.

Indeed, the party's electoral success has underscored the dilemma I face within my party.

In the past, without the presidency, the various wings of the Republican Party in Congress have had some freedom to argue and ultimately to shape the party's agenda. The election of President Bush changed that dramatically. We don't live in a parliamentary system, but it is only natural to expect that people such as myself, who have been honored with positions of leadership, will largely support the president's agenda.

And yet, more and more, I find I cannot. Those who don't know me may have thought I took pleasure in resisting the president's budget, or that I enjoyed the limelight. Nothing could be farther from the truth. I had serious, substantive reservations about that budget, and the decisions it sets in place for today and the future.

Looking ahead, I can see more and more instances where I will disagree with the president on very fundamental issues: the issues of choice, the direction of the judiciary, tax and spending decisions, missile defense, energy and the environment, and a host of other issues, large and small.

The largest for me is education. I come from the state of Justin Smith Morrill, a U.S. Senator who gave America the land-grant college system. His Republican Party stood for opportunity for all, for opening the doors of public school education to every American child. Now, for some, success seems to be measured by the number of students moved out of public schools.

In order to best represent my state of Vermont, my own conscience, and the principles I have stood for my whole life, I will leave the Republican Party and become an Independent. Control of the Senate will soon be changed by my decision. I will make this change and will caucus with the Democrats for organizational purposes, once the conference report on the tax bill is sent to the president.

My colleagues, many of them my friends for years, may find it difficult in their hearts to befriend me any longer. Many of my supporters will be disappointed, and some of my staffers will see their lives upended. I regret this very much. Having made my decision, the weight that has been lifted from my shoulders now hangs on my heart.

But I was not elected to this office to be something that I am not. This comes as no surprise to Vermonters, because independence is the Vermont way. My friends back home have supported and encouraged my independence—even when they did not agree with my decisions. I appreciate the support they have shown when they have agreed with me, and their patience when they have not. I will ask for that support and patience again, which I understand will be difficult for a number of my friends.

I have informed President Bush, Vice President Cheney, and Senator Lott of my decision. They are good people with whom I disagree. They have been fair and decent to me. I have also informed Senator Daschle of my decision. Three of these four men disagreed with my decision, but I hope each understood my reasons. And it is entirely possible that the fourth may well have second thoughts down the road.

I have changed my party label, but I have not changed my beliefs. Indeed, my decision is about affirming the principles that have shaped my career. I hope the people of Vermont will understand it. I hope, in time, that my colleagues will as well. I am confident that it is the right decision.

Acknowledgments

Besides Yvonne and Howard, there were others who were most helpful.

My wife, Liz, my children, Leonard and Laura, and Leonard's wife, Maura, were valuable supporters who helped with their computer skills and their careful reading and patience. I am blessed.

I also must specifically thank two others who were incredibly helpful: Frank Brown—or "Brownie" as we call him—for his helping me recall my years of active duty in the navy, and Dick D'Amato, a member of the Maryland House of Representatives who was on my staff in the House of Representatives. He helped give shape to the important work of those early years.

In Vermont, I am indebted to the dozens of generous people who contributed anecdotes, dug out old letters, provided photographs, and took the time to tell their stories. In particular, I would like to thank Arthur E. Crowley Jr.; former Vermont governor Philip H. Hoff; U.S. District Court Judge Fred Parker; Steve Baumann, the managing editor at the *Rutland Herald*, and Steve Terry, that paper's former managing editor.

Anyone who has experienced as much happiness and fulfillment as I have had the privilege to enjoy certainly has many people to thank. My friends, my colleagues, and my staff (past and present) have all played critical roles in making my life so fulfilling. I thank you all.

Index

abortion issues, 92
Acquilino, Salvatore, 31–32, 41–42, 43
Act 250 (1970), 102, 104, 136, 300
Act 252 (1970), 102–3, 111
Afghanistan, 164
African-Americans, 219, 222
Agency for International Development
    (AID), 149
Agent Orange, 206–7, 208
Agnew, Spiro, 132
Agricultural Lands Protection Bill, 159
Agriculture Department, U.S., 145, 220
Aiken, George, 65–66, 80, 89–90, 94,
    100, 101, 103, 116, 131–34, 136,
    137, 276
Aiken, Lola, 131–32, 276
Aiken, Robert, 94–95
Alaska, 159
Alaska Land Bill, 174
Albany County Jail, 20
Albosta Report, 196n
Albright, Madeleine, 231
Aldrich, Jeffrey Peter, 69–70
Aleutian Islands, 154
Allen, Ethan, 73
Alliance for Progress, 184
All the President's Men, 143
American Medical Association, 233
American University, 230
Amidon, Edward, 91
Amtrak, 178
Anderson, John, 174
anthrax-contaminated letters, 286
Apollo space program, 75, 88

Arias, Oscar, 184
Arms Export Control Act (1976), 201
Army Corps of Engineers, U.S., 100, 226
Ashcroft, John, 203, 229, 248, 251
Associated Press, 263
Atatürk, Mustafa Kemal, 33

baby seal hunting, 152–54
Backus, Jan, 209, 234–35
Bailey, Connie, 133
Balanced Budget Act (1997), 238, 239
Barry, Marion, 224
Basic Instinct, 281
Becker, John, 127, 137
"Before It's Too Late" (John Glenn
    report), 215
Bell, Terrell "Ted," 214, 217
Bennington Banner, 136
Bergland, Bob, 159
Bermuda, 84, 148
Bevill, Tom, 161–62
Bilirakis, Michael, 240–41
billboards, 77, 80–81, 99
Bingaman, Jeff, 289
bipartisanship, 146, 180, 229, 234, 235,
    265
Bishop, Crowley & Jeffords, 59, 62–63,
    67, 72
Bishop, Earle, 59, 62–63, 67, 72
Black, Henry, 107
Blanchard, John, 163
Bloomer, Bob, 63
Blum, Dick, 91
Boca Raton, College of, 171–72, 291

Bogen, Beau, 169
Boll Weevils, 176
Bosnia, 231
Boston, Mass., 48–49, 52, 55, 56
Boston Globe, The, 190
bottle legislation, 110, 126, 144–45
Bowers, Richard, 229
Brademus, John, 141–42
Brattleboro Sane Freeze, 204
Breaux, John, 237, 257, 259–60
Brennan, William, 106
Brigham, Red, 207
Broder, David, 177
Brown, Franklin "Brownie," 44
Bryan, Frank, 275
Buckley, T. Gary, 137
Bulletin of the Atomic Scientists, 232
Bundles for Britain, 9
Burger, Warren, 106
Burgess, John A., 147
Burgess, John "Jack," 117, 120, 134, 135,
    136–37
Burkhardt, Charlie, 161
Burlington, Vt., 46, 48, 53, 54, 56, 67,
    75, 77–78, 79, 111, 134, 135, 137,
    162, 209, 220, 254–55, 273–77,
    279–80
Burlington Free Press, The, 122
Burns, Conrad, 229
Bush, George H. W., 135, 167, 174–75,
    195–97, 202–8
Bush, George W., 119, 181, 237, 251,
    282, 285, 288, 289–90, 305
  education issues and, 264–67, 271,
    298
  tax cuts of, 253–63
Bush (G. H. W.) administration, 185,
    193, 254
Bush (G. W.) administration, 119,
    253–67
Butler, Lisa, 119–20

Cady, George, 17, 25
Cain, Frank, 134, 137–38

Cain, Mary, 138
Caldwell, Peter, 28, 233
Calhoun, John, 91, 115, 128
Calio, Nick, 262
Campbell, Norman, 155
Camp David Accords (1978), 164
Canada, 153–54, 232
Carter, Jimmy, 158, 160, 163, 164–67,
    195–96, 200
Carter administration, 158–67, 192, 195,
    196n, 197, 200
Casey, William, 167, 196n, 197, 198–99
Castro, Fidel, 52
Catholic schools, 116
Center for Strategic and International
    Studies, 149
Central America, 180, 181–86
Central Intelligence Agency (CIA), 35,
    149–50, 167, 200
Central Vermont Public Service
    Corporation, 109, 114
Centrist Coalition, 260
Chafee, Lincoln, 256, 257, 260, 261, 262
Champlain, Lake, 105–8, 128
Champlain, Samuel de, 105
Cheney, Dick, 186, 258–59, 263, 271
Cheney, Kimberly, 128, 131
children's health care, 238–39
China, People's Republic of, 111, 150,
    165, 214, 232, 292, 295
Chou En-Lai, 111
Christopher, Warren, 166
CIA (Central Intelligence Agency), 35,
    149–50, 167, 200
Civil War, U.S., 64, 72
Clean Power Act (2002), 290
Clinton, Bill, 213, 232, 235, 236
  impeachment of, 241–42, 243, 244–46
Clinton, Hillary Rodham, 234, 237, 245,
    285, 287
Clinton administration, 213, 217, 221,
    226, 231–32, 234, 253, 254
CNN, 248, 256, 270, 284
Coats, Dan, 212–13

Coffrin, Albert, 193–94
Cold War, 215
Common Sense Associates, 120, 126
communism, 52, 60, 149–50, 181, 183
Comprehensive Test Ban Treaty (1990),
    203, 232
"Conference on U.S. National Security
    and the Global Environment,"
    305
Congress, U.S., 63, 73, 115–16, 131, 154,
    155, 182–83, 184, 205, 216, 220
    committee system in, 212
    hideaway offices in, 250–51
    increased conservatism of, 178
    partisanship in, 158, 212, 237, 265,
        292
    Republican control of, 209, 253–54,
        272
    success in, 145–46
    Washington, D.C., and, 221–30
    see also House of Representatives,
        U.S.; Senate, U.S.
Congressional Arts Caucus, 180
Congressional Environmental Study
    Conference, 152
Congressional Wind Energy Caucus, 163
Congressional Wood Energy Caucus, 160
Connolly, Ken, 258, 284
Constitution, U.S., 175, 193, 211, 222,
    240
consumer advocate groups, 289
Contract with America, 209–10
Contradoras, 182, 183–84
Cook, George, 68
Cooks, Larry, 177
Coolidge, Abigail, 65
Coolidge, Calvin, 3, 64–65, 73
Costa Rica, 184
Costle, Douglas, 234–35
Cox, Archibald, 132
Craig, Larry, 229, 248, 251, 258, 271
Cree, Albert A., 109, 115
Crowley, Art, 59, 62, 66, 67, 72
Cutter, R. Ammi, 107–8, 128

dairy issues, 141, 145, 147, 149, 156,
    159, 170, 173, 178, 241, 299–300
Daley, John (Jeffords's father-in-law), 77,
    81, 98, 188
Daley, John "Jack" (Vermont Lieutenant
    Governor), 73, 78, 90
D'Amato, Dick, 149, 155, 160
Danforth, Jack, 119
Dartmouth College, 233
Daschle, Tom, 262, 268–69, 286, 289
"Dateline," 244–47
Davis, Deane C., 85–86, 133
    background of, 79–80
    as governor of Vermont, 90, 93,
        95–96, 98, 99–100, 102, 103–4,
        108–9, 115, 117–18, 126, 127
    Jeffords opposed by, 87, 93, 107,
        108–9, 111, 115, 118, 120–21,
        122–23
Davis, Marjorie, 96–97, 98
Davis, Polk & Wardwell, 106
Davis, Tom, 226
Dean, Howard, 233
Debategate, 196n
Defense Department, U.S., 199
deficit, federal, 180
Delaney, Frederic J. "Ted," 56, 57, 58, 64,
    67, 69
Delaney, O'Neill, and Valente, 56
Democratic National Committee, 121
Democratic Party, 123, 152, 160, 161,
    176, 179, 192, 212, 254, 258,
    259–60, 261, 271
    attempted wooing of Jeffords by,
        267–68
    House of Representatives controlled
        by, 140
    in Vermont, 56, 57, 58, 64, 65, 67,
        68, 69, 71, 73, 74, 75–76, 78, 121,
        132, 134, 137–38, 147, 156–57,
        234–35
    see also elections
DeNardis, Larry, 176
Devers, Jacob L., 10

Dewey, George, 73
Dexter family, 206
Diamondstone, Peter, 157
Dietz, S. Marie, 157
District of Columbia, see Washington,
D.C.
District of Columbia Financial
Responsibility and Management
Assistance Act (1995), 224
Dodd, Chris, 235, 267, 268
Domenici, Peter, 251, 256, 258–61, 266
Donne, Jim, 27
Douglas, Stephen, 64
Douglas, William O., 106–7
Doyle, Mavis, 76
drug companies, price fixing lawsuit and,
118–19
drug users, 85, 86
Duberstein, Ken, 176–77

Economic Growth and Tax Relief
Reconciliation Act (2001), 296
economy, U.S., 179, 254–55
Edson family, 4
Education Department, U.S., 214, 217,
227, 242
education issues, 14, 165, 175, 176, 178,
209, 210, 211, 213–30, 241, 282,
283, 288
George W. Bush and, 264–67, 271
government funding and, 213–18,
256–63, 296, 298
Jeffords's national tour and, 218–21,
230
Jeffords's proposals on, 294–96
overview of, 213–15
in Washington, 221, 225, 227–30
Egypt, 164, 292
Eisenhower, Dwight D., 35
elections:
of 1936, 66
of 1958, 67
of 1960, 52
of 1968, 77, 79, 81, 90
of 1970, 103–4
of 1972, 117–28
of 1974, 133–39, 140
of 1976, 147–48
of 1978, 147, 156–57
of 1980, 166, 174–75, 195–96
of 1988, 187, 192
of 1994, 209, 234–95
of 2000, 253
Elementary and Secondary Education
Act (1994), 213, 221
Elk Hills Petroleum Storage facility, 163
Ellsberg, Daniel, 111
El Salvador, 181–82, 185–86
Energy Appropriations Bill, 161–62
Energy Department, U.S., 162–63, 290
energy issues, 158–64, 178–79, 288–90,
298–99
Engler, John, 217
environmental issues, 77, 80–81, 85,
120, 152, 210, 297–98, 305
in Jeffords's Vermont attorney general
tenure, 91, 92, 93–96, 99–103,
104, 105–16, 128–29
Environmental Protection Agency
(EPA), 144–45, 290, 298
Environmental Study Conference, 164
Equal Rights Amendment (ERA), 158,
175, 192, 294
Eritrea, 34
Esquire, 172–73
Everybody Wins! literacy program, 221,
227–29, 245

Farwell, Billy, 14, 25
Federal Bureau of Investigation (FBI),
198, 279
Federal Emergency Management Agency
(FEMA), 284–85
federal judges, selection of, 193–95, 272
Feen, Pearly, 55
Fenton, Wing, Morse, and Jeffords, 3
Fenwick, Millicent, 143
filibusters, 240–41

Finchem, Tim, 229
First, Bill, 237
"flatlanders," 65
Fleischer, Ari, 265–66
FMLN, 185–86
Food and Drug Administration (FDA),
    235, 251
Food for Peace, 149
food stamps, 148, 165, 178
Foote, Ralph, 101
Ford, Gerald R., 132, 136, 137–38, 147
Foreign Operations bill, 185
Forman, Michele, 265
43rd Division, 8, 9, 10, 11
Fox, Jeff, 226
France, 204, 206, 232
Franke, Bill, 45, 127
Freyne, Peter, 270
Friedersdorf, Max, 177
Friends of the Animals, 154
Fuller, Edith, 5

Gano, John, 40, 41
Gebert, Wesley, 32, 38, 40
Germany, 295
Gibb, Arthur, 93–94, 123
Gibb Commission (Governor's
    Commission on Environmental
    Controls), 93–94, 96, 100, 101–2
G.I. Bill, 215
Gibson, Ernest, Jr., 56, 66, 80
Gibson, Ernest, Sr., 66
Gilbert, Bill, 91
Gilman, Ben, 141
Gingrich, Newt, 146, 180, 209–11, 212,
    213, 240, 243
Ginzburg, Alexander, 156
Giuliani, Rudy, 285
Glen Cove, N.Y., 3, 12
Glenn, Jim, 27
Glenn, John, 215
Goals 2000 Educate America Act
    (1995), 217–18
"Good Morning America," 143

Gorbachev, Mikhail, 180–81, 203
Gorton, Slade, 119
Governor's Commission on
    Environmental Controls (Gibb
    Commission), 93–94, 96, 100,
    101–2
Graff, Chris, 263–64
Gramm, Phil, 240–41, 271
Grassley, Chuck, 140, 256, 262
Gray, William, 192
Green, Bill, 176
Green Mountain Park, 76–77
Greenpeace, 153
Gregg, Judd, 212–13
Grey, C. Boyden, 194–95
Griffin, Will, 91
Guatemala, 184, 185, 186
Guild, Arthur, 4
Guild, Jim, 4, 9, 24
Guild, Malcolm, 4, 10, 24, 27
Guild family, 4, 9
Guilford, Rayne, 219
Gulf War, 204–8
Gunderson, Steve, 220
Guyana, 157–58
Gypsy Moths, 176, 177–78

Hackett, Luther "Fred," 111, 117–18,
    121–28
Hackett, Sally, 124
Hagel, Chuck, 260
Hager, Bob, 143
Haiti, 185
Hamilton, Lee, 183, 184
Hansen, George, 15, 16, 25, 46–47, 54
Hansen, John, 91, 94–96, 100, 102–3,
    106, 112, 114–15, 125
Harbin, Thomas, 32, 38–40
Harding, Warren, G., 65
Harkin, Tom, 235, 262, 263
Harmogenizers, 17
Hartigan, John, 17, 25
Harvard Law School, 29, 32, 35, 50–52,
    54–55

Harwood, Madeline, 89, 134–37
Hashemi, Cyrus, 197–99
Hatfield, Mark, 248
Hausman, Doris, 12, 26, 168
Hausman, Laura, 12, 118
Hausman, Nicholas, 4, 11, 12, 17
Haussmann, Baron, 12
Hayes, Ginny, 97
Hayes, Thomas, 79, 90, 97, 103–4
Hayward, Tim, 160
health care, 158, 210, 232–41, 287
Health Care Quality, Education,
    Security, and Trust Act (QUEST
    Act) (1998), 236
Health Care Reform Advisory
    Committee, 233
Hebard, Emory, 74
Heckler, Margaret, 140
Heim, Laurie Schultz, 183
Hemco Inc., 100
Hickel, Walter, 105–6
Hill, Anita, 202
Hill, The, 173, 249
Hills, Carla, 186
Hines, Ed, 6
HMOs, 236–37
Hobson, Julius, 222
Hoff, Philip Henderson, 56, 67, 70–71, 73,
    74, 75–76, 77, 78, 81, 90, 132, 133
Hogg, Douglas, 203
Honduras, 181–82, 184–85
H1B visa program, 215
Hospital Insurance Trust Fund, 238
House Agricultural Committee, 140–41
House Armed Services Committee, 163
House Dairy Subcommittee, 159
House Education and Labor Committee,
    141, 161
    Subcommittee on Employment
        Opportunities of, 159
House Foreign Affairs Committee, 141
House Judiciary Committee, 136
House of Representatives, U.S., 5, 111,
    176, 183, 236, 243

Democratic control of, 140
Jeffords as member of, 133–87, 192,
    258–59, 268, 273
Jeffords's committee memberships in,
    140–41
Jeffords's initiatives in, 146
seniority system in, 140–41, 146
Vermont members of, 67, 111, 113,
    117, 133–34, 265, 292
Washington, D.C., nonvoting mem-
    ber of, 225
House-Senate Committee on Atomic
    Energy, 116
House Ways and Means tax-writing com-
    mittee, 160
Hovis, Guy, 249
H. O. Wheeler School, 220
hunting, 34, 42–43, 152–54
Hussein, Saddam, 204–6
Hyland, Fred, 18–23, 25

Idi Amin, 164
Individuals with Disabilities Education
    Act (IDEA) (1975), 141, 296
political battle over funding of,
    216–18, 256–63, 267
Indonesia, 145, 148–50
International Nuclear Freeze Treaty
    (1988), 181
International Paper Company (IPC),
    105–8, 118, 121, 128–29
Iranian hostage crisis, 158, 165–67
Jeffords's investigation of, 167,
    195–201
Iraq, 166, 204–8
Israel, 164, 195, 201, 208
Italy, 305

Jackson, Henry "Scoop," 156
Jackson, Jesse, 274
Janeway, Edward, 77, 120, 123
Japan, 8, 296
Jeffords, James M.:
    appendicitis of, 6–7

athletics and, 3, 15, 16–17, 20, 24, 26–27, 35, 172

awards and honorary titles received by, 173, 267, 280, 287

birth of, 1, 2

canceled White House passes of, 177, 179

in car accidents, 18–19, 137, 140, 191, 242, 251

challenge to the country issued by, 292–300

childhood of, 2–17

children's relationships with, 60, 83, 144, 169, 171–72, 291

collegiate drinking habits of, 29, 82

early jobs held by, 13–14

education of, 17, 18, 24–29, 32, 35, 50–52, 54–55

failed gubernatorial campaign of, 117–26, 130, 192

financial state of, 4, 24, 35, 44, 52, 56, 142–44, 169–70

first election campaign of, 61–64, 67–71

hitchhiking misadventure of, 17–23

homes of, 4, 57–58, 72, 96, 119, 130, 143–44, 169–73, 190–91, 223, 291

as Independent, 1, 124–25, 267–72, 276

law career of, 59, 62–63, 67, 72, 75, 91, 130

as law clerk, 55–56, 66

as master of the spoken word, 77, 246, 275

as "Mister Dairy," 173

naiveté of, 1, 17–18

naval career of, 23, 24, 25–29, 30–45, 50, 60, 206

obscurity of, 143, 229, 274

physical appearance of, 14, 47

political campaign style of, 16

self-image of, 1–2, 5, 11, 13–14, 15–16, 17–18, 23, 25, 50–51, 81–82, 278

tai kwon do black belt of, 172

as Vermont attorney general, 84, 85–116, 118, 121, 127, 128–29, 138–39

as volunteer fireman, 59, 191

Jeffords, Laura, 142, 173, 190, 242, 269, 271

birth and adoption of, 61

tennis playing of, 171–72, 291

Jeffords, Leonard Olin, 10, 89, 130, 171–73, 175, 190, 268, 269–71, 286

birth and adoption of, 60

education of, 291

Jeffords, Liz, 1, 46–54, 57–61, 72, 75, 77–78, 114, 128, 171, 207, 209, 244, 250, 287, 305

cancer of, 242–43, 291

character of, 47–48, 49–50, 53–54, 81–82, 148, 274

cooking of, 51, 53, 59, 172, 189

Jeffords's letters to, 49, 51, 56

Jeffords's party switch and, 268–70, 274–75, 277, 280

Jeffords's political campaigns and, 62–63, 68–70, 78, 87, 89, 90, 119–20, 124, 134, 192

Jeffords's relationship with, 46–54, 61, 62, 78–79, 81–84, 92–93, 96–98, 103, 122, 130, 142, 144, 148–51, 168–69, 188–92

jobs held by, 46, 47–48, 55, 56, 60, 83

political opinions of, 47–48, 52, 69, 97, 123

substance abuse problems of, 79, 81–82, 97, 130, 134, 148, 150, 189

Jeffords, Marion, 5, 6, 7–8, 11, 12, 56, 61, 68, 83, 130, 144, 148

background of, 3

death of, 168–69

Jeffords, Mary, 5, 6, 9, 12, 15, 24, 83

Jeffords, Maura Blue, 173, 268, 269, 271, 291

Jefford, Olin, 6–8, 15, 16, 17, 19, 20,
 21–23, 24, 44–45, 64, 72, 80, 83,
 148
 background of, 3
 character of, 7, 13
 death of, 60, 98
 health problems of, 48, 50, 56–57, 60,
  168
 Jeffords's relationship with, 4, 7, 9,
  10, 11, 12–13, 81
 judicial career of, 1, 5, 9, 16, 57, 99,
  110, 139
 law career of, 3
Jesuit priests, murdered in El Salvador,
 185–86
Johnson, Connie, 128
Johnson, Lyndon B., 75, 79, 81, 84
Johnson State College, 130
Johnston, Jim, 207
Jones, Jim, 157–58
Jones, Paula, 243
Justice Department, U.S., 132, 136, 195

Kachadorian, Jim, 190
Kassebaum, Nancy, 211
Keefe, Bill, 91
Kennedy, Edward M., 200, 228, 229, 234,
 235, 238, 282, 288
Kennedy, John F., 52, 56, 156, 184–85
Kennedy, Robert F., 88
Kennedy, Walter "Peanut," 111, 137,
 138
Kent State University, 103–4
Key to the Future education summit,
 217
Kharl, Tom, 42
King, Martin Luther, Jr., 84, 143
King Reid Shows, 74
Kinney, Clayton, 72
Klavana, Layton, 91
Knickerbocker News, 22
Kosovo, 231
Kurtz, Bill, 269, 276, 279
Kuwait, 204–5, 207

Larrow, Robert, 67
law enforcement, 87–88
League of Women Voters, 130–31
Leahy, Pat, 92, 133, 134, 138, 157, 185,
 193, 265–66, 286, 292
"Lebanon Crisis," 40–42
Leddy, Bernard, 67
Lefevre, Reid "King Reid," 74, 77, 80
Lewinsky, Monica, 243, 246–47
Liberty Union Party, 137, 157
Lieberman, Joseph, 236, 245
Life, 74
Lincoln, Abraham, 64, 72
Lincoln School, 15
Links to Literacy, 229
literacy programs, 221, 227–29, 241
Long Beach, Calif., 230
Longworth House Office Building, 170
Lott, Trent, 212, 226, 229, 237, 239,
 240, 248–50, 256, 257–58,
 260–63, 271, 282
Lott, Tricia, 269
Love, John, 115–16
Lufkin, Fitz, 41, 42

McCabe, Mike, 164
McCarthy, Eugene, 79, 81
McClaughry, John, 175, 179
McEvoy, Trecia, 265
McGovern, George, 117, 121, 123,
 128
McGreevy, Annie, 119
McGreevy, Harriet, 51, 58, 61, 62, 69,
 75, 78, 79, 98
McGreevy, Kathleen, 63, 119, 153
McGreevy, Paul, 69
Mack, Connie, 248
Mack, Myrna, 186
McLeod, Hugh, 9
McNair, USS, 30–45, 229
McPherson, Al, 17, 25
Mahady, Frank, 111
Mailer, Norman, 51
Maine, 119

Mallary, Richard, 73–74, 109, 110–11, 112, 117, 132–34, 136, 137, 138
Mannetta, Norm, 163
"man overboard" drill, 44
Marcos, Ferdinand, 11
Mares, Bill, 275
Marshall, Thurgood, 201
Martin, Pamela Sue, 153
Martin, Stuart, 127
Maryland, 143, 144
Massachusetts, 119
Maynard, Hull, 59
Maynard, Joanna Taft "Taffy," 57
Meade, Larkin, 72
Medicaid, 178
Medicare, 238, 239
Medicare Home Health Fair Payment Act (1998), 239–40
MediCORE, 233–34
Meeker, Stuart, 44
Mendicino, Jane, 192
Merusi, Aldo, 6
Meyer, William, 67
Michel, Bob, 176
Mikulski, Barbara, 226, 235
Miller, Kelton, 136
Miller, Martin, 91
Miller, Zell, 257
Minnesota, 115
Mintz, John A., 200
Miranda, Georgiana, 91
Missouri, 119
Mitchell, George J., 196, 231, 234
Mitchell, John, 131
Montpelier, Vt., 5, 9, 72, 85, 89, 90–91, 93, 94, 96, 103, 117, 118, 124, 127, 128, 130, 134, 136, 138, 142–43, 144, 155, 205, 207
Morella, Connie, 226
Morse, Russell, 91
Moss, John, 163
Moulton, Elbert G. "Al," 78, 79, 87, 90, 135
"Mountain Rule," 65

Mubarak, Hosni, 292
Munger, Jeff, 276
Murray, Bernice, 119, 123, 124, 130–31, 133, 155
mustang naval officers, 31–32

Naked and the Dead, The (Mailer), 51
National Defense Education Act (1958), 216
National Endowment for the Arts (NEA), 180
National Life Insurance Company, 79
National Security Agency, 199
National Teacher of the Year, 265–66
National Unity Party, 174
"Nation at Risk, A" (Bell report), 214, 215
Native Americans, 218–20
NATO, 231
naval reserves, 45, 60, 206
Navy, U.S., 30–45, 50, 163
Navy ROTC, 23, 24, 25–29
NBC News, 143
Nelson, Ben, 257
Nelson, Bill, 268
Nelson, Garrison, 278
New England Energy Caucus, 161
New Federalism, 178
Newfoundland, 153–54
New Hampshire, 119
Newsweek, 280
New York (state), 106, 107
New York Times, The, 111, 112, 205, 206, 228
New Zealand, 149
Ngawang Choephel, 292
Nicaragua, 181–85
Nichols, Harold "The Hawk," 4
Nichols, Jean, 9
Nickles, Don, 237, 256, 271
Nixon, Richard M., 52, 81, 90, 98, 103, 106, 111, 117, 121, 128, 131–33, 135–36
Nixon administration, 106, 134, 135, 141

North Dakota, 218–20
nuclear arms control, 164, 180–81, 203, 232
nuclear power plants, *see* Vermont Yankee nuclear power plant
Nuclear Regulatory Commission, 287

Oakes, James Lowell, 80, 86, 90, 91, 113
Oak Ridge Boys, 249–51
Oberstar, James, 181
October Surprise, 196–97
Ohio National Guard, 103–4
Omnibus Appropriations Bill (1998), 240–41
Omnibus Emergency Farm Bill, 147
O'Neill, Joe, 56, 69–71, 103
O'Neill, Thomas P. "Tip," 161
One Percent for Education, 217
Operation FitKids, 230
Ophelia Settle Egypt Award, 287
Oregon, 110, 119, 145
Orphaned City, The (Rivlin), 222
Orzell, Andrew, 68
Ottinger, Dick, 163–64
"overseer of the poor," 74

Palmisano, Joseph, 85, 87, 88–90, 99
Parenti, Michael, 137
Parker, Fred, 91, 95, 106, 107, 194–95
patients' rights bills, 236–38
Paul family, 4, 9
Paul Robeson Academy, 219
peace, as national priority, 296–97
Pearl Harbor, 8
Peck, Louis, 91
Pentagon, September 11 attack on, 284–85
Pentagon Papers, 111
People's Church, 157–58
Perkins, Craig, 14–15
PGA Tour, 229
Philippines, 9, 11
Pierce, Glendon, 58
Pierce, Gordon, 58

Pierce, Marion, 58
Pierce, Marjorie, 58, 59, 191
Pierce family, 58, 69, 191
Pierce family store, 58, 191
Pineless, Dean, 194
Planned Parenthood, 287
Plotkin, Mark, 221
"Porker of the Month," 267
Potomac Regional Education Partnership (PREP), 230
Powden, Mark, 208, 260, 269
Pratt, Cora Jeffords, 3, 61
Prouty, Winston, 79, 91, 103, 111
Public Law 100–297, 220
Purdy, Ellery, 68
Pursell, Carl, 176

Rachlin, Robert, 194
Reagan, Nancy, 133
Reagan, Ronald, 133, 164, 166–67, 174–80, 183, 184, 192, 195–201, 213–14, 254
Reagan Library, 200
Reed, Fred, 95–96
Regan (sailor), 37
Reid, Harry, 268–69, 287
Republican National Committee, 120, 135, 276
Republican National Conventions:
   of 1980, 175
   of 1996, 250
Republican Party, 16, 161
   big business control of, 66, 178
   Congress controlled by, 209, 253–54, 272
   increased conservatism of, 209–11, 231, 253, 271–72
   Jeffords's quitting of, 1, 17, 66, 192, 202, 267–77, 287–88, 298, 301–3
   Jeffords's relationship with, 57, 64, 77–78, 81, 87–88, 98, 117–18, 122–25, 127, 135, 137, 152, 174–81, 197, 201–2, 209–12, 216, 243–44, 251–52, 253–72, 282

Jeffords's voting record and, 75–76, 81, 179, 192, 235, 243–44
liberals and moderates in, 65–67, 80, 98, 103, 147, 158, 176, 179, 211, 212, 231, 255
Policy Committee of, 251
reaction to Jeffords's quitting of, 275–83, 305
Senatorial Committee of, 266
in Vermont, 57, 58, 61–63, 64–71, 73–81, 84, 87, 90, 93, 103, 111, 117, 120–29, 131–39, 156, 175, 179, 231, 276
Vermont State Committee of, 77–78, 89, 90, 117, 128, 131, 132–33, 137
see also elections
Rethinking America (Smith), 214, 217
Revolutionary War, 73
Rhee, Joon, 172
Rhodes, John, 146
Ribicoff, Abraham, 156
Rice, George, 91, 130
Richards, Richard, 180
Richardson, Bill, 181–82, 183, 184
Richardson, Elliott, 132
Richmond, Frederick, 180
Riehle, Theodore, 77, 80, 90, 99
Riley, Richard, 217
Rio de Janeiro, 25–27
Rivlin, Alice M., 222
Robert Wood Johnson Health Policy Fellow, 235
Rockefeller, Jay, 271
Rockefeller, Nelson, 81, 136
Rockwell, Norman, 14
Rodriguez, Chi Chi, 229
Roe vs. Wade, 92
Roll Call, 248
Rolling Stone, 281
Rome, Bernie, 16
Romer, Roy, 217
Romney, George, 78
Roosevelt, Theodore, 222

Ross, Charley, 137
ROTC, see Navy ROTC
Roth, William, 239, 240
Rove, Karl, 282
Rudman, Warren, 119, 238
Russ, Jack, 179
Russ, Susan Boardman, 119, 194, 208, 209–10, 260–61, 268–70, 274, 276–77, 279, 284
Rutland, Vt., 1, 24, 45, 56, 59, 62–63, 64, 68–69, 73, 79–80, 83, 89, 91, 136, 144, 148, 168–69, 174, 204, 206
Jeffords's childhood in, 2–17
Rutland County, Vt., 64, 69, 75
Rutland Herald, 6, 8, 10, 15, 86–87, 102, 113, 117, 120, 122, 131–32, 133, 141, 156, 157, 293–94
Rutland High School, 4, 15, 16, 20, 25, 68, 73
Ryan, Leo, 152–54, 157–58

Saddam Hussein, 204–6
St. Albans, Vt., 116
St. John Vienney Church, 54
Salander, Lou, 4
Salmon, Thomas, 103, 104, 121, 124–25, 126, 127–28, 131, 137, 138
Salt II Treaty (1979), 164, 181
Sanders, Bernard, 265, 292
Sanford, Terry, 196–97
Santa's Land, 99
Sargant, John, 3
Saudi Arabia, 204
Schumer, Charles, 285
Scowcroft, Brent, 203, 206
Seal, Judy, 230
seal hunting, 152–54
search-and-rescue missions, 36–37
Secret Service, 199, 207
Senate, U.S., 5, 66, 119, 147, 156, 164, 183, 184
Democratic control of, 271–73
federal judicial appointments and, 193–95

Senate, U.S. (*continued*)
    Jeffords as member of, 145, 185, 187,
        192–300
    Jeffords's committee memberships in,
        196, 211–13, 217, 221, 227, 231,
        235, 238, 239
    Jeffords's threatened filibuster in,
        240–41
    reconsidering of questions in, 262–63
    Republican control of, 202, 209–11,
        253
    Vermont members of, 66, 92, 103,
        111, 117, 131–34, 138, 157, 185,
        193, 292
Senate Appropriations Committee, 239
Senate Budget Committee, 255
Senate Education Committee, 288
Senate Environment and Public Works
    Committee, 1, 286–87, 305
Senate Finance Committee, 238, 241
Senate Foreign Relations Committee, 66,
    196, 231
Senate Health, Education, Labor, and
    Pensions (HELP) Committee, 213,
    234, 235–36, 239, 251, 282–83
Senate Judiciary Committee, 202
Senate Labor, Health, and Human
    Resources Committee, 211–13
Senate Working Group on Mental
    Health and Substance Abuse, 234
September 11 terrorist attacks, 1, 232,
    282, 284–87, 297
Serbia, 231
Serrano, Jorge, 186
Seward, Roland Q., 77, 79, 90, 120, 126,
    128, 147
    background of, 68
    Jeffords opposed by, 113, 123, 132
    Jeffords's political start and, 61–62,
        67, 70
    political power of, 61–62, 68
Shaheen, John, 198–99
Shaw, Natalie, 8–9
Shaw family, 4

Shelby, Richard, 268
Shields, Lee, 170
Shrewsbury, Vt., 4, 57–59, 61, 64, 69, 70,
    72, 77, 78, 84, 85, 98, 119, 130,
    190–91, 291
Shultz, George, 183
Simon, Paul, 228
Singing Senators, 17, 229, 237, 248–52,
    271
Sirica, John, 132
Skipjack, USS, 45
slavery, 64
Smith, Bob, 248, 285
Smith, Hedrick, 214, 217
Smith, Stewart, 128, 133, 137, 147
Smulson, Erik, 248, 261, 270, 276–77, 279
Snelling, Richard, 70, 117, 120
Snowe, Olympia, 176, 238
"social promotion," 227
Solzhenitsyn, Aleksandr, 152, 154–56
Solzhenitsyn, Natalia, 154–56
Soule, Tim, 119, 122, 124
Soviet Union, 52, 145, 152, 154–56, 164,
    180–81, 203, 215
space race, 215–16
Specter, Arlen, 262
Spencer, Jack, 57
Stafford, Bob, 63, 104, 193
    as Jeffords's political mentor, 5, 192,
        270
    political career of, 5, 67, 111, 117,
        187, 192
Stahl, John, 91
Standing Rock Lakota Sioux
    Reservation, 218–20
Stark, John, 73
State Department, U.S., 40, 166, 200
State of Vermont vs. Santa's Land, 99
Stenholm, Charlie, 176
Stepanian, Steve, 55
Stetson, Jackie, 10
Stickney, Sargant, Skeels, and Jeffords, 3
Stone, Sharon, 281
Stowe, Vt., 111–12

Suez Canal, 33, 34–35, 42
Sun Day, 162
Sununu, John, 205
Supreme Court, U.S., 85, 92, 119, 136,
    272, 288
    International Paper Company suit
        and, 104, 106–8
    Thomas's appointment to, 201–3
Switzerland, 49

Tannenbaum, Arthur and Phyllis, 228
taxes, 119, 122
    George W. Bush's cuts in, 253–63
    Reagan's cuts in, 176–80, 192
    in Vermont, 75–77, 81, 93
    Washington commuter tax, 226–27
Teen Center, 15
Teng Hsiao-ping, 165
terrorism, 1, 232, 253, 296–97, 298
    see also September 11 terrorist attacks
Thaddeus T. Parker, USS, 25–27
Third International Mathematics and
    Science Study (TIMSS), 214–15
Thomas, Clarence, 201–3
Thomas, Dick, 90
Thomas, William, 240
Thurmond, Strom, 155
Time, 280
"Today Show," 249
Tomasi, Teresa, 60
Topping, Tom, 30
Torricelli, Bob, 257
Trickle-Down Economics, 178
Tripp, Linda, 243, 247
Truman, Harry S., 66
Tuck School of Business, 233
Turkey, 33–34, 42–43
Turner, Kathleen, 287
21st Century Community Learning
    Center, 220–21

Uganda, 164
United Nations Test Ban Amendment
    Conference (1993), 232

U.N. Security Council 165–66, 204
U.S. News and World Report, 280

Vance, Cyrus, 166
Venice, 35
Vermont, 1–139, 145, 147, 155,
    159–60, 162–63, 174–75, 177,
    186–87, 191, 193, 216, 229,
    233, 241, 300
    character of, 1–2, 73
    credit rating of, 126
    floods in, 72–73, 101, 131
    Jeffords as attorney general of, 84,
        85–116, 118, 121, 127, 128–29,
        138–39
    Honduras as sister state of, 184
    Jeffords's contract with, 211
    Jeffords's failed bid for governorship
        of, 117–26, 130, 192
    National Teacher of the Year from,
        265–66
    Northeast Kingdom of, 87, 100, 122,
        135
    politics in, 56, 57, 58, 64–71, 73–74,
        85–90, 231, 234–35
    population of, 2
    reaction to Jeffords's party switch in,
        275–77, 279–80, 282–83
    Reagan tax cuts and, 178–80
    state income tax in, 75–77, 81
    state sales tax in, 93
    welfare system of, 74, 77
Vermont, University of, 78, 104, 137
Vermont attorney general office:
    Consumer Protection Division of, 91,
        110
    Division of Environmental Controls
        and Local Affairs of, 94
    environmental issues and, 91, 92,
        93–96, 99–103, 104, 105–16,
        128–29
    Jeffords's staff at, 91–92
Vermont Bar Association, 193–94
Vermont Constitution, 64

Vermont House of Representatives,
72–73, 80, 118
Vermont Owner's Manual, The (Bryan
and Mares), 275
Vermont Senate, 127
Jeffords as member of, 62–63, 67–71,
72–81
Jeffords's committee memberships in,
73, 75–76
Vermont State Board of Health, 94, 100,
109
Vermont State House, 72–73, 101, 102,
104, 111
Vermont Supreme Court, 1, 5, 9, 19, 57,
72, 91, 110, 139
Vermont Yankee nuclear power plant,
104, 105, 109, 113–16, 118
Vietnam Veterans of America, 206–7
Vietnam War, 60–61, 75, 79, 81, 88, 92,
98, 103–4, 111, 121, 130, 137,
204, 206–7
volunteer fire departments, 59, 191

Waldheim, Kurt, 165
Wallace, George, 121
Walsh, Lawrence E., 201
Warner, John, 226–27
Warren, Earl, 85
Washington, D.C., 14, 143, 169–71, 191
commuter tax proposed for, 226–27
education issues in, 221, 225, 227–30
Financial Control Board for, 224, 225,
226
Jeffords as Appropriations chair for,
221–27
legal status of, 222–25

Washington Post, The, 177, 226
Watergate scandal, 121, 130, 131–32,
134, 135–36
Water Resources Board (Vermont), 100,
109
Webber, John, 25
Weeks, John E., 72–73
Weingarten, Reid H., 197, 198–99,
201
welfare, 74, 77
Westchester County, N.Y., 94–95
Whalen, Peter, 90
Whipple, Taggert, 106–7
White House, 177, 179
Whitman, Christine Todd, 298
Wild, Kendall, 293–94
Williams-Sweetser, Susan, 175
Wing, Leonard, Jr., 4, 8
Wing, Leonard "Red," Sr., 3, 8–11, 56,
60, 66
Wing, Pat, 56
Wing family, 4
Wolf, Frank, 226
Wolk, David, 265
Wood-Burning Stove Credit, 160
Wood Dog astrological sign, 282
World Trade Center, September 11
attacks on, 284–86
World War II, 2, 8–11, 31, 32, 56, 73,
154
Wu, Shelly, 282

Yale University, 17, 18, 24–29
Yugoslavia, 231

Zermatt, 49

About the Author

James M. Jeffords has been a U.S. senator from Vermont since 1988. Currently serving his third term, he is chairman of the Environment and Public Works Committee. He lives with his wife, Elizabeth, in Shrewsbury, Vermont, and Washington, D.C.